Earth Day raised the level of concern of millions of Americans about environmental pollution and caused them to wonder, "What can I do next?"

Earth Tool Kit provides the answers:

- How to get organized
- Finding money and helpers
- Making the press and TV work for you
- Creating awareness through seminars, teach-ins and guerrilla theater
- The whole gamut of nonviolent protest—from lobbying and law suits to boycotts, picketing, strikes and harassment

Earth Tool Kit examines the "profit and progress" mentality that has given us the highway lobby, air-fouling automobiles, offshore oil spillage and sewage-filled waterways—moving beyond the usual conservation programs to hit the environmental hazards in the factories and the inner city where most Americans work and live.

Finally, *Earth Tool Kit* is a permanent reference source for information needed by every activist:

- A personal checklist of things you can do as an individual to preserve the environment
- A model survey to chart environmental pollution in your local community
- Plus the names, addresses, telephone numbers and group leaders of more than 125 local and national organizations in th~~e~~ ~~~~

EARTH TOOL KIT is an o

EARTH
TOOL
KIT

A Field Manual for Citizen Activists

Prepared by
Environmental Action

editor:
Sam Love

assistant editors:
Peter Harnik and Avery Taylor

PUBLISHED BY POCKET BOOKS NEW YORK

EARTH TOOL KIT

Pocket Book edition published April, 1971

WHO DID IT

Lauren Brown
Wilson Clark
Kathy French
Vicki Garrett
Barbara Herbert
Joan Knight
Eric Little
Betty Livingston
Phil Michael
Marie Nahikian
Carol Oboler
Ginni Puglisi
Barbara Reid
Marc Reisner
Jan Schaeffer
Kathy Stone
Ruth Wallick

description of organization

ENVIRONMENTAL ACTION is an organization dedicated to the non-violent fight for a healthy environment. An outgrowth of the staff which coordinated Earth Day, 1970, it serves as a catalyst to focus public concern on the solutions urgently needed to avert an ecological crisis. The group is currently involved in coordinating lobbying efforts, investigating polluting corporations, and developing local-level actions. Its bi-weekly publication *Environmental Action* alerts citizens to current ecological issues. To do its work, which requires naming the culprits, it cannot have a tax-exempt status; therefore, large sources of funding are closed to it. It depends entirely upon citizen supporters and donations to continue the struggle.

EARTH TOOL KIT

III   Battle Fronts

IV   The Movement: Trial Runs

Appendices

EARTH
TOOL
KIT

introduction

introduction

Contemporary man lives in sealed cubicles. His time at home, in vehicles and on the job revolves within hermetically sealed containers. His air is filtered, humidified, and ionized; water and food is synthesized; and energy is harnessed in efforts to disrupt the natural cycles of day and night. The plastic, steel, concrete and glass walls outlining modern man's realm are creating new spiritual dimensions in which pursuit of progress eclipses previous gods.

Periodically, man must forsake one constructed environment to move to another. Unprotected by plastic, fluorescent lights and air conditioning, his senses are exposed to the assault of filth, noise, and odor. This experience jars all but the dullest consciousness and communicates that something is drastically wrong.

Not imminent death but mutation into a form totally dependent on artificial life-support systems is the threat posed by man's present existence. As ear openings close from exposure to continually increasing noise levels, legs shrink from dependency on motorized transportation, or stomachs shrivel from extensive use of nutrition supplements, a new breed of man may emerge as a small capsule of consciousness totally dependent on a man-made environment for sustenance. But such evolutionary changes take many generations; more possible in the immediate future, with ever increasing exposure to chemicals and radiation, is the emergence of protohuman forms resulting from genetic alterations.

Fear of evolutionary changes must be reserved for future children; today's threats are more immediate. Tomorrow offers only Brave New Worlds, 1984s, eco-catastrophes, atomic holocaust, famines or other hells. Utopia and heaven are no longer guiding visions, but historical phenomena. Unburdened by spiritual direction, man's faith in unchecked material progress propels him forward. Destruction seems inevitable.

How can this be? Man's institutions are constantly adapting to accommodate new technologies. If the answers are found, can't they be implemented to ward off annihilation?

The problem lies not in a lack of answers, but in their implementation. The present environmental crisis is breeding an understanding of the false assumptions which have guided society:

Economics only abstractly values Nature's wealth in gold ripped from the earth's surface. Growth oriented formulas define progress in ever-faster depletion of resources. Air and water exist in abundance and will never disappear.

History reveals Nature's forgiveness. She replenished the earth, replanted the forests, and restocked the rivers.

Western man's spiritual creeds sanctify his pillage. Nature exists to be conquered. Man should be fruitful, multiply and subdue the earth.

Politics dictate artificial boundaries, ignoring ecological features. Legislation dealing with resource management is manipulated by capital interests which convert raw materials into gold.

Culture dictates a convenience-oriented life style that results in rapid resource depletion. Man removes himself from the source of raw materials and begins to view stores and factories as the source of production. Consumption defines prestige.

Many believe that the advantages of our technology compensate for environmental degradation. No other society could claim chemical multiplication of crop yield, massive harnessing of energy, development of synthetics, or other similar achievements. Some have faith that the laboratories that have delivered these miracles can also provide the tools to remedy any problems man may face.

But with technology's gifts to improve man's environment
has come an awesome potential for destruction. Assurances
are constantly offered that our new genies are well sealed in
their bottles and will be unleashed only at man's command.
But what cannot be dismissed from any discussion about
man's new technological toys is Murphy's Law, which states:
"What can go wrong, will go wrong."

The nerve gas disposal problem the Defense Department
faced in the summer of 1970 not only illustrates Murphy's
Law, but it underscores the dangers of creating "technological idiots," which is what C. Wright Mills called the highly trained specialists who have lost the ability to view the entire problem. Someone in the Army decided that the easiest
way to deal with leaking nerve gas shells was to pour concrete over them. That solution soon yielded bigger problems
as the porous concrete began to leak. To complicate the matter, the passage of time made the propellant in the rocket
shells unstable and created another danger—explosion. Before they became too unstable and disposed of themselves,
the Army decided to move them. Every possible scheme for
destroying the shells was considered, including sinking them
at sea, burying them in the earth, obliterating them by atomic
blast, and firing them into outer space. Because the gas neu-
tralized in water, dumping at sea won. The problem then became moving the heavy and possibly explosive concrete
vaults to a dumping site. After a nervous ride by train and
ship, the gas shells found their way to rest at the bottom of
the ocean. Hopefully, the last has been heard from these
shells. The nerve gas incident did not create disaster, but it
did dramatize how easily an eco-catastrophe could occur.

Some scientists and laymen are beginning to question
whether the creation of new potentially dangerous technology
is progress. But progress is now determined by who has the
money to control development. Over 80 percent of the nation's professional scientists and engineers are engaged in research funded by the federal government. Of all research
done, 60 percent focuses on aircraft/missiles and communica-
tions/electrical equipment. These figures reveal the real
priorities of the government. Obviously, scientific advancement can come only in areas where research is being conducted. With rare exceptions, research financed by private

industry is motivated toward work which will result in profit-making ventures for the sponsoring company. Public interest projects receive a low priority. The federal budget dramatically illustrates this. Estimated 1971 expenditure for the Department of Defense is $73.6 billion. The combined budgets for the National Air Pollution Control Administration and the Federal Water Quality Administration for the same year are estimated at $757.4 million, or roughly one percent of the defense budget. America's top priority is death, not life.

While prime importance has been given to development of technology for the military, other inventions could give man the tools for survival. The revolution that has occurred in communications offers tremendous potential for massive education. Unfortunately, its mere existence does not mean that it is being used to forge new sane directions for humanity.

In other nations America is stimulating desires for products that will be impossible to fulfill. An article from the entertainment paper *Variety* titled "Ice Boxes Sabotage Colonialism" explains part of the problem. It quotes Indonesia's President Sukarno saying:

> The motion picture industry has provided a window on the world, and the colonized nations have looked through that window and have seen the things of which they have been deprived. It is perhaps not generally realized that a refrigerator can be a revolutionary symbol—to a people who have no refrigerators. A motor car owned by a worker in one country can be a symbol of revolt to a people deprived of even the necessities of life. . . . Hollywood helped to build up the sense of deprivation of man's birthright, and that sense of deprivation has played a large part in the national revolutions of postwar Asia.

It is important to consider the content of the environmental message currently being relayed to the world. Ecology, pollution, and environment have become catchwords for industry in their advertising. Often they are used simply to try to gain attention. A clothing ad in the *New York Times* (costing about $2,000 for the one-fourth of a page it required) proclaims:

ECOLOGY
IS THE BIG THING THESE DAYS.
AND ONE WAY TO
"KEEP AMERICA BEAUTIFUL"
IS TO WEAR
THE GREAT-LOOKING CLOTHES
YOU'LL FIND IN
COLORFUL PROFUSION
AT GENE LUBIN'S
NEW MAN'S WORLD
IN WESTCHESTER!

There is little danger of these ads conveying a distorted meaning; but they do harm by saturating the public until the vocabulary of the environmental movement is greeted with yawns.

More harmful are the advertisements which deliberately distort to sell their products. Oil companies are furiously advertising that using their new low lead gasolines will fight air pollution. The impression is firmly implanted in the mind of the public that the road to cleaner skies will be built by burning low lead detergent gas so that the more the public drives the cleaner the air will become. But the petroleum industry and their corporate brothers in the auto industry fail to advertise alternative solutions to the air pollution problem.

Soap and detergent manufacturers also practice environmental double-think on the genuine desires of the public for cleaner water. One maker even markets a product tagged Ecolo-G to tap the concern. After high phosphate products received a commercial battering, the industry hurriedly substituted NTA (nitril triacetic acid) and started advertising new pollution fighting detergents. Now, tests are showing that their solution may be as bad or worse than the original phosphate problem.

Access to the mediums of television and the printed page is not open to public interest environmental groups who want to challenge corporate America's advertising. But options for communication of ideas do exist. Leaflets, demonstrations, law suits, elections and other actions can convey a message. It may even be an advantage that environmental activists will have to find other means of combating Madison Avenue's line. A face-to-face debate stimulated by a leaflet may do more to challenge a person's life style and opinions than 60 seconds of prime television time.

Magazine articles and television programs devoted to the environmental crisis are creating a potential constituency for a movement to transform America. As roses wilt from air pollution, the garden club becomes a hotbed of social activists. With increasing fish kills, gray-suited weekday bureaucrats/weekend fishermen become agitators for tough water pollution legislation. Dirtying air over the inner city unites blocks of people against the highway lobby's plans for a new multi-laned freeway. Environmental concerns can force socially and politically diverse groups together to work for a common solution.

The importance of the environmental movement's potential rests not only in what tangible results it can accomplish, but in its acting as a catalyst to start people working together. Alliances possible by organizing around environmental concerns stagger the mind of the seasoned community organizer. Organizations are built around perceived grievances, and pollution problems cross class, economic and social barriers. The dangers of mercury in a city's water supply ignore skin color or economic status.

The interaction which environmental organizing efforts is starting will not stop when the immediate threat is arrested. The process of working together reveals that community harmony is possible among those who do not have vested interest in the source of pollution. Pollution control efforts also define the powerlessness of the average citizen and illustrate the need for strong public interest groups. More people are beginning to understand that decisions with far reaching effects on society are being made without anyone consulting them. Consumers have little say about what products they will face on the television screen. No votes are taken on what additives should be put in food. Drivers have no choice but to drive a smog-producing internal combustion engine. No referendums are held on whether highways should be built through neighborhoods. The American people were never consulted about entering a war in Southeast Asia.

The list of wrongs the individual is suffering as a consequence of bureaucratic decisions could be very long. Realization of personal powerlessness is not a new state of consciousness for many people. "Power to the people" is a recurring battle cry in American history. What is new today are the consequences of the decisions.

More citizens are also understanding the dilemma America faces in the 1970's—its economic and political system is quickly ceasing to operate in the social interest of anyone. The chairman of the board of General Motors, who profits from manufacturing smog-producing engines, must breathe the same air as other citizens. Transportation tie-ups bog down everyone. Chemically contaminated water flows into luxurious new apartments and into slums. No one wins at atomic war.

The realization that all may suffer equally from certain environmental crises must not obscure the realities of power in corporate America. According to a detailed study of wealth in America published in 1962 by Professor Robert J. Lampman of the University of Wisconsin, 1.6 percent of the population owns 82.2 percent of the stock in corporations. That small group controls major decision-making within the corporate structure. Statistics on General Motors provide a look at how mammoth a modern corporate empire can become. Its total annual operating revenues exceed those of all but 12 countries. Receipts from sales are greater than the combined general revenues of New York, New Jersey, Pennsylvania, Ohio, Delaware, and the six New England states. G.M. employs over 700,000 people.

The tremendous financial and human resources of corporations make the creation of organized interest groups at the state and federal level possible. Public relations men, lawyers and experienced staffers can be employed to help influence decisions in a manner favorable to their corporate clients. By building experienced lobbies in Washington, industry can maintain both formal and informal contacts with officials who make day-to-day decisions which affect public policy. Because of this working relationship, job interchange between corporations and government regulatory agencies is accepted practice. It is difficult for public interest groups which do not have the organization, job openings, or wealth to compete with industry for influence. Often the unorganized public does not even know that decisions are being made that might affect it. When public debate is entertained, decisions have usually hardened before the hearings.

Influence is also bought with campaign contributions. The Federal Corrupt Practices Act of 1925 forbids corporations from making political contributions, so officers and directors make them as individuals. How much top corporate officials give is unknown because loopholes in the reporting laws make it impossible to determine accurately donations to candidates. But some information is available because under law donors who are contractors with some federal agencies have to report contributions. According to *Congressional Quarterly*, among the top contributors in 1968 was General Motors, which gave $114,675 to the Republicans and $1,000 to the Democrats.

With such enormous power in the hands of the corporations, the changes needed to circumvent the tragic outcome foreseen by pollution pessimists will not be easily made. Yet, as individuals challenge the structures to circumvent eco-catastrophe, a positive vision is emerging of a new society. Even if environmental groups lose the skirmishes, debate created by efforts to save a park from a six-lane expressway, stop a power plant, or close a source of pollution provides dialogue needed to transform society.

But education by discussion may be too slow a catalyst to affect the quantum alterations in life style required to re-create a livable future. This required shift could happen faster if it were imposed from above by highly centralized authoritarian government. Leading environmentalists are now advocating tighter government controls as an answer. In one of the most widely circulated works, "Tragedy of the Commons" by Garrett Hardin, the solution is "mutual coercion, mutually agreed upon by the majority of the people affected." While his discussion focuses mainly on population controls, the same rationale is used for proposals to ban automobiles in congested cities, drug children to make them better students, and others which would grant the state the exercise of power to curb individual freedom.

The real tragedy of the commons emerges as an increasingly centralized state uses bans to limit the boundaries of freedom. New technologies for control heighten the dangers of allowing the state to impinge on individual freedom. Yet, because the freedom to pollute violates the freedom of others, control must come.

A clear, but more difficult alternative exists to a centralized state dictating change. Corporate and governmental power can be decentralized and citizens at the local level can understand and affect the alterations demanded to combat a lowering quality of life. Critiqued by a respect for life, technology can be freed to serve man, not to enslave him. To accomplish this it must be freed from its dependency on commercial profits for guidance. The first segment that must be broken from financial shackles is communications. Groups offering ideas and positions can then have equal access to the public forum. Ultimately, society can benefit more from advertisements of the advantages of a small family, clean water, and decent air than commercials for chromed automobiles, leaded gasoline, tranquilizers, cigars, and similar commercial items.

Without access to the media, building broad-based faith in a livable future and working to achieve that goal will not be easy. A spirit of pessimism abounds today. For most, facing the realities of genetic engineering, nuclear weapons, chemical and biological warfare, the creation of a society in harmony with nature is impossible. They are accepting, without protest, a vision of a negative Utopia devoid of beauty, peace, and love. To them the task of survival appears so enormous that any individual effort at change is an exercise in futility. Alone it may be, but in unison with millions in a movement, it is not.

To many, it will appear that social actions which challenge growth, power and progress are negative, but these efforts must also be seen as an affirmation of life. If the proper groundwork is done by environmental activists, public support for controlling technology, even if it requires what appear to be negative actions, will develop. It will in part come from the proselytizing of environmentalists, but the largest segment will be generated by individuals rejecting a death-oriented society. The task, then, is not to create a constituency for a life-oriented movement; it is only to give it direction.

A vision of a positive Utopia now exists—a society that respects life. Its realization will come with the creation of a movement willing to struggle to build it.

SAM LOVE

I the foundation

In the face of our seemingly overwhelming environmental problems, the average citizen feels hopelessly inadequate and powerless. Pollution, despoliation and mineral exploitation are in evidence everywhere, and the small "neighborhood" victory seems almost useless when compared with the magnitude of the problem.

Some environmental activists, however, have overcome their feelings of impotency. Major decisions which result in pollution or ecological damage are often local ones—and they can only be fought on that level. Sweeping governmental legislation may be a prerequisite for change, but it is the "neighborhood" victory which really counts. The fledgling organization must begin its work in living rooms, classrooms, and small meeting halls, using borrowed equipment, and rudimentary materials. Money will be scarce and political influence will be slight. General public interest will be minimal. Most likely, everything will go wrong.

No two groups ever follow the same step-by-step procedure, but all successful ones have one attribute in common—a stubborn will to make their presence felt in the community.

strategy

The present alarming condition of our environment reveals a legacy of abuse by industrialists, governmental agencies, and citizens. The problems appear so immense that it is easy to blame the governmental or economic system in general, and difficult to discover what points, if any, can be constructively influenced by citizen pressure.

For people who want to improve the environment, the logical place to start is at home. Life styles must become less consumption oriented. Concerned individuals should familiarize themselves with ways to reorient their consumption patterns.

But that is only a small part of the battle. Industry and government are responsible for most of the major environmental abuses, and serious attempts to improve surrounding conditions must challenge their practices. Diversions from serious anti-pollution drives have been easily manufactured. Millions of dollars from packaging corporations have been poured into anti-litter campaigns to obscure the issue of the production of non-returnables. Auto and petroleum lobbyists support mass transit by buses so that highways will still have to be built.

Almost everyone is against pollution. The task of environmental activists is to tap the general concern and focus it on a specific environmental problem until real changes are made. Too often groups direct their attacks at general targets and never pinpoint the problem that needs a solution. Clamoring for a clean environment is not enough unless the sources of pollution are outlined. Corporate executives like nothing better than general concern because the blame is diffused.

13

Confronting an industry or governmental agency is too big a task for one individual, and he must join with others to generate the required pressure. When considering issues to raise in a community, it is important to select one with which people can identify. If residents are directly affected by an environmental problem, then they will be much more receptive to efforts to fight it. Air pollution outside the plant may not be as immediate a concern to workers as inside conditions. On the other hand, a major fish kill may create general public concern over the wastes of an industry, and present an opportunity to raise the issue of the plant's dumping policies.

Each group should seek to concentrate its attention where there will not be needless competition. With so few resources available for constructive change, rivalry must be avoided. It may be that the worst problem in a community will have to be bypassed because others are already searching for remedies to that particular problem.

It is imperative that a number of people take part in deciding what the focus of a group should be. They should also work together to develop a strategy for attacking the issue. It may be easier to have a small group or one person design a program of action, but involvement in decision making will increase a sense of commitment and unity among participants. Lengthy, sometimes frustrating, debate is often necessary before tactics are planned. But it is important for the education of those involved.

Choosing the right tactics for a specific campaign is difficult. With thousands of tactical possibilities, it is necessary to narrow the field to those that fit the group and can achieve the objectives desired. When thinking about how to approach a target, resources of the participants should be considered. Time, money, equipment, contacts, facilities, and legal help are some of the obvious ones. Others, such as support actions from other citizen groups, are more difficult to calculate.

The possible consequences of any proposed actions should be considered at length. Victory to one person may be defeat to someone else. Environmental groups may celebrate the closing of a plant until they meet the workers who are now out of a job. Another conflict often develops over recycling. Ecology groups collect old newspapers and turn them in to save the trees; poor people collect old newspapers and turn them in to feed their families.

Strategists for a group should not succumb to the temptation to value a tactic by its militancy. Tamer tactics can often achieve the desired objectives. Pollution is violent, and the temptation exists to counter it with violence. But preservation of life is the goal and destruction endangering life is unjustifiable. Anti-pollution, pro-life forces have strong, practical and moral arguments on their side in confrontations with corporations.

When dealing with a diverse group of people—the most potent social force—it is necessary to leave room for a number of actions. The hardhat-student clashes over the war issue should offer an important lesson about the dangers to a movement of alienating certain groups. But fear of alienating some should not temper the zeal of environmental organizers. Roderick Cameron, Executive Director of the Environmental Defense Fund, says, "Being militant about environmental degradation does not indicate one's politics. It only indicates one's desire to survive." Ecological concern shatters traditional barriers of politics, age and race. When health and survival are at stake, people will band together to fight.

Corporations spend millions of dollars on public relations to build a good image in a community. Contracts are sometimes won or lost on the basis of community relations. Actions of an active anti-pollution group, if covered by the media, can endanger images constructed by public relations firms—especially when they are based on half-truths.

The threat of giving a corporation a bad name is a powerful tool, but to solve the problem of pollution, it is not enough. Industrialists must be challenged on the grounds they know best—administrative, legislative and judicial. Without batteries of experts and lawyers that can compete with corporate staffs, citizens are at a decided disadvantage, although past citizen victories have occurred nevertheless.

Corporations may appear at first to be faceless and run by a computerized bureaucracy, but human beings make the decisions concerning plant priorities. It is necessary to determine who can make the changes in production or waste elimination that are desired. After the responsible official is found, pressure can be applied directly at that point.

The eco-activist must build alliances in the community to bring pressure upon public officials. One of the most important groups to involve is organized labor. Workers are at the center of production and industrial pollution. They can be a valuable source of information about the production process, including which plant chemicals are used and released into the environment. If their plant has pollution control equipment, they know if it is doing the job it was designed to do. Some labor unions are becoming aware of the in-plant pollution problem because of its effect on workers' health. Pollution which is only annoying on the exterior of a factory may be deadly on the inside. For this reason, some unions have recently started projects to educate their workers about environmental problems.

Workers have a powerful tool in collective bargaining and, increasingly, plant managers are being confronted with environmental demands in contract negotiations. The Oil Chemical and Atomic Workers and the United Automobile Workers are two of the first unions to make such demands part of contract talks.

Traditionally, workers have felt subjected to exploitation by the owners of the means of production. The rise of labor unions has improved the lot of the industrial worker, but the large gap that still exists between the salaries and life style of top management and workers makes the worker a good source of support for any effort to force a plant clean-up. However, a union may be in a difficult position if the corporate owners of a plant threaten to close it, rather than to pay the price of installing anti-pollution devices. Eco-activists must understand the plight of the union in such a situation, but idle threats or rumors of shutdowns should not stop a campaign. It is one of industry's favorite scare tactics.

Many unionists still remember the McCarthy era (Joe not Gene), and talk of worker-student alliances to crush capitalism will receive little support in factories. Workers, like most people, want more control over decisions that affect their lives. If workers had more control over production decisions, pollution control might receive higher priority.

For any environmental campaign, unions can be a source of money, meeting facilities, and printing. Most unions have funds for social action and access to printing equipment. Other groups which may be of help include:

Health associations such as the Tuberculosis Association. They have offices in most cities and their rhetoric about clean air and respiratory disease is good. These organizations are committed generally to clean air, but may not help wage campaigns against specific polluters.

Churches. In some communities they have provided meeting rooms, money, printing, and bodies.

Women's organizations such as the League of Women Voters. Housewives are financially secure and often have the time to assist as volunteers. They can also apply social pressure to the wives of polluters.

Commercial associations such as oyster and shrimp fishermen. They are often the worst hit by pollution. Other groups which could be helpful include lawyers, doctors, or architects. They can be particularly influential with politicians.

Sportsmen groups. Their members are also very close to the damage done by pollution and most have strong sympathies with a "clean outdoors." (It is probably best to avoid talking about guns.) Many of these groups are surprisingly powerful.

Civic clubs. They are always looking for programs and if they cannot provide bodies for a demonstration they might provide a forum to explain what has to be done. It is advisable that any speaker before a businessmen's lunch club find out if the manager of the target plant is a member.

Some other groups which might provide either money or other assistance are political party organizations, youth groups, and good government associations. Because the makeup and problems of each community are different, a careful look at which groups have been most active on other issues may reveal other possible sources of support. It is important to remember that people who have never been upset about other problems are concerned about pollution and the movement needs fresh people.

Often it is possible for astute environmental organizers to pit business interests against each other. Some corporations have a vested interest in ecologically sound enterprises. Diaper laundry services, for instance, will help spread the word about the harm of throwaway paper diapers. Bus companies are willing to help groups encourage people to leave their cars at home.

While a smoothly functioning broad base is necessary to have social clout, allies which compromise the integrity and aims of a coalition are to be avoided. The goal of any group should be to operate with as much harmony and discipline as possible, because dissension will be used by the other side. Nothing provides better material for a news commentator than a peace group fighting among itself. Discipline is difficult for groups which operate democratically, but it is needed. If someone cannot or will not cooperate with the wishes of the majority, he should be excluded. Possibly, other splinter groups can organize independent support actions.

Because the environmental fight will involve a series of protracted struggles within most institutions which exist today, all actions must be evaluated to see what can be learned from them. Feedback from neutral sources can offer a sound critique. Conversations with taxicab drivers, business associates, classmates, or anybody not immediately involved in the effort can provide a fair assessment of the impact.

If a group's activities are really being felt, trouble in the form of eviction notices, telephoned threats, lawsuits, or similar harassment may develop. If this starts, it is important to find where it is coming from. Sometimes it can be traced back to an angry plant manager, labor union leader, property owner, or politician. Often such agitation, in addition to strengthening the will and spirit of a group, can be publicized and increase a campaign's punch.

The achievement of the original goals is important, but it must also be expected that confrontations with large industries and big government may not always yield victory. Defeat sometimes provides the best education, especially if the lessons learned are used in the next campaign.

collecting information

Collecting the right information is one of the hardest parts of an environmental struggle. Not only does a concerned person need to know technical data about a controversial subject, but he must understand how to discover weak points in the armor of corporations and government agencies.

Wielding the weapon of long-held influence, both rich individuals and big corporations have successfully spun a web of secrecy around much information that environmental activists need. Many products do not list their chemical additives. Drugs are extensively sold under trade names instead of by their true content. Technological advances are kept in the wings for years until the market is ripe.

Owners of stock in corporations can anonymously hide behind a "street name," which allows their stock to be listed with their broker in a fictitious name. Campaign donation reporting laws have so many carefully engineered loopholes that unscrupulous politicians can cloud records of donors so that they escape public scrutiny.

Even basic information on what kinds of pollution are being dumped into the environment have thus far largely escaped governmental scrutiny. In order to formulate standards for effluents, the Federal Water Quality Administration (FWQA) decided in 1963 to inventory industrial water wastes. A questionnaire was designed asking corporations to describe their discharges into the water. In 1970 Office of Management and Budget, which has to approve such queries, finally approved a compromise version of the questionnaire. At issue was the corporation's right to keep its processes a secret. Explained the Office of Management and Budget: "Industry does not like to report effluents . . . [because] there is always pressure from the public to release the federal data and the companies are afraid that the data may get into the hands of the news media."

The Central Intelligence Agency foiled a similar, smaller-scale information search by FWQA several years ago. The water control agency wanted to complete an inventory of waste water on the Potomac River. There is no heavy industry on the lower Potomac. In fact, the CIA has a large establishment along the river, equipped with its own water treatment facility. When asked what pollutants it was dumping into the water, the CIA answered that its effluent is classified.

Industries, backed by patent laws, have long managed to keep ingredients of certain products classified from the public. After the April, 1970, oil spill from Chevron wells off the coast of Louisiana, globs of muck began washing up on the shore. The Ecology Center of Louisiana decided to commission a chemical analysis of the stuff to determine its causes. One suspicion was that it came from detergents used by Chevron to disperse or coagulate the oil slick. The ecology activists asked the FWQA for a listing of the chemicals which had been used so the chemists would know what to look for. The FWQA claimed it could only provide the trade names of the detergents used—not the chemicals, which were trade secrets. This information was the property of the firms that manufactured the dispersants and coagulants, and the Ecology Center was advised to go to those companies.

Corporations have been known to withhold technological improvements—even though these would better public health —in order to protect themselves from outside interferences. The Justice Department filed suit in 1969 against the four major American automobile manufacturers, charging them with collusion to withhold the manufacture and public sale of pollution control devices. In 1955 the major companies had formally signed a "cross-licensing" agreement to share results of research on pollution control devices. They agreed to install such mechanisms only when all parties to the agreement were prepared to do so. This measure effectively eliminated competition among the auto firms in the pollution control field. Industry pressure on the government resulted in an out-of-court "consent decree" in which the industry was let off the hook. Promises were made to end the corrupt practice, but no enforcement procedures were established.

Like industry, the federal government prefers to keep as much of its operations as possible out of public view. A public information official in the Atomic Energy Commission, for example, expressed anger at the charge that she was withholding public information, since she refused to mail to interested citizens a report outlining the way the public may participate in the licensing of atomic power plants. "It's at the public information office of the AEC for anyone who wants to see it," she said heatedly. There is an act of Congress which is designed to give the public access to information when government agencies refuse to give it. The Freedom of Information Act, passed in 1967, promised that, with nine exceptions, all government information would be available to whoever wanted it, at low cost. The wary government has discovered ways to avoid compliance with the act. Some agencies and departments do not collect information which might be useful to the public. The Interstate Commerce Commission, for example, keeps no records of its "requests for voluntary compliance." Or, similar to the AEC example, agencies keep files of some information only in one Washington office. The cost of "searching for a document" is, frequently, $2, and additional charges are made for copying each document. Sometimes agencies deny the information exists at all. Other easy techniques are to delay responding to requests for information or to deny them, which allows the inquiring citizen the right to appeal with written request after written request to ever ascending levels of senior bureaucrats. A more sophisticated approach is to insert public information in the same document as classified material. When these fail, agencies have recourse to a broad interpretation of the nine exemptions listed in the act. Any information that is part of an "investigatory file" is exempt, and some agencies claim that most of its proceedings are perpetually under investigation. "Internal procedures," and "inter- or intra-agency memoranda" are exempt. This allows the Department of Agriculture to withhold minutes of meetings with industry advisory groups.

Although much key information is either unavailable or distorted, the average group can obtain more than it can utilize. Most environmental activists understand the need for good technical data, but research on corporate and governmental groups is often ignored.

The municipal library is a gold mine for the environmental researcher. If the city library is inadequate, other sources such as the nearest university with a business school or a chamber of commerce library can provide the needed publications.

Material which people handle every day often provides important data. Home phone numbers and addresses of plant managers, corporate directors, and politicians are recorded in the telephone directory. In their news stories, city newspapers provide a record of business transactions, scandals, law suits, elections and other tidbits. That type of information is necessary, but other features of the daily paper (which are often considered unimportant) can be valuable. Social pages portray activities of the community's elite. Party descriptions outline who socializes with the "in" crowd, and knowledge of the social connections of husbands and wives can prove useful for interview sources and fund raising tips. Legal notices are hidden in the back of the paper and set in painfully small type, but they provide useful information—notices of commission hearings, city council meetings, election information, transfers of property, etc.

Some helpful material is easily available but not widely circulated. The *Wall Street Journal* is one of the best sources of data on business. It reports pollution stories in depth to inform the business community about the impact environmental issues are having on corporations. Reading back issues allows environmental sleuths to discern trends among industries.

Biographical sketches of people can outline their backgrounds, affiliations, and business interests. *Who's Who in America* and more specialized versions such as *Who's Who in Commerce and Industry* are the best known sources. There are others which may include men missed by the *Who's Who* books. *Current Biography* or the monthly *Current Biographical Reference Service* are two more that might be checked.

Groups which may file law suits can use extensive background on local lawyers. Many law firms are paid retainer fees by corporations in case they are needed to defend the company. Such an arrangement puts lawyers in the employ of industrialists and close relationships develop. A lawyer whose firm is on retainer by a polluting company is not the best source of sound legal advice for an environmental group. *Lawyer's Directory* or *Martindale-Hubbell Law Directory* catalogues legal partners and some corporate clients.

Another source of a person's business interests is the city social register or "Blue Book." It is published commercially and offers prominent citizens an opportunity to disclose their manifold financial holdings, club memberships, etc. What a rich person won't tell the public may be a source of pride to him when revealed to his peers.

Corporate profiles and information should be researched to find weak points of a polluting company's corporate owner. One vulnerable spot of most corporations is their record of pollution control expenditures. They will often quote a lump sum in their advertisements to impress the public with the millions of dollars they are spending to fight pollution. Contrasting the pollution control figures with profits reveals some interesting percentages.

Campaign Against Pollution in Chicago, after researching their local utility, Commonwealth Edison, found that in 1968 the company spent less than .003 percent of revenue on research and development of pollution control devices. In 1969 the percentage dropped to .002.

An even stronger indication of the utility's misdirected priorities was the expenditure in 1969 of $2.1 million for advertising and only $2.2 million on air pollution control. When considering these figures it is important to remember that these are expenditures by a public utility which has no competition. Their advertising money is spent to build an image and create more demand.

One of the first items to obtain when researching a corporation is its annual report. This document contains not only financial statistics, but the names of officers and membership of the board of directors, a description of corporate activities, problems, plans, etc. It can be obtained by writing the secretary of the corporation at its headquarters. The Securities and Exchange Commission also requires copies of annual reports and proxy statements to be filed at its office libraries in New York, Chicago, San Francisco, Atlanta, Washington, D. C., Boston, Denver, Fort Worth, and Seattle. The proxy statement may be very helpful. In it corporations must disclose owners of sizeable shares of their stocks, holdings of the officers and directors, salaries of officers and directors, and any stock options granted to them.

Business directories contain additional information which is important to know. They are found in large city and business school libraries. *Guide to American Directories* indexes and describes all business directories published by corporations, trade associations, chamber of commerce groups, federal and state agencies.

Short corporate descriptions of major companies are available in *Dun and Bradstreet's Middle Market Directory*, which lists over 20,000 firms with sales of $500,000 to $999,999, and *Dun and Bradstreet's Million-Dollar Directory*, listing firms with sales above $1 million. More complete corporate descriptions (three to five pages in length) are in respective volumes of Moody's Investment Service Series: *Moody's Industrial Manual, Moody's Transportation Manual, Moody's Utilities Manual, Moody's Bank, Investment Company, Insurance and Real Estate Manual. Standard and Poor's Corporate Descriptions* is eight volumes and contains additional material. *Poor's Register of Corporations, Direc-*

tors and Executives offers a cross index of the officers and directors of major firms.

Unavailable to private individuals, but invaluable when researching smaller firms that do not make the big directories, is *Dun and Bradstreet's Financial Reporting Service*. Connections in a university treasurer's office, bank, or friendly business may help obtain this source.

The addresses of manufacturing plants and their products for the 1,000 largest corporations are available in *Fortune's Plant and Products Directory of the 1,000 Largest Industrial Corporations*. These location listings could provide the basis for a coordinated campaign by groups in different cities against one company's pollution.

States offer through either their state chamber of commerce or economic development agency an industrial directory which advertises economic attractions and lists all manufacturing firms employing more than 50 workers, their addresses, plants, officers, products, sales, and profits. It is important to find out if the state government through either its tax structure or other laws is subsidizing polluting plants.

Books have been written on some industries and can provide background material. To find them check under the name of the industry or company in the library's card catalogue. The *Politics of Oil* by Robert Engler, published in 1961 by Macmillan, is an excellent example of this type of book.

Corporate research groups are also a possible source of specific information. Because their staffs and finances are limited, their records are only thorough in specific areas. The Council on Economic Priorities, 1028 Connecticut Avenue, N. W., Washington, D. C. 20036, has done an extensive study of paper companies which will soon be available to the public. They also have a regular newsletter which publishes corporate profiles.

Advertising statistics of a company are hard to find, but trade journals and magazines like *Advertising Age* can often be useful. The *New York Times* business page covers Madison Avenue account shifts in detail and these often reveal figures on the amount of a company's yearly advertising budget. Ad information for public utilities is available in the yearly form which they are required to file with the Federal Power Commission in Washington, D. C.

Another valuable statistic to obtain is the amount of political contributions made by top corporate executives. Most states require candidates to report donations to the secretary of state or another official. The Federal Corrupt Practices Act of 1925 forbids corporations from making direct political contributions, so officers and directors give as individuals. Their contributions to senators and representatives are reported along with other citizens to the secretary of the Senate and the clerk of the House of Representatives. Primary records do not have to be reported, only contributions to general election campaigns. Loopholes allow senators and congressmen to list the committees which collect funds for them (instead of individual contributors), so in most cases the Washington records offer little information. But under another law, contractors with some federal agencies (mainly the Defense Department) have to file detailed statements of gifts. These records are evaluated regularly by the Citizens' Research Foundation (CRF), Nassau St., Princeton, New Jersey.

Other data which should be sought, but may be impossible to find, is tax payment records. Some trade journals publish this information yearly. The August 17, 1970, issue of *U. S. Oil Week* contains a listing of tax payments of oil companies.

A breakdown of top management's salaries (which for executives of large corporations run in the hundreds of thousands of dollars) can be useful for mobilizing rank-and-file workers who make considerably less than their bosses. One possible source is the national office of the company's labor union. Many industries pay according to a scale developed by the American Society of Association Executives. Located in Washington, D. C., the group has developed a salary scale which is relative to the annual budget of the company. A group can get a corporation's annual budget from its annual report.

The types of information sources outlined here are all used daily by industrialists in their pursuit of the dollar. They can also be used by environmentalists seeking a cleaner environment.

material resources

After a sufficient number of "people resources"—workers and enthusiastic supporters—are located, the first things any group needs to keep operating effectively are funds and material resources. This does not mean that every scheduled event or undertaking has to result in a large profit, but it does mean that some money and some equipment have to be available for group plans to be put into effect.

Finances can come from a variety of sources, and there are numerous ways to organize fund-raising projects. A group can start a recycling campaign, collecting newspapers, bottles, cans, rags, anything that can be returned to the manufacturers for reuse. Non-returnable aluminum cans will be bought back by some manufacturers, and in an even more unusual example, some junk dealers will buy used motor oil that can be acquired free from many gasoline station attendants. Other materials and objects that would be of no use to the manufacturer but still have several years of use left may be collected and resold to the public in a rummage sale.

Benefits are another way to raise money. Often sympathetic performers will donate their talent and perform without charge. Two things are necessary to the success of any benefit: good location and good publicity. It may make more sense to spend money for a good location, for instance the municipal auditorium, where high prices can be charged, rather than to use a small, free church which is hard to reach and has little prestige. Publicity can be provided by large, colorful, well distributed posters and announcements.

Another fund-raising program is the lecture. A variety of speakers can be provided to attract diverse groups of people who may all become interested in the new cause. Again, a well known personality will attract larger crowds. One disadvantage to charging for the lecture is that those who are not already convinced will neither pay nor become convinced. It may be possible, however, to collect money for a scheduled lecture beforehand by advertising and accepting donations. If collections are made at schools, shopping centers or similar locations, they should be cleared with whoever is in charge of these premises.

Selected mailings may also be used to gather needed funds. Local service groups and liberal organizations may be willing to share their membership and mailing lists. It is always good for any group to keep a record of names and addresses of every contact for future mailings. Certain tactics such as colored envelopes and well designed graphics can increase the percentage of returns, but returns on mailed solicitation generally remain low, between 3 and 10 percent.

A group may always sell objects advertising their cause. Literature, buttons, bumper stickers and posters can all be used as a source of income. The advantage of this method is that it will educate the public and stimulate group involvement as well as earn money. Presumably, the material will also reach many others besides the buyer, since these are all objects for display.

In some cases, a direct plea for money will produce the best results. If asked, another group with the same concern may loan or donate large sums of money to help a new group get on its feet. Well established individuals who are likely to have a strong interest in environmental issues may also be directly approached for funds. It is often very helpful to be specific about the group's needs. A particular expense—payment for a special telephone line, printing costs for an informative pamphlet or office space—may be paid for by one outside individual or organization. Finally, it may be necessary to charge dues or accept donations from members at regular intervals. It is very important for the strength and spirit of a group that no member be excluded because he or she is too poor or not definitely committed. Such exceptions can result in later frictions.

At the same time that financial arrangements are being made, attention must be directed toward acquiring necessary office and program equipment. The best advice on this front is to be inventive; scrounge around and pass around what you have. Almost anything needed for an office can be secured by advertising in a local newspaper where neighborhood needs are emphasized. It is always a good idea to read other ads; somebody might want to get rid of the supplies you need. Old offices that are going out of business will usually throw out large supplies of unused office materials which are no longer needed. Campaign headquarters are particularly good to ask for old supplies; even old campaign buttons can be salvaged and a new label stuck on over the old slogan. Other groups that have decided to buy new equipment may sell their old models very cheaply because of low trade-in value. After all possible sources of free, donated, or purchased equipment are exhausted, it will always be possible to rent the supplies which are too expensive to buy.

Obviously, a major necessity is an office. Initially, a group may be able to operate out of one person's home, a local church, or maybe even a free neighborhood activities center. But eventually additional space will be necessary if the group's activities are to expand and if the group itself is to achieve the larger recognition it will need to successfully encourage environmental awareness. Office space will sometimes be donated by another concerned group; other times a new group might temporarily share the same office with another organization, but the most common solution will probably be to find the cheapest office space to rent. Newspapers, friends and relatives in other offices, and different environmental groups will be the best sources to contact to find out where empty offices are located and whether they are available and reasonably priced.

The next necessity will be office furniture. If not located through advertisements or salvaged out of members' basements and attics, furniture is best found in secondhand stores. Prices will vary so several outlets should be checked before purchasing. Secondhand office supply stores will generally be more expensive than general secondhand furniture stores. Two good sources in any area are the Salvation Army and Goodwill Industries.

One main consideration for any group will be printing equipment which includes typewriters, copying machines, mimeographs, electric stencils, composers, etc. These items may be borrowed from church groups, unions, school newspapers, or other similar sources. Sometimes, two groups with adjoining office space or even office space in the same building can make arrangements to share more expensive printing equipment. The high cost of operating a copying machine, for instance, would make it highly impractical for a single environmental group to rent one; two groups on the other hand might really benefit from the duplications and copies that can be shared.

Paper should be used with care; the amount of paper that can be wasted in one office is incredible. It is a good idea to research the possibility of getting recycled paper from a nearby paper mill or organization handling recycled materials. A local printer might be able to black out or cut off an old letterhead on extra copies of printed material and print a new letterhead or message at a cheaper rate. All wrappers and letters that come into the office should be saved for scrap paper, wrapping up large numbers of booklets, pamphlets or newsletters to be sent out, or even reuse for office letters. Environmental groups, in particular, can get away with crossing out one side of a paper and using the other side for a new message. Furthermore, it is a habit that should definitely be encouraged. Letters and printed material that can be reused at a later time should not be dated, unless necessary. Another innovative idea is to use stationery that can be folded in such a way that one blank side remains for the address; more space is available for a message than on a postcard and any checks or money orders can still be enclosed.

Telephones will also be required, and one expense that can easily be avoided is the additional charge for a colored or push-button phone; the standard black model with the rotating dial will ring just as clearly and handle just as many calls. Installation and monthly rates vary considerably in different cities so it is impossible to give average rates, but it will be approximately twice as expensive to put in two phones with two lines that can be reached on either phone than it will be to put in one phone and one extension with the same number. However, it will be worthwhile for any group to put in several different phones and at least two lines to process all the requests for material and information that they will be likely to receive. Public contact is extremely important and if local citizens are continually frustrated in their efforts to reach a group, their interest and support for the group will probably dwindle.

One alternative that should be looked into is the Wide Area Telephone Service, commonly called a Wats line. Under this system, the United States has been divided into six zones, excluding Hawaii and Alaska. A group may purchase a Wats line to cover any number of these zones, and for a standard monthly charge, they can make long distance calls to any regions within the zones they have selected. A full time charge permits unlimited 24-hour talking time for the entire month; a measured time charge allows any ten hours of talking time per day with a charge for every hour overtime. Rates vary across the country and will be very high if only a few calls are made each day, but a group that undertakes a regional project might find it a more economical method for handling their calls than a regular telephone line. If one group in an area already has a Wats line, they may be very willing to assign another group the hours when the line is seldom used.

Since the telephone bill might easily be the largest office expense, it is a very good idea to keep a signed log book for all long distance calls made on a regular telephone line. If the office is extremely busy with lots of outsiders wandering in and out, one precaution that might be taken is a telephone lock on the dial. When the lock is on, incoming calls can be received, but no outgoing calls can be made, and the problem of many unaccountable calls can then be avoided.

Files are necessary in any office for keeping a variety of records. Any important news articles in magazines, journals, newspapers, and other publications should be filed for future reference and for valuable statistics. Anyone in the office can collect articles and file them in a joint file alphabetically. Addresses of important groups and people should also be filed, and while one person may have a very complete file for everyone's use, it is often best if each person keeps his own cards for specific research or contact purposes. Records of bills and monetary transactions—office expenses, subscription forms, loans, donations, etc.—must be kept for tax records and payment purposes. Expensive metal files are not needed, simple cardboard card files will do nicely, and a converted cardboard box may be used to file printed material.

Odd office equipment which can save much wasted time are a bulletin board, a chalk board, and maybe used carpeting to control distracting noise. A piece of cork big enough to hold any telephone and office messages can do wonders to centralize important information and to keep track of important calls and visitors. Communal equipment such as tape and staplers may be kept on one table for the use of the entire office staff; items such as scissors can even be tied to a drawer handle to prevent loss. One important aspect in any office is the provision of a separate working space for every staff member; in this way, each person's materials will not be lost and methods of concentration and working habits will not be continually interrupted by others groping for their materials or demands that someone be moved.

Program necessities are of a different nature and usually involve a meeting space and sound equipment. Free auditoriums or conference rooms can easily be found with a few inquiries. City halls, churches, public high schools, unions, and courthouses may all have available rooms which they will lend for afternoon or evening citizens' meetings. Any one of these sources can be called and a place reserved. Most universities have very nice meeting halls, but it will usually be necessary to have a local university group sponsor the outside group and have the student organization reserve the space. However, environmental student groups abound so this should not be too difficult. The same sources may also permit a group to borrow their sound equipment. Schools, unions, and courtrooms may have microphones available if not already on the premises; schools may also be able to provide bullhorns for an outdoor meeting in a park that may be twice as effective as an indoor meeting. Imagination should be used to provide an interesting meeting place, but central location, parking facilities, and easy access to the facilities must be considered first. If a meeting seems difficult to approach for any reason—out-of-the-way location, tight knit clique of "in" organizers, or a difficult time period—those that most need to be convinced won't attend. Furthermore, a meeting that is confused by unannounced speakers, faulty sound equipment or disorganized, hasty procedures without background details will discourage those people who made an effort to come to the meeting to learn about something which they did not already know.

A few useful precautions can be taken when choosing meeting space. Make sure that restroom facilities are open and available. Also see that trash receptacles are handy and in sight. It might not be a bad idea to even check out the insurance policy for a building since smoking may be prohibited, but no signs posted announcing this fact.

A word should be added here about group organization. It is very important that everyone feels useful to the group and that the group as a whole feels useful in its social context. The worst jobs—opening mail, changing addresses, and answering telephones, etc.—must be doled out evenly. One person serving as a "workhorse" and nothing else soon feels used and cheated. All antagonisms should be brought out in the open; often constructive criticism can change habits that bother other group members before secretive looks, personal conflicts, or back-biting occur. Often too, a small success will do more to strengthen the group's enthusiasm than an attempt to tackle a major task which is too large to bring any substantial, visible results.

getting the word out

A quip which grew out of the American campus uprisings in the 1960's was, "Three students and a mimeograph machine can shut down any university in the country." While to some the statement is humorous, the general portent is clear —the successful activist group must know how to utilize the printed word. Whether the message is mimeographed, printed in a local newspaper, typed, xeroxed, scrawled on posters, or written in the sky by airplane, it is often the only link a small group will have with outsiders.

After Spiro Agnew's blasts, virtually all Americans are aware of the tremendous success political radicals have had with the press. Environmental groups can use the media to even greater advantage, for there are vast numbers of potential ecological allies among the population-at-large, and widespread coverage can only serve to swell the ranks of the movement.

Newspapers, magazines, and radio and television news bureaus depend upon reportable events for their livelihoods (that is, sales or ratings). Since environmental groups depend upon coverage for their livelihood (contributions or political clout), the relationship is a complementary one and the "alliance," in theory should be strong. In actual fact, the "alliance" is successful only as far as it is cultivated by the individual group. Dealing with the news media is an art, and it should be taken seriously.

Most sophisticated ecology groups are conscious of their images. And most image-conscious groups have one person whose prime or sole responsibility is dealing with reporters. It is he who prepares press releases, arranges press conferences, informs reporters of upcoming actions and provides them with background and support material. He must be knowledgeable, quick-witted, diplomatic, and, in many cases, somewhat aloof from the organization. He must also establish diverse contacts and have a good feel for what is and what is not newsworthy. Most important, he must have a basic understanding of the workings of a news organization, namely, of reporters, photographers and editors.

By and large, reporters are not specialists in any one field. They are sent out to cover events as they occur, and they are trained writers—not environmentalists. Furthermore, they are always under considerable deadline pressure. Thus, everything that transpires—whether active, spoken or written—must be explained clearly and concisely. Since journalists use the "inverted pyramid" style (most important facts first), the press relations person who rambles through a long description may be unpleasantly surprised when the final story appears. Even if the reporter has all the facts straight, his editor (or news director) may not have space or time for the full article, and may cut it half-way through.

Reporters are the underdogs of the news establishment. In general, they tend to be politically liberal, and will react favorably to environmental groups. This bias should be cultivated, and contacts should be developed with at least one newsman from each newspaper and television station in your area. If this is successfully done, reporters will work to get fair and adequate coverage for your group's views, and they will very likely give professional tips on the best way of getting a point across.

Eco groups must also be aware of news photographers and television cameramen. Although groups are never assured of photo coverage in the media, it is something they should strive for, and the theatrical aspect of any action should be considered. A rally or demonstration will be greatly enhanced by "shocking" gimmicks like gas masks, posters, outlandish clothing or unusual sites. If a photogenic situation is likely to arise, let the media know about it beforehand. Keep in mind that one striking picture may be worth many articles.

Unlike reporters, editors may not be overly friendly to environmental groups. The editor is close to the top of the newspaper's hierarchy, and will feel pressure from advertisers and other business groups in the locale if he upsets the status quo too much. Sympathetic articles are often cut down, rewritten, given low priority, or topped by a misleading headline. This is a fact which reporters have to live with, and environmental groups should welcome every favorable article— and protest every misleading one.

Editors rarely write editorials. Editorial writers write them, although a newspaper's or television station's stand on an issue is decided by higher-ups. Since a newspaper will generally come out against pollution (even if it shies away from naming names), a group should attempt to talk to the men who write the editorials to give them ammunition with which to argue. Even if the tone is later watered down, it is these men who will eventually have to write the column.

For the group that has general control over the timing and scope of its own actions, the most important uses of the media will be through the press releases and conferences.

A press release is essentially an announcement sheet—either of an upcoming event (a planned rally, strike, lawsuit, fund-raising drive, corporate challenge, etc.) or a recent occurrence (receipt of a large contribution, formation of a new coalition, etc.) or a statement of opinion (refutation of a company's ad campaign, comment on new legislation, denunciation of municipal practices, endorsement of a candidate, etc.). It is an extremely versatile document, but it must be handled correctly.

The press release is, in effect, a news article. It must be clear, interesting, readable and to the point. In its first sentence (the lead), five questions should be answered—who, what, when, where, and why. Reporters will essentially be rewriting a press release for their articles if there are no other facts at hand, and everything they need should be included.

If the lead is clear and informative, local radio stations may also use it in their hourly reports.

To be effective, the press release must also be timely. One of the media's strictest rules is the deadline, and this must always be taken into account. For morning papers, the deadline is around 7:00 P.M.; for evening papers, around noon; and for evening television news, about 4:00 P.M. Reporters should receive releases substantially ahead of the deadline, preferably by several days if the information is available. Releases should be marked "press release" and should include a release date, or a time when they are to be announced. Groups must also include on every release the name and telephone number of a person who can be contacted for further information or any questions. For best results, the envelope should be addressed to the attention of a sympathetic newsman.

If a complicated situation exists, with new developments several times a week, most groups put out two simultaneous news releases—the first, a brief one containing the new information, and the other giving added explanation, background material and analysis. Although the press will not usually print the long version, reporters may pick and choose from the more extensive fact sheet.

Press releases should be sent to every newspaper, television and radio station in a community. (These can be checked in the yellow pages of the telephone book). If time permits, deliver them by hand. A press release might look like:

PRESS RELEASE

Contact: (spokesman's name)   For release: (time
    (telephone number)   and date)

Activists from a coalition of five different environmental groups convicted the Cram Computer Company of polluting the Kawatawga River with chrome wastes today (March 15), climaxing a two-hour mock trial in the Village Square. Activists' Coalition for the Environment (ACE) will culminate the trial tomorrow at 8 P.M. by sentencing the company at St. Stephen's Church.

Today's trial charged that Cram's wastes, dumped directly into the Kawatawga, are damaging the town's sewage treatment process and have even been discovered in the drinking water of Harleyville, 24 miles downstream.

One of the witnesses, biologist Julie Piper of State University, testified that the chrome killed the bacteria which treat the town's waste in the sewage plant. Other witnesses pointed out that similar discharges have destroyed sewage plants in other parts of the country.

According to Harleyville's deputy mayor, James Douglass, the town's water has tasted and smelled bad over the past three months. "It's getting so that we receive ten to fifteen complaints a day now," Douglass testified.

Eric Hatcher, the black-robed "justice" found the company guilty on separate counts of trespassing, public nuisance, and violation of the 1965 Water Quality Act. After the trial, he commented, "The company is slowly destroying the river and our town. We want to publicize this fact in the hopes that someone in the mayor's office will finally take some responsible action."

The trial was the latest effort to get the computer manufacturer to install adequate filters. ACE currently has collected 5000 signatures condemning Cram for pollution, and the group has indicated that it may file suit.

* * *

The press conference is the other major tool that the environmental group should learn to master. Unlike the press release, which can be used as often as possible, the press conference should be reserved only for extraordinary occasions.

In some respects, the press conference is merely a glorified press release, but it has major advantages because it can be photographed and televised, and because, as an actual happening, it warrants greater attention and coverage. It does, however, put greater strains on the press relations officer and the media.

The press conference should only be called for a major announcement, such as the start of a campaign which would affect many people in the community, state or country; the decision to begin a campaign for (or against) a candidate for office; or the filing of legal papers against a larger polluter.

A press conference can be called virtually anywhere, providing there are adequate facilities for television cameras. The outdoors can provide a good setting if the weather is right and if electrical outlets are within reach. Press conferences should not be held outside if there is too much bright sunlight or wind or if street noises would interfere with the microphones. Indoors, meeting rooms are adequate if there is reasonable access to them (a three-story walk-up, for instance, is out of the question). Universities and churches will almost certainly have facilities available, and may be quite willing to let them be used.

For city groups which only have small, cluttered offices, one of the best alternatives is to rent a hotel meeting room for a couple of hours. This will rarely cost more than $25, and all the necessary equipment—chairs, tables, a podium, and decent electrical connections—are there. Environmental Action learned this lesson the hard way. In its early days, it attempted to hold a press conference in its offices in a rather old building. As the action began and all the television camera lights were turned on, the fuses blew.

To inform the media of a press conference, it is usually necessary to call each newspaper and station separately, giving exact time and place, and directions to the place if they are not generally known. In some larger cities, Associated Press and United Press International have city wires which are connected to all the news agencies. By contacting these two organizations, the word will be spread, although it is still advisable to call elsewhere.

At the press conference room, everything must be set up ahead of time, as the crews will be under time pressure and may have to leave soon. Speakers and anyone who may be on camera should be ready, and the press relations officer must circulate, greeting newsmen and answering any questions. A press release, which should include the entire prepared statement, as well as the correct spellings of all the participants' names, should be prepared and distributed to all newsmen.

Big name speakers or participants may help to give the press conference greater coverage, but care must be taken that the more famous person does not obscure the fact that the ecology group has organized and arranged the proceedings. Since newsmen tend to play up personalities, this is a very real risk and should be carefully considered.

Another type of press conference is the "background conference." This is far less common than the other kind, and generally is not given for the public's immediate benefit. The background conference is called by a group to brief reporters on certain important facts and background information, and rarely involves television cameramen and newspaper photographers.

The background conference is generally utilized when a group knows that it will be starting a campaign or other project in the near future which will probably receive wide press coverage. If reporters have a good understanding of the issues and facts at stake, they can write better articles more easily, and the eco group will benefit from the greater coverage.

Procedures for arranging a background conference are similar to those for the press conference, although provisions do not have to be made for cameras. Information should be available for reporters to keep, including relevant statistics and newspaper and magazine clippings. The discussion should be concise and detailed, and some indication should be given of what is to come.

There is another aspect to dealing with television stations, although it has little to do with the news department, and is certainly not marked by the cordiality of the press conference. It involves making the television station adequately serve the public interest.

Under the Federal Communications Act of 1934, all television stations are required to operate "in the public interest." Although the term is not clearly defined, television stations must have licenses to operate, and these licenses are subject to renewal every three years. The Act specifies that the station must demonstrate that it is carrying out certain minimum provisions, and, if it is not, its license may be revoked.

Under the ruling, environmental and other groups can challenge stations for not devoting enough time to the problems that surround them, for presenting biased or fraudulent shows and news reports, and for denying equal time for editorial rebuttals. If environmental groups combine forces with other groups (such as civil rights organizations) and can demonstrate that the station has been negligent across a wide spectrum of issues, the chances for victory are increased.

The Federal Communications Commission (FCC) is not likely to revoke a license merely on limited or circumstantial evidence. The general renewal procedure is a quick, uncontroversial matter, and the challenge group will have to make a very strong case to win. In Jackson, Mississippi, a station, WLBT, was challenged by a citizen's coalition for the station's use of derogatory remarks in reference to minority groups. The FCC ruled in favor of the public interest group and revoked the license of the operating company. A "comparative hearing" will decide who the new licensee should be and until that decision is made it will be operated by a nonprofit group.

The procedure for challenging is difficult and future legislation may make it impossible, but it can pressure television stations to be more considerate of the public interest. For challenges, quantities of evidence must be accumulated, including tape-recordings of offensive shows. Then some group must be established which could demand the license and prove that it would be capable of running the station. Then the case must be won.

So far, no case has been won conclusively, but that is no reason not to try it. The publicity which a group would create and which the station would be subjected to is enormous, and may bring about better results than even winning the case would. It would also serve to remind all the other local stations that environmental and other activist groups "mean business" and must be reckoned with.

Although the newspaper page, the radio set and the television screen reach the eyes and ears of most Americans, they are not the only forms of communications—and may not even be the best. Grass roots issues are always very "people-oriented," that is, they thrive on or even depend upon personal contact and a feeling of true involvement. The mass media is effective at providing publicity, but not at instilling a feeling of "belonging."

To announce a meeting or a rally, the established media should not be ignored (if they are willing to provide such information), but less "official" methods should also be used. Signs should be placed in neighborhood shop windows if the owners are amenable, particularly such often frequented spots as markets, laundromats, pizza and sandwich shops, drugstores, hardware stores and bookstores. They should be clear and colorful but not so big as to interfere with window displays. If there is a community or university bulletin board, the use of it is highly recommended.

Flyers, leaflets or pamphlets can also be effective. They should be handed out during peak shopping hours in areas frequented by many persons, or left in a neat pile in places where they are likely to be seen. Sometimes newspaper stands provide good locations, and the leaflets should be clearly marked "free" or "take one," if that is the case.

If a local minister is sympathetic, an attempt should be made to get him to make an announcement for the group during the service. Other civic organizations can be tapped for free publicity, too, such as the P.T.A.

For an extended campaign, two effective devices are the button and the bumpersticker. Of course, these objects have been used for many years by hundreds of different groups pursuing different goals, and they must make up for lack of originality by being appealing to the eye. Their use presents basic philosophical dilemmas for the eco-activist, too, since they are potential polluters and they definitely waste materials that could be used for a better purpose. However, their use is often justified if the potential victory they help assure aids Nature more than the buttons or bumperstickers harm it. The environmentalist should also be aware of the possible contradictions posed by the automobile which carries the sign "Stop Air Pollution," or the discarded button which says "Don't Litter."

Ecology forces should not become too obsessed with the inconsistencies in our daily life since the whole fabric of American civilization rests on premises which go against the concept of "harmony with nature," but they should consider ways to minimize the contradictions. Despite the ecological harmfulness of most written communications, groups should recognize the different possibilities they have in publicizing their actions and their meetings. The printed word is the most effective way of stirring up general interest in a move-ment or an organization, and its effectiveness should not be passed up.

II tactics

Concern about the environment leads many individuals to take small, personal steps to bring their old life style into closer harmony with Nature. But after placing a brick in the toilet tank to save water, changing to white tissues to fight water pollution, and walking to work to clean up the air, they notice that conditions are not improving. This period of enlightenment dramatizes the need for social as well as individual action.

What general tactics are available to the individual who is ready to join with others to work for a cleaner environment?

building awareness

Social movements require a broad base of support to achieve their goals. Awareness of the need for change can be created by events such as assassinations, depressions, and wars. In non-crisis times, it may also be developed by effective communication of ideas.

Speaking is the simplest method of heightening public consciousness. Depending on circumstances, it can take the form of discussions, forums, debates, lectures or mass gatherings. Although a speaking engagement offers no guarantee of communication because it is a passive experience for the audience, the event can be stimulated by planting someone in the crowd who will ask the speaker controversial questions.

For large gatherings, "big name" personalities tend to attract people more than lesser-known experts. A careful combination of the two types of speakers will help ensure a large turnout and hopefully increase understanding. A question-and-answer period is often the key to a successful meeting. The audience is made to feel a part of the situation, and generally the true feelings and opinions of each speaker are brought out in areas which he may have avoided in a prepared talk. Involving outside speakers in informal discussions with interested individuals will help break down the mystique that can surround a national reputation. For most groups the biggest problem will be finding the money to pay travel and honorarium expenses. Massive recycling drives offer not only a possible source of funds, but can also advertise the appearance.

Speeches can be given almost anywhere and any time. College and high school students generally prefer afternoons; housewives and working people are usually less busy in the evening. In the spring and summer an outdoor rally will often lure many otherwise-unconcerned community members to see what is going on; downtown parks at lunchtime usually attract businessmen eager for a change from their office-work. Generally outdoor speeches do not require permits, although local ordinances should be checked. (New York City, for instance, has an old rule requiring speakers to display an American flag near them.) In most cases, incitement that might set off violence should be carefully avoided, because it can be grounds for arrest.

Variations of the one-speaker program are possible. Panel discussions can be organized with proponents of opposing positions. These sessions can be electric and if anything coherent is expected from the panelists, they should present their position in a designated amount of time at the beginning of the session. Other possibilities for program presentations are films, tapes, slides, and speeches delivered via telephone.

While speeches are good for reaching large crowds of people, workshops with a small number may prove to be the key to successfully stimulating awareness of issues. With a group of about 10, participants can talk personally about how they feel concerning the topic. The workshop or seminar format works best with the group seated in a circle. Resource people who can add to the discussion, not leaders, are required in this situation. One-session workshops can be useful, but meeting on a weekly basis over a period of time could create a hard core of individuals who can form a nucleus for later action. If action is considered, it is important to discuss with each member what they would be willing to do.

Teach-ins can also be used to inform people about environmental issues. The first ones were conducted to stimulate discussion about the Vietnam War. Originally, they consisted of college professors pondering a problem before an audience, but they have evolved into a far more diversified format. As the Environmental Teach-In on April 22, 1970, demonstrated, the limits of the human imagination are now the only boundaries for definition of a "teach-in." Activities scheduled during the day included earth-rock concerts, auto burials, lectures, community pollution inventories, dump-ins of non-returnable containers, street closings, television programs, clean-ups, and many others.

The teach-in starts to bridge the gap between rhetoric and

environmental action. Many effectively used guerrilla theater, a short skit or social confrontation which uses satire to dramatize certain societal follies, to prick consciences about problems. A group in Miami, Florida, organized a massive "Dead Orange" parade on Earth Day to comment satirically on the city's yearly Orange Parade. They included hand-pulled non-polluting floats constructed from trash, dead oranges and other items which illustrated what the Orange Parade might look like in the future if destruction of the environment continues. They capped the ceremony with the crowning of a "Dead Orange Queen."

Waste, overconsumption, profit, affluence and other social abuses are difficult concepts to confront, and guerrilla theater is often the only way groups can challenge these sacred subjects. To be effective it must be understood as a method of communicating an idea. It is important that the performance not be so obscure or distant that the target audience questions the sanity of the performers rather than understands the point.

Because imaginative skits are very visual, they offer photographers an opportunity to shoot unusual pictures. Even a conservative editor or program director can rarely resist the public appeal of scenes like a baby wearing a gas mask, an automobile being buried, or mourners carrying a coffin filled with broken appliances. Such pictures convey powerful visual impacts to the millions of people who were not present at the demonstration.

Since television can reach thousands of people at the same time, anti-pollution forces should capture air time at every opportunity. Some stations will permit citizens to rebut staff editorials or provide material for a local interview show.

But, for the most part, corporations continue to pour out their propaganda in advertisements, while environment groups have to beg for time. One tactic is still open: citizens may challenge a station for equal time to answer advertising by polluting companies. Three public interest groups—Friends of the Earth, the Environmental Protection Administration of New York City, and Citizens for Clean Air—asked the Federal Communications Commission (FCC) for the same amount of time that petroleum and automobile companies buy to run anti-air pollution spots. The FCC ruled that the request did not meet the requirements of the

"Fairness Doctrine" which gave equal time to anti-cigarette spots. But in a dissenting opinion, one of the FCC commissioners, Nicholas Johnson, argued strongly that the petitioners should have the right to "present an alternative to the siren call of the oil and auto establishments." He believes that television must show not just the glamour depicted in the auto commercials, but also the "warts, the wrinkles" because "they, too, are an important part of reality." One day his position may be accepted.

But TV stations themselves do not have an inalienable right to their licenses. They must operate their channel in the public interest. It is possible that written complaints sent to both the television station and the FCC will persuade the broadcast manager to grant a challenger time to present his view rather than risk the chance that the FCC will question the station's license at renewal time.

Educational television stations are another possible outlet. Some stations have used films and programs produced by local environmental organizations themselves or with the aid of university film-making groups. Once broadcast, educational television programming can also be used as a source of instructional material for classrooms.

Curricular changes or additions should not be overlooked when considering the stimulation of environmental awareness. Material for classroom teaching of ecology and related subjects is becoming readily available through educational supply channels.

High school classes and community organizations are constantly looking for speakers, and environmental groups should provide them. A speakers' bureau should be established with a central phone number for program chairmen. Post cards or phone calls to other groups can announce the service.

When attempting to create awareness about an issue in a community, it is important to reach as many people as possible. Activities should be planned which stimulate discussion about the topic in all social circles. Bumperstickers, buttons, and posters should all be considered, although some may object to the outdoor advertising approach because of its visual pollution.

It is important to start people talking to each other about the problems facing the environment. One tactic which some groups have used to achieve this is the mock vote. Tables can be set up outside polling places on regular election days and public referendums can be conducted on issues which otherwise might not be subject to a vote. Citizens could cast their ballots on highway, power plant, industrial and other construction projects. The result of this vote might give a group strong ammunition to argue that the people are not in favor of a proposed project.

Another activity which has been used at exhibits to stimulate thinking about pollution control is simulation. Games can be created which develop real-life situations. They are easily constructed with imagination and readily available materials. Names to fill in squares, drawn on old sheets, can be those of local villains, good guys, and pollution control agencies. Dice or numbers in a hat can be used to determine how many squares an individual who steps on the board should move. A condensed version of a typical board game might look like:

Regardless of what activities are used to mold public opinion about an issue, it must be remembered that the job will be easier if people can relate to the topic. In sparsely populated states it is difficult for anyone to understand the urgency of population control; yet, if it is a mining area, ecological damage resulting from strip mining may be easily understood. In a similar manner urbanites may have a hard time relating to the hazards associated with a massive program of fire ant eradication, but they can relate to the evils of the auto.

political involvement: lobbying

Contrary to high school civics and typical Washington reports, not all of the world problems can be solved through the "political process." Part of the problem is just that political process. Lobbying for environmental issues will not bring about the new ecological man, or instill within the population

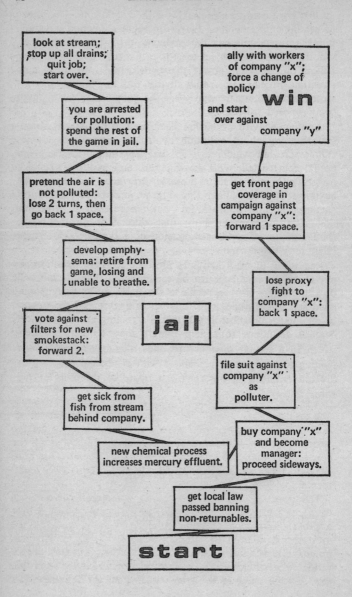

a new consciousness, but taking into account all of its built-in limitations, this tactic can achieve certain successes.

One might wonder, why bother with the letter to the Senator or Congressman, or why bother with legislation at all? There are some positive aspects that make it worthwhile. Citizens' lobbies can activate the grass roots, give direction to local group activities and provide a focal point for publicity and action on a particular issue. Legislation dealing with environmental issues can demonstrate a societal interest and commitment to a better quality of life; therefore educating citizens to the need for new directions and priorities. Environmental legislation (even if it fails to pass) can act as an educational tool for legislators and citizens. The debate, media exposure, and local agitation in favor of such action can create significant forces for behavioral change in individuals and corporations.

There are many environmental issues, particularly those that involve enforcing existing technical possibilities, which can be directly and positively affected by legislation. For instance, the technology exists to produce a clean automobile engine, but certain corporations have made a conscious decision not to employ that technology. Congress has now enacted a law (Clean Air Act of 1970) which will require a 90 percent reduction in automobile emissions by 1976, thereby forcing Detroit to make use of the know-how available to reduce air pollution.

Citizens' lobbying also creates a "righteous opposition" which reveals the operation methods of the other side—special influence, high powered lobbying, etc. Publicity exposed and diluted the impact of the appearance in the Senators' offices of top automobile executives who were trying to gut the strong clean air act that had just been reported out of the Senate Subcommittee on Air and Water Pollution. This public watchdog function can be the most vital service environmental lobbyists perform.

Demonstrating massive public interest support for an issue to counter private or special interest lobbying is not a new approach. However, environmental lobbying is certainly the most recent attempt to create a citizens' lobby. Tough anti-pollution legislation is generally opposed by powerful corporations and often by the government bureaucracy, and this can only be checked by demonstrating to the legislator that his political life (his re-election) may hang in the balance of his decision on support. Such a demonstration can only come when his constituency translates their concern about an issue into action. The activity of citizens at the local level will educate the legislator to the depth and extent of public interest.

There are additional activities which can educate a legislator. A knowledgeable group in any field can sway opinions through presentation of intellectual or scientific findings. While this may have some influence over a politician, nothing speaks like people power.

The environmentally concerned group's influence can be amplified by the creation of coalitions with others. Some conservation organizations have been waging the fight for years for more wilderness areas, national parks, proper land use, fish and wildlife protection, timber supply and soil conservation. It is only within the last year that environmental issues have come to be identified in the public mind with urban concerns. Debate has increased on such issues as air pollution, municipal sewage disposal, industrial plant siting, highways, and solid wastes. Concern is also being generated on the systematic effects of chemicals such as pesticides, herbicides, food additives, and industrial materials. With the increase of these concerns has come the possibility of new broad based coalitions. Labor unions, consumer groups, urban organizations, minority groups, suburban housewives, and student activists are banding together to work toward goals in which they feel a common interest.

If this is the case, one might wonder why environmental legislation has not had clear sailing through Congress and state legislatures. The SST came within 14 votes of being beaten in the House of Representatives in 1970, but it won. The Highway Trust Fund still exists. The rape of the land goes on. Part of the reason lies in the diffuse nature of people power: it is not really organized yet. Citizens must not only be involved, but involved at the right time, during the crucial legislative maneuvers. Organizers who are experienced are in short supply; funds to conduct the necessary lobbying, media and local campaigns are not easy to find; and enough people are not educated about how to act within the present political process.

If lobbying efforts by citizen groups are to be successful, they must be backed by people who know the legislative process. Most of the action does not take place on the floors of the House and Senate, but in committee. Every bill goes to a committee which can rewrite it to make it tougher or weaker. Unless there is strong opposition on the floor, every bill reported out favorably by a committee will pass. A bill disliked by the committee can never be reported out.

It is important for citizens who want to make their position felt to know what committees their Congressmen and Senators are on. Environmental issues connected with these committees should be the top priority for local groups. Bills of interest in other committees can also be influenced by writing your representative and asking him to testify in person at the hearings on it. Individuals and representatives from local civic groups should also testify.

The following is a partial list of committee jurisdictions of the 91st Congress prepared by Friends of the Earth:

Joint Atomic Energy Committee:	Nuclear power plants, nuclear testing.
House and Senate Agriculture Committees: (Subcommittee on Forests.)	Forestry, soil conservation, pesticides.
House and Senate Interior Committees: (Subcommittees on National Parks and Recreation, Indian Affairs, Public Lands, Irrigation and Reclamation.)	Parks, wilderness areas, dams, grazing, mining on public lands.
House Merchant Marine and Fisheries Committee: (Subcommittee on Fisheries and Wildlife Conservation.)	Protection of estuaries, fish and wildlife.
House Govermnment (Operations Committee: Subcommittee on Conservation.)	Investigations, structural changes.
House and Senate Public Works Committees: (Subcommittees on Roads, Rivers and Har-	Highways, dams, dredging, destruction, air pollution, railroads.

bors, Flood Control.) (The Senate Committee considers air pollution legislation, the House Committee does not.)

House and Senate Appropriations Committees: (Subcommittees on Interior, Public Works, Transportation.)	Appropriation of federal funds.
Senate Finance Committee:	Tax incentives (not to pollute, not to have babies, etc.).
House Ways and Means Committee:	Same as above.
House Interstate and Foreign Commerce Committee: (Subcommittee on Public Health and Welfare.)	Sometimes air pollution, population.
Senate Commerce Committee: (Subcommittee on Energy, Natural Resources and the Environment.)	Estuaries, wildlife, transportation.
Senate Labor and Public Welfare Committee: (Subcommittee on Health.)	Population.

It is important for constituents to know how a legislator can support a bill. Trading favors is the most effective way, but that is invisible. There are other more public ways. If it is his own bill, he can send a letter to all of his colleagues asking them for co-sponsorship; he can testify before the committee that receives his bill; and he can try to get press coverage about the bill. During floor debate, speeches in the *Congressional Record* can be helpful. If it is someone else's bill, he can co-sponsor it, testify before or write to the committee holding hearings on it, and make a floor speech in support of it.

Groups should also remember that any activity about a piece of legislation in a representative's home district may be noticed. Articles and editorials in local papers are important. Publication of the roll call vote on an issue will publicly reveal his position and could be a lever in the future.

One tool the citizen can use to register his feelings with a legislator is the personal letter or telegram. The best time to write is just before a decision has to be made by him either in committee or on the floor. During this period he will ask his staff what side of the debate his mail favors. Separate letters are much better than one with several signatures. The following points are good tips for letter writing:

1. Write a short, concise letter in your own words, on your own stationery (never use form letters). Write as a private citizen. Use official organization letters to let your representative know a group position.

2. Discuss only one subject per letter. Address remarks to a particular bill (giving bill number or title) and state the subject and your position in the first paragraph. Ask him for his opinion (whether *for* or *against*).

3. Educate him to your point of view, using local examples of the problem or explaining why the community will benefit. Ask that your views be presented to the committee handling the legislation.

4. Remember the most effective letters are those that appear while a bill is being considered by a committee (called a mark-up session), or when the bill comes up for action before the full body for a vote.

5. Most letters are not seen by the Congressmen themselves, but by their legislative assistant handling your area of legislative interest. However, the content, tone and the number of letters are passed on to the Congressman at the end of the day.

6. Use common sense, i.e., being rude, offensive, threatening will bring the same reaction as if you used that tactic on your next door neighbor.

7. Use positive reinforcement and congratulate him when he has done good things, voted right, publicized an issue, or sponsored a bill. You can always tell when this happens by publicity in the local newspaper.

8. Using the phrase "as a citizen and a taxpayer" is not a good tactic. He assumes that you are not an alien and ALL of us (including him) pay taxes.

9. Telegrams called Public Opinion Messages (POM) can be sent to any elected official day or night for $1.00 (a limit of 15 words per message body, address not included). They can be billed to your telephone number by calling Western Union. A barrage of telegrams can be an extremely effective tool and they are always considered more important than letters.

Information on specific legislation is most easily available through your Congressman's office. His staff will usually have ready access to most relevant information, and it is there to serve his constituents as well as him. Letters to Representatives and Senators of other states or districts are rarely effective, for they are routinely forwarded to that district's Congressman.

For groups truly interested in the day-to-day proceedings of the Senate and the House, the *Congressional Record* is an invaluable document. It provides, perhaps, a bit too much reading material for the single citizen who wishes to keep informed, but it is extremely useful for reference material in a group's library. The subscription fee is $3.75 a month or $45 a year, payable by check (in advance) to the Superintendent of Documents, Government Printing Office, Washington, D. C. 20402.

Congressmen are free to include anything they wish in their floor discussion, and it is reprinted in the *Congressional Record*. This has often included long articles from national magazines and even copies of speeches that have been given around the country. Thus, environmentalists who come across material which they feel is relevant should send it to Congressmen who are interested in the field and who might include it in the *Record*.

For more detailed information, each committee prints its own Legislative Calendar which lists virtually everything that has happened or that is scheduled to happen to a bill in the committee's jurisdiction. This is available free from the relevant committee.

The Congressional Directory, a hard-cover book issued yearly by the government, contains a wealth of information on literally every aspect of Washington's political scene. It is available for $4 from the Government Printing Office.

One of the best sources of legislative and general background information is the weekly *National Journal,* published by the Center for Political Research, 1730 M Street, N. W., Washington, D. C. Most Washington observers consider it a valuable commentary on a wide range of subjects; unfortunately a subscription costs $450 a year ($200 for tax-exempt organizations). However, it is available at most large libraries, and is worth referring to.

For the less affluent, the League of Women Voters also publishes some valuable materials concerning the workings of Congress. The pamphlet "You and Your National Government," (#273, 1962) costs 25 cents and contains a section detailing how a bill becomes a law. Another good one is "When You Write to Washington," (#349, 1969) which costs 50 cents. Both are available from League of Women Voters, 1730 M Street, N. W., Washington, D. C. 20036.

Another excellent pamphlet which helps the citizen find his way through the intricacies of Congress is the "1971-1972 Guide to the 92nd Congress," prepared and distributed without charge by the United Auto Workers. The 48-page booklet is available from the UAW Washington Office, 1126 16th Street, N. W., Washington, D. C. 20036.

Once the citizen has assimilated enough information to understand a situation or an upcoming piece of legislation, he will want to translate this knowledge into action. One approach is to come to Washington and register your feelings with your Senators and Representatives. For the vast majority of Americans, however, this is an unfeasible alternative because of the time and costs involved. Their only recourse, in that case, is to let groups and persons in and around Washington do their lobbying for them.

There are at present four environmental lobbying groups in Washington which are national in focus and are legally incorporated to spend a substantial portion of their time engaging in political action. Because of the structure of present regulations, this means they are not tax exempt, and depend upon public contributions for support. The groups are:

> Environmental Action
> Room 731
> 1346 Connecticut Ave., N. W.
> Washington, D. C. 20036

Friends of the Earth
917 15th Street, N. W.
Washington, D. C. 20005

Zero Population Growth
917 15th Street, N. W.
Washington, D. C. 20005

Citizens Committee on Natural Resources
712 DuPont Circle Building
1346 Connecticut Avenue, N. W.
Washington, D. C. 20036

There are, as well, a number of other major conservation organizations that keep up-to-date on legislation concerning the environment. They are tax exempt and not permitted to lobby for bills, but they do participate in Congressional testimony and they keep their members informed on the status of pending legislation. Among these groups, the most active are:

The Wilderness Society
729 15th Street, N. W.
Washington, D. C. 20005

The Sierra Club
235 Massachusetts Avenue, N. E.
Washington, D. C. 20002

All of the above groups publish newsletters.

It should be remembered that lobbying is a two-way street. Lobbyists depend on information, for the most part, to persuade congressmen. Any information which a citizen thinks might be useful to one of the groups that is working to preserve the environment, should immediately be sent to Washington. Even a small newspaper clipping might add enough ammunition to a lobbyist's argument to change a few votes.

In return, groups which lobby generally have access to exactly this wealth of information which has come in from around the country. Citizens who are in the midst of a local pollution battle should feel free to turn to the national organizations for written material and help. Usually there will have been some precedent elsewhere which a national lobbying organization may be able to cite quickly.

political involvement: elections

Most successful politicians have two guiding principles: to gain power where they don't have it, and to retain power after they get it. To get power they must make realistic, credible promises and build up a base of support. To maintain power, they must keep their constituents satisfied. When the environmentalist moves into the realm of political action, these are the rules he must understand.

To the politically naive, idealistic citizen who is primarily concerned with living a life free from environmental abuse, the rules of the game seem harsh, unfair and irrelevant. Actually, this is far from the case. Legislators and other elected officials need their constituents more than their constituents need them. As soon as the citizen realizes that it is he who rules his representative, and not vice versa, the battle for good government is half won.

Since the vast majority of the population is politically apathetic, the small but well disciplined environmental group can wield power disproportionately greater than its size would indicate. Phone calls, telegrams and letters indicate citizen interest—and to maintain his power, this is not something a politician can ignore. The more the politician is conscious of citizen awareness, the more accountable he is and the less hypocritically he is able to vote.

To write letters, one must be informed. And keeping informed is a year-round activity. It means keeping track of a legislator's voting record, his committee assignments, the bills he sponsors and the floor fights he leads for (and against) legislation.

Keeping track of voting records can be a tiresome task. Local newspapers, even the best of them, report the details of a vote only when it is an important issue. At other times, when the media spotlight is off, the legislator should be watched even more closely. The only way this can be done, on a day-to-day basis nationally, is with the *Congressional Record*, the daily journal of the activities of the House and Senate. The *Record* is difficult reading filled with the complexities of parliamentary procedure and congressional trivia, but it is an accurate record of everything that goes on. Reading it keeps one informed about the introduction of bills, committee reports and roll call votes.

The hard work of keeping up with day-to-day happenings in Washington (and the state capitol) is obviously valuable throughout the whole year since an effective eco group must be able to react quickly. It really bears fruit, however, in the months immediately preceding election time. That is when the real pressure begins—to support those who voted well on environmental issues, and to oust those who didn't. For groups who are unable to "keep up" with the issues all year long, or who find holes in their research, there are still options available. At least five national research organizations have Congressional information available for those who request it. These are:

The League of Women Voters
1730 M Street, N. W.
Washington, D. C.
(or a local branch)

Americans for Democratic Action
1424 16th Street, N. W.
Washington, D. C.

Citizens' Research Foundation
245 Nassau Street
Princeton, New Jersey

American Friends Service Committee
on National Legislation
245 2nd Street, N. E.
Washington, D. C.

League of Conservation Voters
917 15th Street, N. W.
Washington, D. C.

Once the material is assimilated, it is time to use it profitably to influence voters. And it is in this realm that groups have to define their goals and methods carefully, to avoid surprises from the Internal Revenue Service.

A group which openly engages in partisan political activity is not granted a tax-exempt status—which means that contributors may not deduct contributions. This generally makes a great deal of difference to the organization's money-raising capabilities.

To qualify for a tax-exempt status, an organization must be rated non-profit and educational. This does not exclude politically oriented groups, but it does prohibit them from engaging in partisan activity. Under the guidelines of education, however, a great deal of pseudo-political work can still be done. Questionnaire surveys are perfectly legitimate, as in the publication of research into voting records. The Environmental Council of Arizona, in Tucson, for instance, released a detailed summary of the major Arizona candidates' environmental positions in October, 1970. Among the questions asked were: Should we emphasize environmental over economic factors in the use of federal land? How can we improve federal laws to better control air pollution? Are you in favor of diverting money from the Federal Highway Trust to mass transit?

Tax-exempt organizations should refrain from making positive (or negative) endorsements during a campaign, and should not make their own resources (money or equipment) available to one candidate.

If a particular situation renders the tax-exempt status too great a burden, groups have another option. A new, temporary coalition can be formed for specific political purposes. This would not be tax-exempt and would have to raise its own money and keep separate books, but its operation would last only until the election and then fold. This alternative is not difficult, it is flexible and legal. If any questions arise, however, consult a lawyer.

After the information is gathered and the group's structure is determined, it is time to form a base for political power with which to defeat a foe. All his "wrong" votes should be publicized throughout the district or state. Coalitions with other concerned groups should be formed, and a bad environmental record should be clearly linked with other issues, such as defense spending, civil rights and domestic priorities. It is significant to note that a good portion of those politicians who have not gotten the environmental message have also failed to face up to the wider range of pressing social concerns.

For the hard-hitting ecology group, a candidate's campaign finance provides a juicy area for investigation. Theoretically, all national candidates for public office must disclose campaign contributions of $100 or more. Unfortunately, there are so many loopholes in the current legislation covering the field, that it is virtually impossible for outsiders to find anything at all helpful or revealing. Environmentalists should press for more stringent controls on what must be disclosed, and anything financial that is discovered should be played up to the hilt, as it is certain to be merely the tip of the iceberg.

As a primary or an election approaches, one of the most effective tools to focus public attention on environmental issues is the endorsement. In 1970, Environmental Action had good success with its "dirty dozen" campaign which named 12 environmental "bad guys" and publicly called for their defeat in the Congressional elections. They were carefully chosen on their total record on the environment, including the Vietnam war, civil rights, conservation, and domestic priorities. Their vulnerability in their districts was also considered. Their opposition and local groups used this negative endorsement to good advantage. Seven of the incumbent congressmen were defeated.

While negative endorsement tends to make more headlines, positive endorsement can also be effective. Marion Edey of the League of Conservation Voters, for instance, spent many weeks in the summer of 1970 putting together a comprehensive list of the voting patterns of each representative, weighing each vote as to its importance and noting absences and other relevant factors. The League then endorsed (and financially supported) several congressmen and also aided the campaigns of a few promising challengers.

There are other areas in which environmental groups can help to elect good candidates. Environmental data, background and issue analysis can be provided for speech material and education of the candidate. Fund raising, either on a personal basis or in the form of parties or movies, can be pursued in various neighborhoods. Especially during primaries, this could prove crucial because of the shortage of money.

Volunteers should be recruited to canvass and to man telephones and headquarters. Local appearances of the candidate should be arranged so that he receives as much exposure as possible.

Finally, of course, environmentalists must help to get the vote out on Election Day. It is upon people who want a clean environment that an environmental challenger depends. His opponent will very likely have more money and more industrial support—and this can only be overcome by concerted action on the part of the citizen.

petitioning

A good introduction for people who want to do something about environmental conditions is the solicitation of signatures for a petition. It is also a good excuse for starting dialogue on a person-to-person level.

In the state of Washington, citizens collected a record number of 189,524 signatures to place a bill on the ballot banning the sale of non-returnable drink containers. It lost in the November, 1970, elections, but publicity surrounding the drive stimulated discussion of the subject.

While few petitions have any legal backing, anti-war forces in Massachusetts developed a unique tactic to pressure the U. S. Supreme Court to hear a case. It involved the constitutionality of a state statute which forbids any Massachusetts citizen from serving in a foreign war which has not been formally declared by Congress. The signatures were made part of an "Amicus Curiae" (friend of the court) brief asking the Court to hear the case. Because the Court did not hear it, the legality of the petition effort was never judged.

Petitions may be submitted to anybody, but they will have a greater impact on officials who are closer to the signatories than President Nixon. For petitions which have no legal standing, some impact on policy decisions can come from the publicity generated by the drive. Attempts should be made to get the press to cover kick-off announcements of petition efforts. After the signatures are collected, they should be presented personally, if possible, to a government official with representatives of the press present. If the press does not show up, dress a friend like a reporter and have him photograph the presentation. After a few photographic flashes, the recipient will at least know that somebody has it recorded.

Before a group decides to solicit signatures on paper for a cause, certain considerations are important. If the signatures are needed to call a referendum, do the signers have to be registered voters? Are there any state or local regulations controlling petitions?

Petition statements should be as short as possible and printed on each page. They should also be composed of words and phrases readily understood by the person who will be asked to sign. Blue collar workers use a different vocabulary from college faculty members.

Research done by G. A. Miller at Harvard and P. C. Wason at University College, London, offers some guidelines for drafting statements. They discovered that the time required to respond correctly to a sentence varies directly with the grammatical structure employed. Affirmative, active and declarative sentences are most readily understood. Qualifiers such as "unless," "providing," and "except" are troublesome to the reader. Also, phrases using "never" and "always" are hard to understand. They found negative sentences take longer to understand than positive ones.

Before petitioners hit the streets looking for signatures, they should understand the issues involved in the campaign. Discussions should be held to clarify any questions that they might be asked by people on the street. When the signed petitions are returned to the coordinator, an effort should be made to find out how the public reacted to the statement.

law suits

Pollution battles represent many different conflicts between public and private interests. Some may be resolved by legislative or private initiative, but others will be decided in the courts. Environmental law suits are expensive for citizens to pursue, require extensive preparatory research and frequently take years. Once a suit goes to court, it is essentially a legal battle between lawyers. It will be of only limited educational value to the public. For these reasons suits should never be the first or only concern of citizen environmental groups.

Some court decisions are only temporary; a later appeal can rescind the citizens' victory and the pollution, momentarily abated, will continue. Legal battles may be court victories, but, nevertheless, environmental failures—money damages will be awarded but the pollution unabated. Once in a while, a successful suit might succeed in setting a new precedent in environmental law; for that it is to be commended. But the average environmental law suit is a long, slow struggle toward what must be considered a minor victory in the overall battle to combat polluters and to protect our natural resources. Citizens' efforts, then, should really be directed to all those steps preceding the law suit where public opinion and public action may be strong enough to convince a polluter to change his attitude and methods before a lawsuit becomes necessary.

This is where a lawyer can serve his most important purpose. Tony Roisman, a partner with the Washington, D. C. law firm Berlin, Roisman & Kessler which has handled numerous environmental suits, sees the lawyer as a strategist, a doctor of social problems. In this role, he serves as an important preliminary advisor to an environmentally concerned group, suggesting what people to contact, in what order, at what time. Then, if it does become necessary to go to court, the citizens' case will have been prepared correctly.

The cost to the plaintiff or persons bringing suit in an environmental law case is often prohibitive. If the defendant, the person or group being sued, is a corporation or government official, and most likely it will be, defense funds will be virtually limitless. Furthermore, corporations can write their legal fees off of taxes as business expenses. Citizens, on the other hand, must be ready and able to put up thousands of dollars—or more—for several years before the initial battle is completed. And, unless they can prove their fees to be business expenses, which is unlikely, the tax write-off is unavailable to them. Occasionally, when a suit is successful, the court directs the defendants to assume the court costs of the plaintiffs, but the sum to be paid is usually only a fraction of the total costs involved in maintaining the suit. Furthermore, after the initial suit there may be an appeal and several new legal battles to finance.

Legal costs, then, are one very important reason for citizens to act as a group rather than as individuals in environmental work. If a suit is large enough for several private attorneys, the expenses can run well over $100,000. By comparison, the cost of legal advice is minimal, the lowest fee permitted by most bar associations being $30 an hour. Considering that ten hours of advice over several months may provide an acceptable solution for $300, this price is more than reasonable.

A good lawyer is not going to try to push a case into court. He wants to find the easiest and most permanent solution just as much as his clients. For this reason, he may suggest a constant lobbying effort as the most effective means to influence the officials in power, many of whom won't have the time or interest to attend a courtroom battle. Or he may suggest a massive picketing effort which can inform large numbers of other citizens of the problem at the same time that it hopefully embarrasses the polluters or environmental offenders.

The citizen's first move then is to find a good lawyer. One of the best known environmental law groups is the Environmental Defense Fund (EDF), 1910 N St., N. W., Washington, D. C. 20036, and 162 Old Town Rd., East Setauket, New York 11733. (Another office is expected to be opened in San Francisco shortly.) Started as a science group and supported by national membership and small foundation grants, EDF handles, without charge, environmental cases which they feel are of scientific importance. Representative cases in which they have been involved include suits against DDT, nerve gas, and a barge canal planned to cross the state of Florida. EDF also offers legal assistance for citizen suits if there is a worthwhile and substantial case. It should be noted that according to new Internal Revenue Service guidelines for public interest law firms, they can only handle those cases involving broad public interest—cases of such large size, urgency, or very general nature that they would not normally be handled by private attorneys. A suit to ban DDT, for instance, could not be successfully argued by a single irritated citizen. However, EDF feels strongly that unless a citizen group collects some money, they are not sufficiently interested in a law suit or fully aware of its cost in time and effort. Most of their cases are handled in conjunction with private firms that are being paid some money.

The National Environmental Law Society, Stanford Law School, Stanford, California 94305, offers the public a list of over 25 affiliate environmental law societies across the country. Although these societies are joined together under a board of directors, they are organized and run separately by concerned law students on different college campuses. Consequently, actions and advice will vary. Stanford's Environmental Law Society directs most of its efforts toward research projects rather than handling citizen suits and they will probably direct citizens to the California Bar Association to find a qualified environmental lawyer. The Environmental Law Society at George Washington University in Washington, D. C., operates a referral service for lawyers interested in public interest work. It also does legal research for specific cases, such as one suit to restrain the Federal Power Commission from constructing a pump storage plant in Marble Valley, Virginia. If contacted, the nearest Environmental Law Society will offer either legal assistance or referral.

If an Environmental Law Society is not nearby, the dean of the nearest law school or its professors will probably know several practicing lawyers who will handle legitimate environmental grievances.

In the northeast, the Conservation Law Society in Boston

and the Natural Resources Council in New York and Washington, D. C., know of good lawyers.

Any competent lawyer can handle an environmental lawsuit, provided there is a substantial legal case. If a lawyer is interested in helping but feels unqualified in the environmental field, he may be interested in subscribing to the *Environmental Law Reporter,* a cumulative loose-leaf monthly on problems in environmental law, published by the Environmental Law Institute, 1346 Connecticut Ave., N. W., Washington, D. C. 20036. They have also published an *Environmental Law Digest* which lists recent environmental law cases with a description of the problem, the plaintiff's suit, and the court's decision. While the case information might be useful and interesting to the citizen, the service is primarily designed to aid the lawyer and most information is presented in technical, legal terms. It is an excellent source for attorneys.

It is important to remember that each lawyer's approach will be different. One attorney may be best qualified to handle a strict legal argument; another might be better for taking imaginative steps in an unusual case. A word of advice is offered by Roisman: "Don't give up after you have only tried one lawyer. If you think something's wrong, chances are there's a legal answer." Whichever lawyer takes the case, he will be greatly aided if citizens provide him in the beginning with a simple, non-biased explanation of the problem, not the answer. A short, clearly written description of what the citizens are objecting to, without the added opinions of outside professionals or other consultants, can go a long way in clearing up any confusion, misinformation, or missing facts before advice is offered and tactics planned.

After all other tactics fail and it becomes necessary to begin a law suit, several qualifications must be met and important procedural decisions made. It is important for citizens to understand which legal avenues are open to them and the limitations of lawsuits. The following will explain, in laymen's terms, many of the legal questions with which citizens will be faced.*

---

* We are grateful to Professor Arnold Reitze of the George Washington University Law School for his help in collecting and explaining the legal information in this section.

Selecting the proper court is the first step, and this is probably one of the most difficult things to understand. Put very simply, the problem is to decide whether or not a suit is qualified to go to a federal rather than a state court. While it is usually no problem to find a state court that can legally hear your case, numerous legal technicalities have been established to minimize the number of federal law suits brought each year. And unless precise qualifications are met, a case can be thrown out of the federal court, regardless of the number or importance of the citizens' injuries. Therefore, the citizens' lawyer must be careful to present enough evidence justifying why the federal court should be legally permitted to handle the case; otherwise, it is best to take the suit to a state court.

When a government administrative agency, state or federal, is responsible for the citizens' injuries, the right to appeal the agency's actions is usually provided in the rules governing that agency or in administrative procedure acts. For federal agencies, section 10 of the Administrative Procedure Act normally provides for judicial review. The best policy is to review the regulations governing the specific agency at fault to see what rights citizens have to bring a law suit against it. It will usually be easier to sue local governments or specific districts than the state. It is also easier to sue for commission of an act rather than omission. For example, a government is more likely to be held responsible for damages caused by the spraying of harmful pesticides than it is for damages caused by not having a spraying program.

Once a law suit has been filed in the proper court, plaintiffs must have proper "standing" in order that the case can be prosecuted. In other words, they must be judged to be the correct parties to bring the suit having directly or indirectly received a legal injury. In state courts, standing, like jurisdiction, is rarely a problem. It has only been contested a few times, and most of the decisions broadly interpreted the required legal injury to find proper standing.

In federal courts, standing is tricky and often has to be defended. For a long time, definite economic injury had to be proved to comply with standing requirements. Then, in December, 1965, the United States Court of Appeals found the Scenic Hudson Preservation Conference to have proper standing in their suit against the Federal Power Commission

(FPC). In this case, an unincorporated association of conservation organizations challenged the FPC's grant of a license to Consolidated Edison Company of New York to build a pumped storage hydroelectric project on the Hudson River at Storm King Mountain. The Court found that:

> . . . those who by their activities and conduct have exhibited a special interest in such areas (aesthetics, conservation, and recreation), must be held to be included in the class of "aggrieved" parties . . .

But two things made this case easier than most. First, the public has always had more rights to intervene in licensing cases than in cases involving other government activities. Secondly, the plaintiffs could refer to a specific law guarding their rights, namely, the Federal Water Power Act, which states that public use of the land to be developed must be considered.

Several other cases have established that in order for proper standing to exist, there must be some injury, economic or otherwise; a case or controversy must be evident; and the interest sought to be protected must arguably be within those interests normally protected by a statute or constitutional right. Intelligent application of these qualifications should make it easy for almost anyone to comply.

However, care must be taken. In June, 1969, the Sierra Club filed a suit in the United States District Court against Walter Hickel, then Secretary of Interior, and Clifford Hardin, Secretary of Agriculture, for injunctive relief restraining the Forest Service from issuing special use permits for construction and operation of a private ski resort on 13,000 acres of Mineral King National Forest land in California. The plaintiffs had strong, well detailed arguments showing that the Forest Service had not had a required public hearing, had granted permits in excess of their jurisdiction, and had acted in violation of the Protection of National Forests Act by proposing a use which would destroy Mineral King as a National Game Refuge. Temporary injunction was granted on June 23, 1969. But on September 16, 1970, a ninth circuit Court of Appeals held that the Sierra Club had failed to show sufficient evidence that it had been "aggrieved" or "adversely affected" within the meaning of the rules of standing.

As Professor Arnold Reitze of George Washington University Law School points out: "The case makes it important to include as plaintiffs a local organization of residents of the area affected by administrative action."

Even to achieve standing may not be sufficient. After the Scenic Hudson case, the FPC was told to reconsider their original plans, the result being that on August 19, 1970, the FPC ruled against Scenic Hudson. The case continues, and the cost to the conservationists is now astronomical. Meanwhile, the construction delay has caused Consolidated Edison to expand fossil fuel plants in New York creating more air pollution for New York City. Standing, therefore, is only part of the total legal strategy necessary to achieve an environmental goal.

In public interest as opposed to private law suits, a group of citizens can legally represent the rest of the public, and there are several classifications under which these groups may receive legitimate standing. The first is a taxpayers' suit. In most state courts, taxpaying citizens have the right to seek an injunction prohibiting the spending of public money. Often, money need not even be specifically involved in the case. In one suit in Middlesex County, Massachusetts, in 1960, the court ruled that the taxpayers had legal standing to demand a *writ of mandamus,* a court order directing the defendant to act, in this case forcing public officials to protect the shores and woodlands of Walden Pond.

Another possible action is to file a class action suit where a few class members can legally defend a right belonging to the entire class. It must be possible to specify who is in the class being represented, such as the landowners around a lake or workers in one factory, and it must be understood that the interests of the plaintiffs are in no way contradictory with the interests of the entire class. One variation of the class action suit is a shareholders' suit against a corporation; shareholders are likely to have rights to challenge corporate practices that ordinary members of the public do not have. Unfortunately, corporations will be at a considerable advantage in such suits with their extra funding and numerous legal rights but, in spite of existing limitations, citizens must sue chronic polluters when other alternatives have been exhausted.

When procedural difficulties are resolved, the plaintiffs must decide what claim they can plead to achieve relief. This claim can be based on common law doctrines, property law, state or federal statutes, or constitutional rights. The plaintiffs may seek money damages and/or equitable remedies such as an injunction ordering the cessation of an activity or a *writ of mandamus* forcing a public official to do something. Often, if the clients have limited funds and the attorney thinks that they have a good chance to win their case for money damages, he will accept a contingent fee as his payment, taking nothing if the case is lost, and a certain percentage, commonly 30 percent of the awarded damages if the case is won. This can greatly lessen the available cash needed to be raised by the plaintiffs.

The three basic common law doctrines are nuisance, trespass, and negligence. While these remedies have evolved through court decisions, successful suits based on these doctrines usually depend on applicable statutes for support. For instance, an air pollution statute might state that an odor which adversely affects a given percentage of those exposed to it is unreasonable. The presence of such an odor could then be considered a nuisance. At other times, a statute may include standards, the violation of which constitutes negligence. Statutes may also determine the amount of proof needed, the person responsible for the proof and the defenses which can be used.

Environmental nuisance suits are not new. In 1611, it was ruled that odors from a defendant's hog sty constituted a nuisance. There are two types of nuisance, public and private, and they have separate legal definitions, but they often overlap. The plaintiff's lawyer should therefore plead as many legal claims for relief as he can. Then if the plaintiff's injury is judged not to fit under one doctrine, it may still fit under another.

A private nuisance is defined as an interference with land rights, and a substantial invasion of property rights must be proved. This is easy to do if the invasion is physical, but if the interference involves subjective annoyance such as aesthetics or inconvenience, proof may be very difficult to establish. The court must "balance interests"; considering that one man's use of his property will necessarily affect his neighbors to some degree, the court must decide whether his use is "reasonable." In one 1904 landmark case, *Madison v. Ducktown Sulphur Copper and Iron Company*, farmers were seeking property damages from a mining processing enterprise. Since an injunction to stop the damages would require closing down the plant which would result in massive unemployment and greatly decreased property value, the court allowed the defendants to in effect buy off the plaintiffs with money damages. According to Professor Reitze, this result occurs with depressing frequency and underlines the weakness of the "balancing process": the large polluters will never be stopped until they injure an equally large economic interest.

But this need not be the case. In the past if a community wanted industry, it had to accept pollution. Today, however, pollution control devices are available, and companies can afford to buy them. Professor Reitze warns that a corporation's defense of technological impossibility and cost limitations must be anticipated by the plaintiff's lawyer and refuted. Damage to the health of citizens must also be pointed out since it is becoming one of the few environmental abuses to override economic interests in the balancing process.

Public nuisances must affect an interest of the general public as opposed to that of only a few individuals. At the same time, the plaintiff, in order to maintain a private action, must show that he has suffered "special damages," different in kind (not degree) from other citizens, and he must also show that this damage constitutes violation of a particular legal right. It does not matter whether the injury was intentional or caused through the defendant's negligence. Under this reasoning, physical injury, even if a large number of people suffered similar physical injury, seems to be the best way to show unique personal injury and the easiest claim to protect under the public nuisance doctrine. However, because physical injury is often the result of private nuisance, the citizen's lawyer normally pleads both causes of action.

Monetary losses can also be remedied by a public nuisance claim, but only those suits that can prove direct interference with a small community group or a similar claim are likely to succeed. A general loss affecting an entire community, such as when pollution from the only factory in town creates a substantial decrease in tourism, will not hold up in court under a public nuisance claim pressed by private citizens. Similar qualifications limit recovery for interference with use of land as a public nuisance claim. Substantial blocking of access to land is a valid plea; however, interference with the public right of passage by the use of detours is not legally considered to be a public nuisance, since some alternative access is still available. Again, the court must balance information to determine whether the defendant's interference is substantial and whether a plaintiff has received special damages.

There are three remedies for nuisance: money damages, equitable relief by injunction requiring the nuisance to cease, or "abatement through self help." The acceptance of money damages is dangerous in so far as it may allow the nuisance to continue. In at least one case where a defendant refused to obey a court order to abate a nuisance, the court judged that the nuisance was unabatable and awarded money damages to the plaintiff in place of an injunction. A large polluter, then, is quite capable of dragging a citizen group with limited funds into a long-drawn-out legal battle, knowing that even if he loses the suit, he will probably only have to pay money damages equal to the loss in the plaintiff's property value or loss of income from that property. As Professor Reitze points out: "If an industry must be allowed to continue operation for the economic good of the community, a court should at least use its equity powers to assure that the best equipment that can be procured is used to reduce the harm from a defendant's operation. A careful showing by plaintiff's counsel that such equipment is available could help assure that courts will make orders requiring its use."

There are many possible injunctive measures. If citizens can prove that irreversible damage is likely to occur in the near future, the court can grant a temporary restraining order which forces the defendant to cease his injurious activity immediately. The temporary restraining order will last for only a short period, during which time the defendant must seek to avoid the predicted damage. Secondly, there is a temporary injunction which forces the defendant to stop his actions until the court comes to a final decision regarding his activities. This measure is effective only while it lasts. If the citizens' case is thrown out of court for any technical reasons or if the citizens lose their suit, then pollution can continue. Finally, the court may grant a permanent injunction, requiring the defendant to cease his activity permanently. For example, permanent injunctions have been used to limit the dumping of mercury into waterways.

"Abatement through self help" is the legal term for a citizen "taking a problem into his own hands." If, for example, a factory is illegally dumping mercury into a local stream and dead fish float to the surface in large quantities, one citizen might attempt to locate the drainage pipe and clog the pipe mouth or otherwise succeed in stopping the leakage. If the company then takes that citizen to court, he may be found to be legally within his own rights, but only if he can prove that he had insufficient time to press charges and that he only used the minimum amount of necessary force to stop the nuisance. Most courts, however, require a notice of abatement to be given to the offender responsible for the nuisance before self help is exercised.

Trespass has rarely been used in environmental cases. It is easier to prove than nuisance, in theory, since actual damages need not be shown. The invasion of an interest, usually property, constitutes legal damage in itself. But pollution from industry—noise, solid and chemical wastes, fumes, etc.—is more easily seen as a nuisance than as trespass. However, several pollution suits have been based on liberal interpretations of trespassing. In a series of fluoride emission cases against Reynolds Metals Company in Washington and Oregon, plaintiffs claimed direct invasion of property by particulates carried in the air. In the fourth suit, the court allowed the jury to consider punitive money damages on top of the regular court damages for the company's failure to act after the previous three cases.

Negligence suits are difficult to prove since the plaintiff not only has to show that an applicable "standard of conduct" has been breached but also that this failure to maintain a certain standard is the direct cause of the plaintiff's injury. The harm caused by pollution is particularly hard to prove since it is diffuse, slow to manifest itself, and often the result of exposure to a wide variety of pollutants that may come from several different sources. A standard defense move is to show "contributory negligence" from the plaintiff as well as from other sources. Smoking, for example, can make the plaintiff negligent, and if the plaintiff is even one percent negligent, he may not recover damages from a polluter who is 99 percent negligent.

As our society becomes more technological, new approaches to proving injury are being developed. One is to shift the burden of proof. If the plaintiff can provide enough facts to leave no doubt that one particular defendant is responsible for damages, then the responsibility of proof shifts from the plaintiff to the defendant who must now prove that he is not responsible for the injury. Another approach is to allow multiple defendants in one suit, making them jointly liable for an injury. Needless to say, it is extremely difficult to hold several individuals or corporations legally responsible for an ambiguous mass of pollutants to which they have all apparently contributed. But if the plaintiff's counsel can show injury was caused by a pollutant, he should be able to obtain a judgment. One other new approach is to prove that if the defendant had had the best technological controls available, injury would not have occurred. Standards in negligence cases are being based more and more on conditions that would exist if the best control equipment were in use. Therefore, failure to have this equipment would be basis for a negligence suit. It is clear that imaginative legal theorizing must be developed in the environmental fields and accepted by the court if we are to secure environmental protection.

Certain rights are more applicable to a specific environmental suit than others. For example, water pollution can be attacked by specific water laws. Owners of land in the eastern half of the United States and along the Pacific Coast, directly adjoining a water course, have what are known as "riparian rights" to reasonable use of the water as it flows. Each court must decide what is meant by "reasonable use," and though application of riparian rights has not yet been very effective, stricter interpretations of the term "reasonable" in the future may lead to successful suits against polluting companies who dump their wastes in water courses. Appropriation rights, a doctrine used in arid areas, grant a certain quantity of water to individuals, often requiring that it be returned to the water course to be reused. Thus, if one individual or one company returns the water in an excessively polluted state, others holding the same water rights should have grounds to sue.

Damage to property from highway construction or airport noise may be argued under what is known as "inverse condemnation." Although the land has not been formally condemned or confiscated, it may be considered "condemned" by injurious location, and citizens can sue for loss in property value.

Public Trust Doctrines assume that people have a legal right to government protection of the natural resources held by the government. In one famous case in 1892, the State of Illinois sued to prevent the city of Chicago from giving away most of the city harbor to Illinois Railroad and the transfer was prevented. However, use of the Public Trust Doctrine is complicated by co-existing rights to the same territory; while the federal government has a legal navigational interest in a water course, the riparian owner and the state also have separate legal interests in the same body of water. Protecting one interest, therefore, can be detrimental to other legal interests. Furthermore, Public Trust Doctrines do not protect any land that the state does not hold for public purposes; in other words, land acquired to build a government building cannot be saved from development by pleading breach of public trust.

That citizens have a legal constitutional right to a decent environment has often been argued—but never successfully in court. The fifth, ninth, and fourteenth amendments have all been claimed at one time or another in support of an environmental suit, and these theories have even been stretched to include environmental rights as civil rights. But the extremely vague and ambiguous relations between personal and environmental rights as they are currently defined make it considerably more advantageous to citizens to support and make use of those statutes with well defined environmental connections.

However, one case worth mentioning is a suit brought by the Environmental Defense Fund against Hoerner Waldorf Corporation in Missoula, Montana, November, 1968. EDF sought an injunction restraining the defendants from operating a pulp and paper mill emitting many toxic substances in the air. For a number of technical reasons the defendant won a motion to dismiss the case from court. However, at that time, the judge issued a dictum or statement of opinion, indicating that the court:

> . . . had no difficulty in finding that the right to life, liberty and property are constitutionally protected . . . and surely a person's health is what, in a most significant degree, sustains

life. So it seems to me that each of us is constitutionally protected in our natural and personal state of life and health.

Hopefully, this statement will have impact or bearing on future environmental suits claimed on constitutional grounds.

Specific statutes providing legal rights will be of more
practical use than will general constitutional theories. A statute can do one of two things. It can provide a legal right
which, when violated, is cause enough for legal action. Or,
more commonly, it can provide a standard, which, when not
maintained, can be used to show a right to recover damages.

One statute of considerable environmental importance is
the 1899 Rivers and Harbor Act (also known as the Refuse
Act) which prohibits dumping of any refuse of any kind into
navigable waters without a permit from the Army Corps of
Engineers. By 1970, after 71 years of the act's existence, only
266 of these permits had been granted; presumably, every
other industrial plant and factory currently dumping wastes
into our rivers and streams is at fault and should be fined.
The Act provides for fines to be levied for even the smallest
amount of dumped material, accidental dumpage. Furthermore, citizens providing information leading to conviction
are to receive one-half of any fine levied. Usually this fine is
set and collected by the federal government. But the possibility does exist for a citizen to file a *qui tam* action in court to
recover his share of the fine directly, even though no successful precedent using this action has been set.

Unfortunately, however, the Justice Department has issued
a statement that certain practices will be exempt from the
provisions of this act. Those manufacturers who discharge
toxic materials during their manufacturing process, and who
have already made agreements with the Federal Water Quality Administration to gradually stop these discharges over a
certain time period, cannot be prosecuted under the Refuse
Act. Needless to say, this decision permits some of the largest
and worst offenders to continue to pollute our waterways.

Care must be taken so that recent and future environmental
legislation is not rendered ineffective by conditional provisions
or subsequent laws. The National Environmental Policy Act
of 1969 is potentially a powerful statute to protect environmental conditions. Section 102 requires every federal agency
to prepare a statement outlining the environmental impact of

a proposed plan and listing alternative methods. The statement must then be made available to certain government agencies, the Council on Environmental Quality, and the public. This right of citizens to be informed about all proposed environmental changes and their ability to intervene in the decision-making process has tremendous possibilities for future law suits.

However, a serious weakness exists in the failure of the act to mention *when* each group must receive the environmental policy statement. Already a dangerous precedent has been set with Congressional approval of the Omnibus Rivers and Harbor Act of 1970. Passage of the act was upheld until the House and Senate Committees received their copy of the statement. But a copy was not made available to the public until after the Congressional hearings were completed and the act approved. If public review and criticism can continually be avoided in this manner, the Environmental Policy Act of 1969 will have failed to secure the citizen rights it was intended to protect.

By far the most important step in any environmental law suit is the follow-up, regardless of which court was used, what statutes employed, or which injuries claimed. Award of money damages only indicates one court's favorable reaction to the citizens' viewpoint; it does nothing to support the citizens' future actions or to limit those of the polluter. A temporary restraining order or a primary injunction only establishes a limited time period during which the polluter is legally required to change his methods; how much change or by what methods it is to be accomplished need not be specified. It is particularly important for citizens to make every possible effort to prove a polluter's actions unnecessary and harmful during this time period. Otherwise, the offender will essentially have been granted free time in which to convince public officials of the necessary and unavoidable nature of his methods and actions, and a second court is likely to rule in his favor.

The battle over the environment is a long and hard one that neither begins nor ends in court. And citizens must be willing to work at all aspects of the struggle if the final outcome is to have any permanent environmental effect.

corporate challenges

Most pollution fights pit public interest groups against businesses which have an economic investment in the status quo of either their products or their manufacturing plants. In theory major corporate decisions are controlled by a board of directors which is elected by the shareholders at an annual meeting. In practice little is decided at the stockholders' meeting because stockholders are presented one slate of individuals picked by the incumbent board of directors. The myth of the shareholders having the power to make fundamental decisions about who shall run "their" corporation for a year is called "shareholder democracy."

A good place to vocalize challenges to a company's corporate policies is at the annual shareholders' meeting. It is extremely unlikely that any motion which is opposed by the board will be passed, but the annual meeting does provide an excellent forum for discussion. Press coverage, especially by influential newspapers like the *Wall Street Journal*, is virtually assured, particularly if the challenging group adopts unusual or shocking tactics. Some groups have been able to gain widespread attention and stimulate broad-based support for their causes.

With only a few shares of common stock, Campaign GM captured national attention in 1970 with a proxy fight to make General Motors more responsive to its constituency—labor, automobile dealers, and consumers. The challenge came in the form of a motion to add three directors to represent the public interest during its board meetings.

Campaign GM, attempting to operate without large amounts of capital, discovered the practical limitations of a stock challenge in a capitalist society. GM has over 1.2 million stockholders, most of whom own only a small number of shares. One mailing of a challenge ballot and material would cost over $100,000. Direct mailing by challengers may not be necessary because of federal regulations governing proxy fights. If resolutions are submitted to the board at a meeting at least 60 days previous to the annual shareholders meeting and rejected, they must be included in proxy materials mailed out by the corporation.

Because Campaign GM only had 12 shares, it tried to involve institutions such as churches and universities which have large stock holdings. Most of the institutions had not been confronted about their stock voting power before and usually allowed firms which hold their shares to vote their block with management. Some when asked by their students or members to vote with Campaign GM did so, but others refused.

Rival business interests have always waged stockholder battles. The emergence of the Campaign GM-type fight which raises public interest questions is relatively new. While challenging the social responsibility of corporations, the citizen efforts are also raising fundamental questions about the nature of corporate decision-making. The evolution of Campaign GM from the 1970 to the 1971 "model" offers some insight into this. In the kick-off press conference for the 1971 General Motors challenge, Philip Moore, the group's coordinator, stated that the first effort "focused on the social impact of corporate decisions," but the second will "focus on who makes the decisions and how they are made." Involving the public in a process that was designed by a minority for control by a minority will challenge some basic assumptions about the governance of corporations.

It will also question the policies of many institutions which consider themselves neutral in society. Churches, universities, and retirement funds will be increasingly confronted by members to use their proxy power to pressure corporations to become more socially responsible. But from Campaign GM and other challenge attempts, certain structural blockades have been uncovered which highlight the difficulty citizens face in a corporate battle. Among these is one which challengers uncovered—that institutions do not have to reveal their stock holdings. Only the government can get that information.

One way citizens are supposed to be able to find out is through a Securities and Exchange Commission rule requiring corporations to reveal to any "stockholder of record" 10 days before the annual meeting, a list of their stockholders. That would make it appear that any challenge group who had a share of stock could get the list, but it is not that easy. Most institutions and rich individuals own stock in "street name" or the name of their broker. The street name might be fictional and registered with the Internal Revenue Service, but not available to someone who requests it.

This loophole creates a situation where only a few even know who wields power. Environmental groups can attack this problem by pressuring universities, churches, and similar institutions to reveal their holdings. This stock and its proxy power can be used to challenge corporate policies. Having the support of a large university or a church can also give a campaign greater credibility.

If institutional support cannot be mustered, the likelihood is remote of a serious challenge to corporate policies developing from a group controlling only a few shares. All may not be lost, however, because the ownership of a few shares allows access to all company mailings. A stockholder may also have the right to other information (unless it is a trade secret) so that he will know how "his" company is being managed.

When considering the stock challenge as a viable tactic, it must be remembered that a corporate meeting has space for only a limited number of participants who are subject to the ground rules of the company at its meeting. Therefore, groups should not only contemplate what can be done inside its closed doors, but also outside. A "people's stockholders meeting" could offer sharp contrast to the company's formal affair. Annual meetings also present a prime target for rallies and civil disobedience.

Regardless of size, the right combination of assaults on a corporation can create a climate for change. It took everything from harassment of campus recruiters to a stock challenge to convince Dow Chemical to stop making napalm. The production of napalm did not stop, but at least now it is not being made by Dow.

boycotting

Because money is powerful in society, the wallet is an excellent target for environmental activists. One method to pressure companies or individuals is to boycott their products or business establishments. In theory it appears easy to convince enough people to stop buying a product long enough to create pressure for social or environmental change, but in practice a successful boycott is rare.

An informal boycott against several laundry products began in reaction to a massively circulated list which ranked detergents according to their phosphate percentages. A subsequent drop in the sales of some of these products resulted in almost the entire industry considerably lowering their phosphate levels or switching to alternative chemical compositions. The reasons the companies capitulated are complex, but the public concern over water pollution made evident by sales shifts was a major factor in the change.

For years, civil rights groups and labor unions have used boycotts against companies and individuals to win victories for their cause. The Caesar Chavez victory over grape growers after a prolonged national boycott proved its value as a tactic. The persistent refusal of consumers to buy grapes season after season, aided by frequent picketing and leafleting by concerned citizens in front of their neighborhood markets, helped Chavez to win recognition of his agricultural union. Furthermore, it brought widespread public attention to the farm workers' strike, helping the laborers to build their movement.

Analysis of the grape boycott can provide valuable guidelines for what it takes to make the tactic work. The ideal product may not exist for boycotting, but grapes come close.

They are highly perishable; therefore, there were peak times when activity was required to focus public attention on the campaign. The threat of millions of bunches of grapes rotting each season gave the strikers powerful leverage against growers and renewed public interest. Grapes are also a luxury item. People desire them but do not have to have them. By being an underdog, Chavez could also tap sympathy from the public.

Whereas the nature of grapes made them an excellent boycott candidate, many products that harm the environment are almost impossible targets. In a city without adequate mass transit, it is difficult to convince people to walk miles to work to boycott motor vehicles. Telephone service, electric power, and garbage collection are necessities for which there are no feasible alternatives.

Certain business changes also create problems for environmentally oriented boycotts. The small independent grocery store could be pressured by a boycott into stocking only returnable bottles, but the chain store operation, because of its size, can resist all but the strongest public anti-purchase campaigns. Even if pressure can be mounted to cripple one polluting company, it may turn out to be part of a larger conglomerate composed of many corporations. The others can continue to earn enough to cover sales losses of one operation until the consumer campaign is over.

The immense purchasing power of state and local government agencies must also be considered when evaluating the boycott as a possible tactic. The grape strike was almost broken by a sudden, unusually high purchase of grapes for military bases.

When all of the factors have been considered, a boycott may not seem worthwhile. But while it may not bring a company to the negotiating table because of sales losses, the boycott can serve definite educational and organizational functions. For example, a boycott of new internal combustion engine-powered vehicles may not be successful in forcing Detroit to market a new automobile. But it could prove educational to a large number of people. Most Americans do not know that their family chariot is an ecological demon. Madison Avenue advertisements only outline promised improvements in a person's sexual prowess or status that purchase of a new car offers. Enough money does not exist among ecology groups to compete with General Motors for prime time on television, but a boycott on big over-powered cars could mobilize thousands of people to communicate their evils.

Successful campaigns may take months and require extensive activity, but this can help build an organization. Because a decision to boycott leaves open the question of how it will be executed, a group can choose from a large number of tactical possibilities. These range from leafleting to blocking trucks delivering selected products.

Publicity surrounding a boycott can attract new people to an organization and strengthen it. But unless community support exists for the effort, an adverse reaction of support could be triggered for the company or individual merchant. In that case their sales and profits go up.

picketing

When a group is ready to progress beyond the letter-writing stage, picketing could be the right action. It is highly visible and can help focus public attention on a cause or an individual. It does not require a high degree of commitment to environmental activism, but is an activity which can encourage its development.

Placards for picketing can be constructed from almost any material. Scraps of art board, cardboard, plywood, and stretched canvas are available cheaply and can easily be painted. Good signs should withstand moderate winds and moisture without becoming illegible. Wind resistance can be reduced by cutting holes in signs. Before they are mounted on sticks, local ordinances should be checked to see if there are any regulations governing how they must be mounted and whether wooden supports are permitted.

Signs should be kept simple and must be readable from a distance. If photographs or cartoons are used, they should be understandable at a quick glance. When making signs, it is important to consider how they might appear on television, since the group may get coverage. Reds, blues and greens will show up better than other colors such as chartreuse. Slogans or symbols should be easily understood and lettering should be legible. Placards can be printed, but handmade ones have a greater impact.

Picketing may require a permit or prior notice in some places, but the courts have prohibited interference from officials. It is important to check local ordinances which might apply. For example, an Illinois law bars picketing in front of private residences. Regulations in Washington, D. C., require that a sign carried in front of federal buildings be no wider than the body of the person carrying it. Generally, any privately owned thoroughfare used by the public is fair game for picketing. Most police insist that picketers keep moving, but they can only be arrested for refusing to obey a police order to keep moving if traffic is blocked.

Answers to expected questions like, "What's this all about?" should be debated before the demonstration by the group and a spokesman should be available to the press to explain the action. People passing the picket line should be given a leaflet outlining the points of protest. After it is over, the area should be checked for discarded leaflets.

When most people think of picketing, they picture a line of placard-carrying demonstrators, but other forms should also be considered. Anti-war forces have used the silent vigil to create a haunting reminder to officials of the price of the Vietnam conflict. Vigils can consist of one or more persons waiting for a period of time in a conspicuous place such as an outer office waiting room or on the steps of a building. As a tactic, it attempts to communicate a sense of moral concern about a problem.

In either pickets or vigils, it is a good idea to assemble somewhere close to the selected target and move to it in a group. This could prevent the embarrassing situation of one lone picketer standing in front of a building.

marches and rallies

A gathering of people in support of a cause can generate a feeling of power among participants, unexcelled by any other experience. The sheer numbers that rallied and marched on Earth Day, 1969, communicated a sense of massive concern that could not be ignored by business and governmental structures. Teach-in activities in Philadelphia and New York drew crowds of approximately 100,000 people each.

Planning a march is not difficult and the event can go smoothly if the organizers take care of a few important details. Mobilization of participants is essential and can be carried out by the usual means of publicity and personal contact. A broad-based sponsorship will generate a larger turnout. Sponsors should be responsible for planning march activities and routes.

Singing, chanting, and clapping build enthusiasm. The best spirit will be spontaneous, but some control can be attained by mixing people with the crowd who know what type of chants and songs marchers will pick up.

If material is needed for the march, such as candles for a night demonstration or black arm bands to symbolize death, someone must be responsible for their acquisition and distribution. If marchers are expected to bring the materials with them, it is still good to have more available for those who forget or were not informed. If signs are used, extra ones should be on hand and if the march is for a specific cause, it is important to have informative signs in front.

While most public thoroughfares are fair game for peaceful demonstrations that do not block traffic, some cities require a permit. If a parade is scheduled which requires access to the street, a permit is almost always required. Though

good reasons have to exist for denial, standards of reason-
ableness are still in a state of flux in the courts. Most lawyers
advise groups to apply for a permit, then if the application is
rejected, a better defense can be developed in case of arrest.

Marches may be any length, but shorter ones will usually
attract more people and have fewer drop outs. Leaders
should set the pace at a rate that will not create too many
stragglers.

Parades and marches are good to assemble people for a
rally. It provides an opportunity for speakers to convey their
message to others. The educational value of rallies lies not so
much in who speaks but in the dynamics of the crowd. Complete with rock bands and folk singers, they can be a great
source of education and entertainment.

Sponsors should make sure that restrooms are available
and open, sound equipment works, trash cans are provided,
and transportation is planned for the speakers and bands.
During the Earth Day rally at the Washington Monument, a
tense situation developed because of bad coordination. Organizers did not know that the Park Service was going to
turn off the electricity to the stage at midnight because the
permit for the event had legally expired at 10:30 P.M. In the
middle of Pete Seeger's performance to over 10,000 people,
the electricity was shut off and the sound died. Riots have
started with less provocation.

Public parks almost always require permits for assemblies.
Some even limit the size of the crowd. Applications for permits may have to be made a specific amount of time in advance (usually 24 hours, but it can be two weeks). Someone
in any environmental group that might plan a demonstration
in protest of the next eco-catastrophe must find out who is in
charge of issuing permits, what time limits exist for assemblies, and whether there are crowd size limitations.

One of the most important, and often overlooked, pieces
of equipment at any demonstration is the sound system. Portable bull horns are necessary for leading chants and controlling the crowd. For occasional demonstrations without music,
it may be a good idea to use only bull horns to save money.
However, for larger rallies, the stage platform in the assembly area should be adequately equipped with a mike, ampli-
fier, and speakers that work. The necessary sound equipment
can be rented in almost any city. Because of its theft poten-

tial, however, dealers usually charge exorbitant deposits on the equipment, bull horns included (deposits can run as high as $75 for a single bull horn). For that reason, it is a good idea for a guard to be posted at the stage during and after the event.

Crowd control is the hardest part of organizing any large, outdoor event. It has become almost a science not only with police, but also with movement groups. One of the best systems developed so far is the marshal plan. Marshals are ordinary demonstrators who voluntarily accept responsibility for the tone of the demonstration. They serve as intermediaries with policemen and demonstrators. They also give essential information to participants, convey confidence to the crowd, and co-ordinate activities. They can be divided into classifications such as legal, medical, and crowd marshals.

Marshal training takes place before a planned event in order for the volunteers to understand the goals and strategy of the march or rally. Training procedures have been outlined in a manual which is available from the Friends Peace Committee, 1520 Race St., Philadelphia, Pa. 19102 for 35 cents. Stress is placed on anticipating what might happen and preparing for it. One of the best ways to do this is to create role-play situations which simulate possible occurrences. Individuals are asked to pretend they are other people in different tense crowd situations and to play out their feelings.

When conducting role play it is important to:

1) present each scenario quickly and vividly to all participants;

2) give special instructions to each role separately;

3) allow participants a few minutes to develop strategy;

4) stop after the essential issues have emerged;

5) let the entire group evaluate what happened.

Sample role-play situations might be:

Scenario	Rally
Roles	Group spokesman; speaker; demonstrators; 3 hecklers

Special instructions	Hecklers should be loud, obscene and threatening a speaker with violence
Discussion	What tactics should be used with heckling? How does the group decide?

* * *

Scenario	A peaceful demonstration is planned at a plant site to protest dumping of chemicals into a river. The company has warned that while demonstrators have the right to march on the side of a public road, anyone crossing onto plant property will be arrested and company guards will use tear gas to disperse demonstrators.
Roles	Demonstrators; splinter group
Special instructions	Splinter group should climb company's fence and start hassling guards
Discussion	What to do? How is the decision made?

* * *

Scenario	A peaceful march to protest defoliation in Vietnam
Roles	Marchers; onlookers
Special instructions	A fight starts between several demonstrators and several onlookers
Discussion	What to do?

After role-playing situations, marshals should be given some situations which require quick decisions. For example:

1) A man approaches a demonstration of 30 people and says that he represents a group of 40 and wants to join.

2) Someone appears with a bull horn and starts chanting provocative slogans.

3) Someone in the back of the crowd starts throwing rocks at the police.

4) March stalls, people become impatient.

5) Marchers harass marshals.

6) Disrupters come to take over platform.

Continual communication between marshals is needed so that if any changes in plans take place, word can quickly spread throughout the crowd. Small battery powered two-way radios are excellent for this purpose. If they are used, who can talk on them should be limited and they should be evenly distributed.

When planning any activity that involves a large number of people, little time should be left open. Alternative plans must be ready if a vacuum occurs so that the original purpose of the demonstration is not obscured or lost.

Marshals must also understand what to do if tear gas is used by the police. They should be equipped with information on antidotes for the various types of gas. The impact of standard tear gas can be lessened by covering the mouth and nose with a wet cloth or tissue. Some gas that causes burning of the eyes should be treated with water, some should not. Jars and canteens of water should be on hand if there is even a remote possibility that gas will be used to break up a crowd.

If a crowd is routed at the first shot of tear gas, it is important to calm them so that people do not get trampled. If possible, marshals should move in front of running people, link arms, and start chanting "Walk, Walk, Walk."

In attempting crowd control, demonstrators should never feel coerced. The goal of organizers must be to develop a delicate balance between control and freedom. While structure and preparation are important, it must also be remembered that some of the best events of any demonstration are spontaneous and unplanned. Therefore, plans must be reasonably flexible.

strikes

As a general rule, the strike is the most effective tool a worker has to effect change—either in the wage structure or in working conditions. For many years now, the union-called strike has been protected by law and the various aspects of bargaining and picketing have been regulated. The fact that this type of strike is legitimate, however, does not help those who are not unionized, those who can't persuade the union to call a strike, and those who have localized grievances.

Although the typical issue over which workers have traditionally struck is wages and monetary fringe benefits, this is changing. Workers by and large work amid some of the worst environments, and strikes are beginning to be valued as legitimate tools to attack what has been previously considered a "fact of life."

Some unions, for instance, are calling for safeguards against injury from excessive and continuous noise and from dangerous chemicals. Others are demanding an end to the noxious and harmful smoke, gas and soot that continually surrounds the workers.

The wildcat strike is one which is called without notice by non-union workers or union workers in defiance of their union. This tactic is more often used to protest working conditions than pay scales, and generally is the result of a gradual build-up of tension. The wildcat strike is illegal, but it is likely that it will be used more and more frequently as workers become concerned over the issue of occupational health. In the past, unions have tended to use health issues as bargaining points and occupational safeguards have often fallen by the wayside. The field is ripe for an environmentalist-worker coalition, and apparently a beginning has already been made.

In Ecorse, Michigan, in June, 1970, automobile workers at the Dana Corporation left work and staged what is probably the first demonstration of its kind. The men, members of the United Auto Workers, wore gas masks and protested the clouds of red smoke pouring from the chimneys of the neighboring plant of the Great Lakes Steel Corporation. The workers stated that they would not return to work until the smoke cleared away and until they received a commitment that the problem would not recur. The workers returned to their jobs after the offending company promised to clear up the problem within five months.

In the cases where workers are not permitted to strike, there are other approaches that they can take, particularly by calling in "sick," and by going to work but carrying out their duties slowly and inefficiently. The most publicized case of a work "slow-down" came in the spring of 1970 when air controllers at major airports protested their harassing working conditions. For years the controllers had been handling planes as fast as they arrived, although this was technically against Federal Aviation Administration regulations. Because of the heavy workload, they began to stick to the letter of their authority by restricting planes to the prescribed three mile safety margin, and forcing the rest to maintain holding patterns. Naturally, air traffic was severely affected, especially around New York City, yet the action was completely within the limits of the law.

In England, in December, 1970, the nation's 150,000 electrical workers staged a similar slow-down, although theirs was purely for increased wages. For years England's power industry had relied on overtime work for its employees to provide enough electricity for the country. When their wage demands were refused, the workers merely decided to "work to rule"—not accepting any overtime. Although the country was not blacked out, each community was forced to go through periods of up to four hours daily without electricity. (After about a week's harassment, however, the workers had to retreat from their militancy since public hostility against them began to increase markedly.)

Slow-downs are applicable to a variety of environmental issues. Traffic policemen, for instance, could wreak havoc during the rush hour by stopping cars in both directions for long periods, with the explanation that the air they are forced to breathe in the intersection is poisonous. Subway engineers could drive their trains at slow speeds to protest the danger of the continual noise to which they are exposed.

The possibilities for environmental strikes and slow-downs are virtually limitless. The main fact is that, in many cases, workers and environmentalists can struggle together against common problems. Strikes, coupled with boycotts, can be potent weapons with which to confront the power structure.

harassment

The possibilities for a group using creative harassment to annoy environmental villains are tremendous. But to be a viable tool, it should never be used simply to destroy. It is only effective insofar as sufficient delay or inconvenience forces polluters to realize the impact of their actions. Simply to annoy environmental offenders misses the point; they must understand the environmental objections. Too much harassment can backfire and create the temptation for irate corporate officials to retaliate rather than change their attitude or methods. As with any action, it is important to let a respect for all living organisms dictate activity.

No manual for harassment exists, but environmental movement lore is becoming filled with inspiring examples. Sierra Club members are fond of telling the tale of how an anti-litter hike set back planners of a recreation and ski resort in California's Mineral King Valley. In 1969 surveyors were staking out a road to the new site. Conservationists, upset that the construction would destroy the scenic valley, announced a hike to pick up litter in the valley. To the shock of the engineers, the hikers, in addition to collecting the beer cans and paper, accidentally picked up all surveying stakes, thus delaying the project until the area could be surveyed again.

In the same spirit of constructive harassment, a concerned citizens group in Santa Barbara, California, Get the Oil Out (GOO), staged a fish-in off the coast at a site slated by Sun

Oil Company for a new drilling rig. When the floating platform reached its destination, dozens of small boats blocked
the desired location (one member even rented a helicopter
from which to dangle her hook). The fishing craft succeeded
in frustrating attempts to locate the oil company's equipment
for days.

While these examples are dramatic, some of the best require considerably less effort. But it must be remembered that
harassing a corporation could violate certain laws. One very
vulnerable spot is a large corporation's computer department.
Bills or checks prepared on computer cards can be altered by
adding a random hole. If it is the same size as the others in the
card, and if the punch hits the right place it could change
the amount recorded on the bill. Even if the machine rejects
the card because of the additional hole, an employee will be
forced to deal with it manually, thus taking up company time.

Another way to harass a company is to pay their bill for
slightly more ($.05) than the computerized card indicates.
This will either force them to record the extra amount and
deduct it from the next bill or refund the customer. Any creative student of computer programming can suggest other
ways to tie up an accounting department of a company which
has replaced employees with a machine.

Another electronic marvel which can provide considerable
headaches for a corporation is the telephone. The home
phone number of a company president can be a pipeline to
flood him with complaints. A few dedicated callers can tie up
an office switchboard for hours, thus isolating businessmen
from incoming business deals. Callers can either register a
lengthy complaint with an official or apologize for dialing the
wrong number.

Selecting the right sore spot to aggravate within a corporation is the key to annoying them. For example, if a company
uses their smokestacks for incineration at night, a group
could illuminate the problem by securing a spotlight and focusing on the belching smoke.

While such actions may not stop a determined corporation's plans, their impact may be greater than anyone in
industry is willing to admit.

perturbance of systems

With our life-support systems such as highways, electric lines and communications networks increasing in complexity, their vulnerabilities increase also. Thus while electric utilities normally promote the use of every kind of electrical gadget from back scratchers to bedwarmers, a *Village Voice* writer's suggestion in the summer of 1970 for everyone to turn on their lights and appliances during a power shortage drives Consolidated Edison up the wall. A sudden increase in demand at these critical periods could darken New York City.

With or without knowing it, the *Village Voice* staffer suggested a tactic becoming known as "perturbance of systems." Its success depends upon someone detecting a weak point in a complex system. When the weakness is exploited to its maximum potential, it collapses, bringing the entire operation to a grinding halt.

While using electricity to stop electricity and thereby force a reevaluation of energy consumption sounds like something overheard from drunk electrical engineers, the perturbance of systems idea has potential. Draft-eligible men flooded their boards in the summer of 1970 with letters outlining events, ailments, attitudes, etc. which might affect a change of their draft status and almost bogged down the selective service system with paperwork.

If enough people are involved, perturbing systems has interesting possibilities for environmental activists. Automobile salesmen and dealerships could theoretically be financially crippled by individuals taking up the time of sales personnel by demanding pitches on new cars, and even going through the preliminaries of ordering. After considerable time debating color, engine size, radios, wheel covers, upholstery, model, gear shift, etc., the environmentally concerned non-customer can voice his objections about automobiles and leave. However, because some salesmen work almost entirely on commission, it is important to find out whom such an action will hurt.

intervention

When all legal, administrative and political appeals for change are exhausted or when results are too slow in coming, it becomes necessary for environmental activists to use civil disobedience or direct action tactics which break laws. Conservationists, after diverse attempts to save giant redwoods from logging operations in California, sat in front of the log trucks, thereby not only stopping them, but also dramatizing their cause. Public support increased for more redwood protection and new legislation resulted.

A definition of direct action is difficult, but it is usually understood to be action undertaken without any intermediate steps and with a specific objective in mind. It can be violent or non-violent and if it is the latter is called civil disobedience. The effectiveness of these tactics is a subject of much unresolved debate, although it is clear why people resort to them. They occur when advocates of change believe that appeals within the system will not produce necessary results, either fast enough or at all. While the motivation for direct action is created by frustration, its execution like other tactics requires patience and planning.

For direct action to achieve any results it must not only reflect the convictions of those immediately involved, but it must also generate support sentiment among a larger number of people.

But achievement of concrete results is not the only reason direct action is used. It can serve to alert and educate people to the issues of a cause. To do this the action must have a clear purpose. Press statements and leaflets should be very specific and focus attention on the issues. Other organizations should be contacted so that they understand the nature of the action and the reason it was felt necessary. Most people will interpret any disruption of the normal order of business as a negative action, so it is important to explain the positive motivation.

Justifying civil disobedience when the end is a better quality of life is easier if the means utilized reflect the goal. Building take-overs are dramatic, but material damage to the facility should be carefully avoided, because it could result in press coverage which obscures the demonstration's purpose by leading to debate over the use of violence. In any situation where confusion over the use of direct action may occur, it should be stressed to reporters that all actions of the group are subject to the critique of respect for all living organisms.

Direct action is not new to environmentalists. Its roots reach deep into the past and touch the actions of individuals such as Henry David Thoreau. Thoreau understood that economic values could not dominate environmental considerations. In *Walden* man assumes a role integral with Nature. One passage reads:

> Flint's Pond! Such is the poverty of our nomenclature. What right had the unclean and stupid farmer, whose farm abutted on this sky water, whose shores he had ruthlessly laid bare, to give his name to it? . . . I respect not his labors, his farm where everything has its price, who would carry the landscape, who would carry his God, to market, if he could get anything for him; who goes to market *for* his god as it is . . .

Thoreau knew also that society's laws exist for the good of the Flints, not the pond; therefore certain actions to protect the pond may require breaking the laws of man.

In addition to Thoreau's philosophy and life style, he also provided a tactical example of civil disobedience—tax refusal. In modern times, with governments still squandering money on weaponry, an individual can still follow Thoreau's guide. In addition to protesting war, other possibilities for using tax resistance to dramatize a cause exist. This year, our tax money will have to buy poison to eradicate fire ants ($7.6 million in 1971), finance the Army Engineers' earth-shaping projects (at least $600 million for 1971), and perhaps even subsidize the supersonic transport ($290 million for 1971). Individuals can withhold from their tax return their contribution to these projects, and the money withheld could be sent to organizations working to readjust national priorities.

In theory massive tax resistance could be a tactic to bring about new social pressures for a change, but in practice it becomes little more than a device to stimulate discussion of a problem. Even if enough people could be persuaded to risk jail by refusing all or part of their tax payment, most do not really control their taxes. Because the government requires employers to withhold a percentage of each employee's paycheck, the Internal Revenue Service has collected a large amount of its money by the April tax filing deadline. An individual's refusal to file when he has a large amount withheld could result in the government actually collecting more money.

Although the government's practice of withholding taxes makes tax refusal difficult for most persons, there are other forms of civil disobedience which can be utilized. The most famous is the sit-in and its more exotic offshoots. While some activists consider the sit-in to be an outmoded approach which has lost its initial impact and shock value, the tactic continues to prove itself under a variety of different situations. Like the anti-war sit-in, the environmental sit-in can be highly effective because it places the machine in stark contrast to a helpless humanity.

There is virtually no limit to its application. Government offices have been the scene of lengthy take-overs, and private offices have had their share of dissidents, too, most recently in the context of women's liberation. Sit-ins can be used against ships, trucks, and trains. Bulldozers have repeatedly been blocked, both by anti-highway and anti-mining forces.

The successful sit-in requires a well disciplined group which is willing to let one person serve as a spokesman. Participants should be reasonably orderly and take pains to keep the demonstration aimed at one or two specific problems. Keeping in mind that much of the sit-in's purpose is to provide publicity is important, and curious bystanders should be informed closely about the purpose of an action. Even if an observer at first appears hostile, a haughty or flippant demonstrator will only reinforce his antagonism. Orderliness does not necessarily mean silence (although that can sometimes be very successful), and singing or chanting generally provide better results than random shouting. Singing is also very useful for building spirit. A demonstration disrupted in the middle of "America the Beautiful" has the potential to provide good copy for a news story.

If possible, groups should pay special attention to becoming as ethnically, racially and sexually diverse as possible and including members from different age groups. In some instances this will protect demonstrators from excessive police violence if the group is attacked, and in any case, it will make the demonstration a more "respected" one in the press.

In addition to office sit-ins, a harmful process can be temporarily halted by the interposition of bodies. Just as the Sierra Clubbers stopped the logging operations in California during the redwood cutting controversy, sit-ins can tie up business operations, transportation arteries, and recreational facilities.

Direct action can encompass other tactics, in addition to tax refusal and the sit-in. In Kane County, Illinois, polluters are being harassed by a man who calls himself "The Fox." Few people know his identity, but whenever he blocks a plant's drainage pipe, seals its chimney, dumps dead fish in a lobby, or leaves a dead skunk on the porch of an executive, he leaves a signed note explaining his actions. According to a *Chicago Sun-Times* interview with the mysterious "antipolution Zorro" he slips onto private property to wage his crusade. During his exploits, "The Fox" has been chased by plant guards, crawled through drainage pipes, climbed roofs, and has had shots fired in his direction.

In the interview it is revealed that "The Fox" is an ordinary, soft-spoken citizen approaching middle age. In explaining his philosophy he said:

> I decided that even if I was only one man, I'd do something. I don't believe in hurting people or in destroying things, but I do believe in stopping things that are hurting our environment. So I have been doing something. I want them to know why it is being done, so I always leave a note suggesting that they clean up their mess, and I sign it "The Fox." That's because of the Fox River.

When asked how long he plans to continue his crusade, he answered:

> Oh, I know this all sounds silly and dramatic, but I'd rather hear a frog croaking or see a flight of mallards cutting through a sunset than hear some guy talk about increasing profits, when he did it by killing nature. So I'll be "The Fox" until I see results.

The possibilities for "Fox"-type tactics are only limited by the creative power of the human imagination. For example, after the massive Gulf of Mexico oil spill caused by Chevron's drilling leaks, protesters created a large oil spill, complete with dead seabirds, in a fountain in front of the company's San Francisco office.

Because direct action is not the type of activity with which most people are familiar, it is advisable to meet before a demonstration to discuss it. The reasons for an action's necessity and the possible consequences should be clear to everyone. Someone should be familiar with the physical layout of the demonstration site and he should describe it. It is also a good idea to simulate situations which may occur so that when they do, the participants will know how to react. If anyone in the group has been involved in a demonstration broken up by the police, he should relate what happened. If there is a danger of physical contact, everyone should be reminded to remove glasses and jewelry.

Because most direct action violates law, everyone should understand there is a good possibility that participants will be arrested. It is also important to make arrangements for securing bail money and a lawyer before the demonstration. If arrests occur, participants should understand the hazards of not cooperating with police. Even if an arrest is later declared illegal, the act of going limp or sitting down during it could result in charges of resisting arrest. These charges could be separate from those related to the demonstration and could remain. If a trial results from the action, it could present an opportunity to publicize the issue being protested.

While spending a night in jail to save the environment may be appealing to some, respect must develop in an organization for each member. Getting arrested should never be equated with commitment to the cause.

III battle fronts

Virtually every aspect of our modern existence inflicts severe environmental damage in one form or another. Progress has turned into overproduction, consumption into waste, and quality into artificial obsolescence.

What follows is a description of 14 major problem areas that our civilization must come to grips with—soon—if we are to survive the 20th century. Each section contains a description of what tactics might be applicable to individuals and citizen groups who are concerned. Obviously, these sections are inadequate to describe fully the extent of our ecological crisis, and the suggestions and anecdotes are not enough to win every battle. The concept that war, for instance, is by far the most ecologically harmful activity that man can pursue is only occasionally touched upon because the subject is so vast as to fall outside the limits of this book. It is to be hoped that environmental awareness will include the understanding that war is a disaster—ecologically, psychologically, economically, politically, morally and otherwise—and is, perhaps, the first of many problems that need to be faced and countered in this country.

Ecology, as a science, is a relatively modern field of endeavor. Ecology, as political action, is only beginning to take form. This part has been titled "Battle Fronts" because that is the nature of the present struggle.

highways

• *Many cities devote over 50 percent of the land in downtown areas to the auto and its supporting facilities, like garages, parking lots and auto salesrooms.*
• *The American Association of State Highway Officials (ASHO) has requested that $320 billion be spent on highway needs over the next 15 years. That is just under the national debt ($375 billion).*
• *There is one vehicle for every 2.4 persons in the United States, and one mile of road for every square mile of land.*

Highway pavement covers approximately 4 million square miles of land in the United States. Each mile of freeway consumes about 24 acres of land. There are also millions of square miles devoted to the storage and service of automobiles and trucks. To construct these facilities gravel, sand, asphalt, and other materials are scraped, gouged, and drilled from the earth—ruining untold additional acres. The Department of Transportation actually brags about the sheer immensity of its road-building impact. They point out that:

To construct the Interstate System *alone*, total excavation will move enough dirt and rock to blanket Connecticut knee-deep. Sand, gravel, and crushed stone for the construction would build a mound 50 feet wide and 9 feet high completely around the world. The concrete used would build six sidewalks to the moon ...

Once trolleys were a very satisfactory way to travel in most cities, and cross-country travel in Pullman sleepers was considered a luxury. Today Americans who travel in Europe

103

and Japan are delighted by the efficient high-speed train systems. The automobile and concrete manufacturers would have us believe that the sad fate of our unsubsidized mass transit is somehow "progress."

Is the automobile really an improvement? Consider the following facts: One highway lane can carry approximately 3,600 passengers per hour in cars. The same highway lane can carry 60,000 people in buses—and this assumes that the buses are only one-half filled. A train, using the same amount of space, and again only one-half filled, can transport 42,000 passengers in an hour. Although it is not as fast, if the space were used for bicycles or even for walking, the number of people reaching their destination would be greater than the number that would be able to get there by car.

Land-use planning is of great interest to ecologists. Every square mile of land that is devoted to the automobile is ecologically wasted. In fact, it is ecologically destructive. Those who study the benefits of mass transportation as compared to the private automobile can cite alarming statistics about air pollution, and fuel consumption, as well as space consumption. Is freedom of mobility in the form of the automobile worth it—ecologically speaking?

The "greatest" achievement of the highway-builders is the United States Interstate Highway System. When the program was first conceived in the early forties, it was considered a major transportation breakthrough, and through the fifties and the early sixties, people joyfully took their customary vacation trips in half the time they once required. The Interstate System was not planned to go through cities; it was supposed to bypass them, and a 1956 issue of the magazine *Automotive Industries* predicted that:

> . . . neighborhood units will spring up—pleasant residential areas, made up mostly of medium-sized apartment buildings located close to modern factories and office buildings, thus eliminating the need for a great deal of commuting . . . transportation will no longer be a problem, . . . and walking will once more be safe and pleasant . . . The city would become a pleasant place to work in and live in.

Now, however, the people who traveled these roads with such pleasure are beginning to find out their true price. As the highway routes come near their neighborhoods, they see that a highway will bring them more than "increased mobility." It will also bring the hidden costs of noise and air pollution. Plans were made in New York City for an expressway to cut through Lower Manhattan, at a cost, incidentally, of $100 million per mile, but the plans were dropped when the New York Department of Air Resources found that the existence of the expressway would raise the carbon monoxide levels in the area to 125 parts per million. The National Academy of Sciences and the National Academy of Engineering have found that increased rates of death among persons with cardiovascular diseases can occur when the carbon monoxide levels reach 10 ppm or higher.

Hidden costs of highways also include social factors. Highway forces in Washington, D. C. seem determined to pave over the city in order to lighten rush hour traffic from Maryland and Virginia. Approximately 25,000 families will be displaced. Ninety percent of the evictees will be black, displaced for a "white man's road." The District of Columbia is already financially crippled, and yet land that is a valuable tax base for the city will be turned into an economic loss, as most displaced businesses relocate in the suburbs. The highways will be relatively useless except during the four hours of the day when suburbanites are commuting, and even then the lanes on one side of the road will not be necessary. Once the cars get downtown, they gobble up land voraciously. In the downtown business area, D. C. land is more than 60 percent devoted to the movement and storage of automobiles.

The effects of highways are most evident in the cities, but wild areas suffer as well. So many tourists drove their cars into Yosemite National Park that in the spring of 1970 congestion and air pollution forced the park officials to ban autos in the Mariposa Grove of Giant Redwoods. Visitors now leave their cars in a parking lot and see the redwoods in a sightseeing rig hauled by a truck.

With highways so costly, who has the responsibility for building new roads? Who decides where they will be? In most cases it is the State Highway Department. Major arteries are supposed to be part of a general plan for a given region— drawn up by a planning commission. But, in effect, the highway department's plans are usually the ones that the planners adopt. Highways have generally determined subsequent development of an area. The ecological disaster known as "sub-urban sprawl" is the result of the highway builders' brand of "planning." The 1970 annual report of the Council of Environmental Quality states: "Development moves out from the city, . . . branching out from the highways and expressway interchanges."

Whether or not roads are built depends basically on the availability of funds. Most major highways are built with the aid of federal money. The state highway departments must show a "need" for a new highway in order to qualify for funds. This "need" is defined as the number of cars and trucks that are projected to use the road if it is built. This is circular reasoning at its best, and of course ignores the detrimental effects of the proposed road.

It is interesting to study how "needs" for new roads develop in direct proportion to available federal funds. The Interstate Highway System (by the highwaymen's own admission) would not have been built if it was not for the fact that the states receive $9 of federal money for every $1 that the state contributes. Other major highways receive 50 percent federal aid. (The Federal Highway Act of 1970 contains a provision upping it to 70 percent.)

Most federal allocations such as those for education, housing, and agriculture, are reviewed and revised by Congress each year. Thus, the resources of the nation can be redirected if and when our priorities change. This is not so with money for highways. Taxes from almost all auto-related retail transactions go into the sacrosanct Highway Trust Fund which is earmarked almost exclusively for new road construction. The theory is that highways are thus paid for by those who use them (the "user-tax" concept). But as Helen Leavitt, author of *Superhighway-Superhoax* points out, the logic is bad. It is like using taxes on alcohol to expand the liquor industry. One might say it makes as much sense as reserving all federal estate taxes for use of the deceased.

The Highway Trust Fund is accumulating huge amounts of money while poverty and education programs go begging. About $5 billion rolls automatically each year into the trust fund coffers.

Once a road is built, local municipalities are burdened with the formidable task of maintenance. These expenses average about 10 percent of the cost of the original construction of the road. Such financial obligations are no joke to local tax-payers.

The activities of state highway departments are coordinated and reviewed by the Federal Highway Administration which is part of the Department of Transportation (DOT). The Administration was established to carry out the general mandates of Congress concerning highways and DOT is charged with the responsibility for all types of transportation. While all forms should be considered, Secretary of Transportation John Volpe and his assistants (occasional pleasant rhetoric excepted) show little desire to change the emphasis on the automobile as America's dominant mode of transportation.

DOT sometimes sponsors "pilot studies" and "demonstration projects" that show the effectiveness of alternative transit methods. But in the meantime, the railroads are going bankrupt and existing commuter tracks connecting suburb to city continue to rust in spite of an ever-louder citizen clamor for transportation sanity. Exactly what is the situation for mass transportation at this time? How badly off are the bus and train industries? Two recent legislative developments, some feel, will help the industry get back on its feet.

A $3.1 billion mass transit subsidy act which is designed to help cities revive or build subway and bus systems has been passed. This amount will be released over a five year period. With the federal government handing out almost $5 billion in a single year for new highway construction, however, this amount for ailing mass transit systems is trifling. (The mass transit industry claims that its minimum capital equipment requirements over the next decade will be $20 billion.)

The other interesting recent development is the establishment of a National Rail Passenger Corporation. The existing railroad companies will turn over their passenger service to the new corporation. This new corporation will receive some federal subsidy, but most of its money will come from the railroad companies themselves. They will be obliged to purchase stock in the corporation in return for its taking over their passenger service. Thus, any improvements that may be evidenced in inter-city public rail transportation will be the result of novel management techniques. Infusion of "new" money into the rail industry as a whole will not occur in any substantial amount. Again, it is an interesting development, but when viewed in comparison with the Highway Trust Fund, it is not very meaningful. The administration has now proposed that, as a first step to "improve" the nation's rail service, more than one-half the trains that are running today will be discontinued. Several cities presently serviced by some passenger train service will be severed entirely from the system. It appears that the effort to revive intercity passenger train service may be doomed to failure at the start.

Entirely new forms of public transportation could entice people away from their cars. Innovations, such as the "dial-a-bus" system which scientists at the Massachusetts Institute of Technology have been working on for years, could be an important step in a transition away from the automobile.

Computer-directed mini-buses would pick up passengers at their doorsteps and deliver them to other sections of the city. For critics of the privately-owned automobile this system is of great interest. But last July, when the demonstration phase of the project was to begin, the head of the Urban Mass Transit Administration, Carlos Villarreal, withdrew federal money. The MIT scientists are bitter: one stated, "I don't know whether it's politics or incompetence, but Villarreal is killing off every innovation in mass transit."

Despite minor gains on some fronts, the future for public transportation does not look as if it will be significantly different from the past. It's a little like trying to hold your own by walking up a down escalator which is moving too fast.

In some very real ways our present transportation policies smack more of the macabre than anything else. The poor urban dweller, particularly, is caught in the midst of a three-pronged attack on his health and sensibilities. At best, he is merely tormented by extreme pollution of the air, primarily caused by the automobile. He is also plagued by a lack of adequate public transportation. Finally, he is under the threat of being evicted by new highways designed primarily to shuttle suburbanites across the city. On top of this, although he probably does not own a car, he sees his streets crowded with suburbanites' cars during the working day. Moreover, the street which is closed off from cars is rare and even parkland is being encroached upon by parking lots and roads.

Citizen groups, especially in urban areas, are beginning to strike out against these injustices. Some groups are concentrating on reducing air pollution by pressing for stronger laws and better enforcement; others are attempting to exert pressure on those in power to improve and construct mass- and rapid-transit systems. The largest numbers of people, and those with perhaps the most at stake, are fighting against what many regard as a city's cancer—the highway.

On all three fronts, groups are hovering between some successes and some defeats. All three issues are, of course, closely related, and to reorganize a city's priorities and even its life-style, the combination of the three-pronged attack will be necessary. In New York City, for instance, automobiles are banned from Central Park on weekends and bicycle riding is on the general increase, even among businessmen, yet the city is still among the most polluted in the nation.

Before embarking on the crusade, many citizens find it necessary to sit back and reconsider their own attitudes toward a new life style. Is there a paradox in being an eco-activist and owning a car? Which is a greater status symbol: a Cadillac, a Volkswagen or a bicycle? Is a five-mile walk in a city park more enjoyable than a 100-mile drive in the country? Should a suburban businessman form a car pool with three of his neighbors, or is it too much of a complication? Answers to questions like these are often difficult to find, though they may prove very helpful in analyzing one's attitude toward environmental considerations.

The next step—and it is a very big one—is political and legal action. Changes in life style affect only those who decide to make changes; political action, when successful, affects everyone—the road which is stopped in the courts is stopped, now and in the future.

The citizen who discovers that a new highway is projected to go through his house or his neighborhood is generally not too pleased with the revelation. His first step should be to find out all he can about the road—where it will go, where it is coming from, how much it costs, how it is being financed, who determined that it was necessary, why the site was chosen. After the information is gathered, standard organizing techniques, as described elsewhere in this book, should be pursued. Form a group, print a newsletter, distribute petitions, posters and flyers, and stage demonstrations, news conferences, and teach-ins. Involve local and state elected officials.

If citizen pressure fails and local officials refuse or are unable to help stop the highway lobby, it is time to turn to the courts.

There are specific legal tactics* that can be utilized. For each road receiving federal aid two public hearings are required. The first hearing is to consider the "need" for the road and the general location. The first hearing must be held "before the route location is approved and before the state highway department is committed to a specific proposal." The second hearing is on specific location and design factors. The one important question which must be kept in focus at all times—during *both* hearings—is whether the road should be built at all. The highway department representatives will try to divert attention into alternative locations or perhaps alternative designs.

Citizens in San Francisco decided they did not want an automobile-dominated city. Experts pressured officials to reject the interstate money and build a rapid transit system which they saw as a more "feasible and prudent" alternative.

If the road is to go through a park or historic site, opposition can be based on the 1966 Federal Aid Highway Act. It specifies that a road cannot be built through parks or historic sites unless there is "no feasible and prudent alternative," and unless there is "all possible planning to minimize harm to the area." Don't let anyone forget that the most "feasible and prudent alternative" may well be no road at all.

Environmental objections to highway construction are given some legal sanction under the 1970 Highway Act. A copy should be obtained from a representative to see if some of the ecological and social safeguards spelled out in the act can be used as a delaying tactic. The National Environmental Policy Act requires detailed statements on ecological consequences of any proposed project. If they have not been submitted in accordance with section 102 of the act, the court may grant an injunction until they are completed. If they have, it is important to obtain a copy from the Federal Highway Administration because it may contain information that can be used against highway advocates.

Spokesmen from a variety of organizations are valuable assets at hearings. Clean air groups, housing agencies, potential

---

* Editor's note: see Sections 135 and 136 of the Federal Aid Highway Act of 1970.

displacees, bicyclists, economists, conservationists, historical societies, etc. may all have reasons for opposing a new road.

The testimony of "experts" arguing in favor of a highway should never deter citizens opposing its construction. Experts tend to be narrow-minded at best and their testimony should be challenged by others. A "traffic flow expert" ignores parking and dislocation problems generated by new highways. He can be embarrassed by questions about this. The citizens of the District of Columbia scored a success when they questioned the director of the Maryland State Roads Commission about the displacement of Washington citizens by Maryland commuters entering D. C. The limitations of his views were obvious when he stated, "My job is to build the road up to the state line. What happens from then on is none of my business."

If after the hearings, rallies, letters, and other demonstrations of public sentiment, the decision is made to build the road, the filing of a law suit could stop its construction. Groups have successfully used the courts to block highway construction in Washington, D. C., New Orleans, New York, and other cities. In New York, the Lower Manhattan Expressway was blocked because of the air pollution the road would bring. In Washington, D. C., construction of the Three Sisters Bridge, a vital link to a freeway, has been delayed because the hearings were incomplete. Many suits are pending. Baltimore's Society for the Preservation of Fells Point has sued the federal government to save the oldest area of the city from the ravages of interstate highway construction. In Memphis, the Citizens to Preserve Overton Park are bringing suit on the basis of both inadequate hearings and the "feasible and prudent alternative" clause.

Construction of over 135 miles of highways in over a dozen cities has been halted by sheer public outrage. Building the pressure required demonstrations, law suits, balloting, and petitions. The projects now in dispute represent almost $4 billion in contracts.

Another area of citizen involvement which has been largely overlooked in the past is improving public transportation in the community. Attention of citizen groups should be focused on the inadequacies of bus and/or rail systems. Agitate for new routes, express buses, lower fares, responsible fiscal management, etc. Where there are old commuter rail lines lying idle, demand that service be restored. This is most important, since putting existing lines back into use is the least disruptive way to improve public transportation quickly. Many of these existing but unused railroad rights-of-way are bought by the road-builders for the construction of new highways.

In London, public transportation will soon be free. The transit company will be financed by taxation, the average taxpayer's contribution being about $65 per year. This is less than he would have paid in fares because fare collectors, accountants, etc. are no longer needed.

In New York City, Mayor John Lindsay wanted to collect additional tolls from commuters at bridges and tunnels, and use the money to aid the subway system. The city studied a proposal which would have charged full cars (four or five passengers) a low rate, and cars with only one occupant as much as $3 per trip, but the opposition of Governor Nelson Rockefeller has precluded any implementation thus far.

There is now under study in DOT a plan which would create separate bus lanes on highways, principally those which are heavily used by commuters. The principle behind this is that a continuous stream of buses flowing into and out of a city during rush hours would cut down on automobile traffic and provide a viable alternative for commuters who drive to work. According to DOT, less cars means less pollution and less congestion.

But, wait! Will the builders expropriate one of the already existing lanes of the highways? No, they are going to add a new lane! Furthermore, they will add new, complicated access ramps and overpasses so that the buses will not have to cross regular traffic upon entering and leaving. Thus, as soon as the buses start running, all the commuters will look out their windows and see three unclogged lanes beside them, simply waiting for the man who likes to drive or hates buses.

Basically, of course, this plan is just another justification for urban highway construction. Train tracks and rights-of-way lie unused while the highway and bus lobbies dream up "impossible schemes" to tackle. And subway systems, while they are destructive when they are being built, ultimately serve the public much more adequately. Everyone can use a subway; it is fast and more ecologically sound, and it does not tear apart or isolate neighborhoods.

The most important contribution citizens can make to the national scene right now is to use local issues to increase awareness of the transportation crisis—which is basically the same everywhere. There are already enlightened and aroused citizens' groups all over the country. The National Coalition on the Transportation Crisis (Box 4529, Washington, D. C. 20017) publishes a newsletter to keep groups informed on major developments. The national conservation organizations are also printing information in their newsletters and magazines.

Alternative transportation modes to highways offer definite social and ecological advantages citizens should keep in mind when considering the question of highways. Beautification and anti-litter drives should not be confused with substantive ecological issues. Billboards and litter may be unattractive, but ecologically they are relatively harmless. The real threats are poisons in the air, waste of natural resources, such as petroleum, and destruction of the land.

The general public tends to feel that if and when the automobile engine is "cleaned up" the crisis will be over. A clean engine in the long run will only increase reliance on the private automobile. Cars will still need space for storage. Roads with their major ecological, sociological, and psychological side-effects will still be necessary. Those who can't afford cars, the young, the old, and others who don't drive, will still be the victims of America's infatuation with the automobile.

automobiles

• Conventional automobiles and other vehicles powered by the internal combustion engine generate 60 percent of the nation's air pollution: 92 percent of the carbon monoxide (CO) produced, 63 percent of the hydrocarbons (HC), 46 percent of the nitrogen oxides (which react in the presence of sunlight to create photochemical smog), and 8 percent of the particulates (pieces of solid matter such as carbon and lead).

• Since 1945 the number of cars, trucks and buses in the U.S. has increased more than three-fold from 30 million to over 100 million. Estimates suggest that there will be 30 million more motor vehicles by 1980. Virtually all vehicles now on the road are powered by internal combustion engines.

Over the past quarter century no single machine has played as powerful a role in shaping the way Americans live as the automobile. The nation's economy is enslaved by the car. Autos have determined the physical development of suburban communities. Shopping centers, motels, drive-ins, restaurants, movies, banks, stores—are manifestations of the automobilized society. Some also hold the car accountable for a revolution in social behavior. Today's American has territorial and sexual mobility far surpassing his parents'.

Only within the last 10 years has the general public begun to recognize the automobile as a social villain. The car is a murderer. Fifty-five thousand people each year die from auto accidents. Autos attack humans in more subtle fashions as well. Vehicles powered by internal combustion engines create at least 60 percent of the total air pollution in the U. S.; in some urban areas the figure rises to about 80 percent. Motor vehicles account for 85 percent of the noise in urban areas, and auto noise can cause permanent hearing loss. Auto-related uses claim enormous proportions of land in cities. To accommodate the car, highways pave over people, homes, businesses, rivers, forests, farms and mountains. The auto's gift of mobility is bestowed only on the physically and financially able, however. Twenty-five percent of the adult population—the elderly, the infirmed, the disabled, the poor, and many women—cannot drive, although all social classes suffer the ill effects of automobiles.

Some of the health hazards resulting from automotive air pollution are fairly well documented, but studies of what happens to humans when they breathe air-borne contaminants are incomplete. Single causal agents are hard to isolate. Effects of smoking, for instance, are increased in the presence of carbon monoxide. Urban traffic regularly produces enough carbon monoxide to impair vision and hinder the speed of drivers' reactions to traffic stimuli. Hydrocarbons and nitrogen oxides play a part in producing smog, which damages plants, irritates eyes and the respiratory tract, and limits visibility. Nitrogen dioxide, produced from nitrogen oxide emissions in the photochemical smog reaction, can in high enough concentrations cause respiratory diseases known to be fatal to man. Recent data indicate that air-borne lead is definitely detrimental to human health. Links are believed to exist between respiratory ailments and pollution from rubber tires and asbestos brake linings.

Even if the internal combustion engine (ICE) can be successfully modified to lower emissions, within a few decades air pollution is expected to increase beyond present limits due to the rapid rise in the sheer number of vehicles. Since 1945 the number of cars, trucks, and buses has more than tripled. Detroit predicts that by 1980, they will give birth to 41,000 cars each day, almost a doubling of the present rate. During the period since World War II the population of the U.S. has grown by only 46 percent. The growth rate of autos does not depend on population expansion; population control won't necessarily curb auto growth.

In terms of material accoutrements, the U. S. has the highest standard of living in the world. Naturally it is also the biggest car consumer in the world. Half the world's cars are registered in the U. S. It holds the world's record both for number of cars (85 million) and for number of cars per person (1 car for every 2.4 persons). California's more than 10 million automobiles top the total in any single foreign country except West Germany, Britain and France.

Cars move the nation's economy. One-sixth of the business firms in the U. S. are estimated to be part of the auto industry. Almost 20 percent of the labor force works in auto-related jobs. Twenty percent of the steel produced in the U. S., 60 percent of the rubber, 30 percent of the zinc, and 10 percent of the aluminum are directly used by the auto.

Since so much of America's industry is tied to the auto, it is little wonder that auto makers and related groups fight governmental attempts to clean up the car, or that these interests have formed one of the most powerful lobbying groups in Washington. Shifting production to a non-polluting engine involves some gambles and may deflect the car makers' steady stream of profit. Even riskier is the switch from the private-auto-dominated market to a balanced transportation program offering efficient, convenient and comfortable public transit. However, this must be the direction of the future, if we are not all to be entombed by one big traffic jam, each encased in his own two tons of auto, mired in beds of asphalt and concrete.

Because the private auto is convenient and it has been backed by a tidal wave of federal money for highways, a steady demand for it is assured. But as the auto became king, it took its toll on public transportation networks. Now that the car is established, it will not be easy to force the processes of government and industry to change. Yet strong enough pressure must come from the public to force either government to regulate the auto industry or the corporations to reshape their product.

The history of government's relationship to the auto companies reveals the difficulty of securing change. Only within the last dozen years has the auto industry even admitted the casual connection between automobiles and smog. In 1950 Dr. Arlie Haagen-Smith, a professor at the California Institute of Technology, discovered the relationship. The motor companies in 1953 publicly denied it. Said a GM official in a letter to a Los Angeles County supervisor: "The information that is available to us does not indicate that carbon monoxide is present in harmful amounts in the Los Angeles atmosphere and so we have not been concerned about the imminence of a serious health problem from this source."

California initiated regulations effective in 1961 to force the auto makers to do something to control emissions. Not until 1968 were these requirements established nationally. The industry negotiated delays time after time by begging that it would be technologically impossible for pollution control progress to be made at the rates which first the state of California, then the federal government had in mind. Meanwhile industry argued that pollution control was the job of the consumer. The managing director of the Automobile Manufacturers Association, Harry Williams, said in a speech:

> What I want to discuss today is something which, so far as I know, no other industry has ever been called upon to do: namely, to concern itself with how the consumer uses or misuses the product long after its sale to the public ... In eliminating smoke from vehicle exhaust, much progress has been made. True, there is room for improvement, but mostly this must come from the [car] owners, who are alone responsible for the maintenance of their vehicles.

Behind the backs of the public during the fifties and sixties, the industries were collaborating on a scheme that withheld pollution control innovations from the market. The Justice Department filed suit against the four major companies in January, 1969, charging them with collusion on pollution control devices. Specifically, they cited the companies' practices of eliminating competition by sharing technological breakthroughs among themselves, holding back on production until each member of the agreement was able to produce. The injunction was settled in fall of 1970 with a "consent decree" in which the companies agreed to end the conspiracy, but no method of enforcement was set up. A suit challenging the decree was subsequently filed in a U. S. District Court in California, but it was speedily turned down.

The U. S. government took on the job of regulating auto emissions in 1965. Congress passed a clean air bill that year which authorized the Secretary of Health, Education and Welfare to set limits on carbon monoxide (CO) and hydrocarbons (HC). In 1966 the National Air Pollution Control Administration (NAPCA) adopted standards for 1968 model cars; again in 1968 modifications were announced to apply to 1970 cars. In November, 1970, new limits were set for 1972 cars. Standards for emissions of oxides of nitrogen (NO_x) for 1973 cars have been discussed, but no limits have been finally agreed upon.

Theoretically, the industry has since 1960 achieved an 80 percent reduction in CO emissions and a 70 percent reduction in HC. At least one industry official has decided that the "battle" for a clean car "has been won." This simply is not true. The engine modifications used throughout the sixties to reduce HC and CO (which basically involve improving the crankcase valve and increasing the temperature of combustion, thus making possible more complete combustion) actually increase NO_x. Using catalytic mufflers makes it possible to deal with all three pollutants quite effectively, but presently only a few such devices are being used.

Catalytic mufflers are delicate mechanisms. Lead is poison to them. The industry's push to get the lead out of fuel is based not on environmental concern but on the auto makers' need for lead-free fuel in order to use the catalytic muffler.

NAPCA is in charge of carrying out a testing program to assure the effectiveness of Detroit's pollution control program. Unfortunately, it is a farce. Tests are carried out on specially tuned prototype models—not on production line vehicles, and not on cars which have ever been in the hands of the public. Manufacturers, it is suspected, develop and drive a fleet of carefully groomed prototype cars and offer up only the best performers when the time comes for a test. Should a model fail the test, NAPCA sends it back for retuning. According to the Ralph Nader-affiliated task force which produced the report *Vanishing Air,* some cars get third and even fourth tries before they pass the test.

Vanishing Air reports the findings of a NAPCA-sponsored check on their testing process. Emissions of over 100 Hertz rent-a-cars were measured. A study subsequently conducted by the California Air Resources Board supported the Hertz results. NAPCA Commissioner John T. Middleton admitted before a Congressional subcommittee in March, 1970, that 75 to 80 percent of new cars tested on the road failed to meet national emission standards by a margin of 15 to 25 percent. The authors of *Vanishing Air* conclude: "Every study the Task Force has been able to find which was conducted by persons outside the automobile establishment indicates that any connection between the standards and actual automotive performance is purely coincidental."

Even though the mechanisms are not all the industry promised, one should nevertheless shop for a car with pollution control devices. Buy a car which is low to moderately powered. The horsepower should coincide with the weight of the car and the load it is pulling; cars should be neither grossly overpowered nor underpowered. Most important is to maintain a car well. It should be tuned twice a year, during spring and fall when the seasons change. (In the South where the seasons remain virtually constant, once a year.) The mechanic should have a reputation for good work and thorough knowledge of your model automobile. Often a reputable dealer is the best bet.

Pollution control packages are available to clean up old cars. They sell for about $10. These inexpensive kits do not treat NO_x, however; and the catalytic converters which do, cost around $200. When shopping for a used car, find out from the dealer what its emissions ratings are. California, New Jersey and Washington, D. C. offer free emissions testing services. California's is a mobile unit run by the state's Air Resources Control Board. New Jersey has designated a number of inspection stations which are scattered around the state. There is one testing agency in the District of Columbia. Emissions tests carried out by private testing laboratories are prohibitively expensive—approximately $500. Drivers should pressure their state and municipal pollution control agencies to follow California's example.

The only certain way to clean up the automobile is to replace the ICE with an alternative non-polluting power source. The only way to increase the mobility of all people, to reduce congestion, and to stop highways from raping the land is to develop mass transit systems which work well enough to compete with the privately owned auto. But these alternatives do not exist now, and most citizens have no choice about their relationship to the auto. Until another engine is available or until adequate mass transportation is constructed, most people will drive their cars. If they do, there are steps they can take to use it in the least destructive manner.

Oil companies' advertisements claim that by using low-

leaded or lead-free gas the driver can combat air pollution.
Contradictory claims in other ads, as well as those which ex-
hort drivers to clean the air by using gasolines with detergent
additives, have smogged the gasoline issue to the point at
which even intelligent and questioning consumers are confused. What kind of gasoline should be put in a car?

The facts about lead are clear: lead is toxic to humans.
Leaded gasoline emits lead particles into the air. There is the
most lead in the air where traffic is heaviest. An increasing
number of scientists are warning that we may no longer have
to chew old paint to acquire the headaches, weight loss, dizziness, convulsions and blindness that characterize various
stages of lead poisoning. We may get it from polluted air.

Lead advocates like the Ethyl Corporation, oldest manufacturer of the tetraethyl lead which is added to gasoline, cite
studies which say that there is no conclusive evidence of
harm to humans from air-borne lead. However, J. Buxbaum,
M. D., chairman of the New York Scientists' Committee for
Public Information, has pointed out that most of these studies suffer from: (1) a lack of sensitivity of the testing
methods; (2) insufficient numbers and variety of subjects; or
(3) the assumption that there is a certain level at which the
amount of lead in the body becomes dangerous to health. In
a September, 1970, report, Dr. Buxbaum cited recent studies
that raise anew the health hazards from breathing our daily
lead.

Other scientists have discovered that one of the additives
put in leaded gasoline to clean lead deposits from spark
plugs, trimethylphosphate, may be a factor in causing
deformed and aborted births. The additive, known in the industry as a "scavenger," was linked to an abnormally high
percentage of early deaths among unborn fetal mice in experiments reported in the November, 1970, issue of *Science*
magazine.

In the process of making gasoline, oil is refined until it is
of suitable composition and quality to be used as an automotive fuel. Different types of engines require different quality
gasoline. High compression engines need gasoline with a high
octane rating ("premium" gas, 100 octane) to operate efficiently and without knocking. Low-powered, low-compres-
sion engines can get along with lower octane gasoline ("regular" gas is 94 octane). High octane gasoline can be obtained

by blending in organic chemicals, hydrocarbons, during the refining process or by adding inorganic tetraethyl lead.

In widely circulated advertisements Ethyl Corporation claimed that lead-free fuels increase emissions of hydrocarbons, which in turn increase smog. As evidence, the firm cites studies which examine relatively high octane lead-free gasoline. However, 9 out of 10 cars produced in 1971 are supposed to have such low compression engines that they can use gasoline with even lower ratings (91 octane) than regular gasoline. According to Ethyl, smog is increased by the organic additives which replace lead in the process of raising octane ratings. In low octane gasoline, none of these additives are necessary, so no increases in smog-producing emissions are incurred.

Several oil companies have initiated massive national advertising campaigns for their new "low lead" (not no-lead) gasoline because "engine tests show some lead is needed to prevent possible valve damage" (Esso) in high compression cars already on the road. The National Air Pollution Control Administration has said in rebuttal that to put enough wear on an engine to damage the valves with unleaded gasoline would require sustained speeds of 100 mph for 100 hours or its equivalent—pulling a heavy trailer across the country, for example, or driving at sustained high speed over the Rocky Mountains. In such relatively rare instances, the motorist is well justified in using low-lead high octane gasoline. The rest of the time, even his high compression car could operate as well with no lead at all.

In general, car owners should check with manufacturers to learn the octane requirements of their engines, and then should experiment with lower octane gasolines to assure that the manufacturers are correct. One obstacle confronting the driver who wishes to use low-octane gas is the fact that oil companies do not ordinarily announce the octane ratings of their products. Sunoco's dial-a-blend pump does. Other companies should be required by law to list the octane number on the gasoline pump.

Use the lowest octane gasoline possible in your car. Lead-free is best, and if high octane gasoline is necessary, choose Amoco lead-free premium or other such premiums, should they be introduced. If it is at all possible use the new unleaded 91 octane regular gasolines.

Several leading petroleum industry spokesmen, including Union Oil Company President Fred L. Hartley, have proposed lowering compression ratios even on present cars by such relatively minor changes as installing thicker engine head gaskets. This would permit use of a low (91) octane lead-free regular and a lower-leaded (97) octane premium that would meet the needs of both new and older car models.

Some charge that unleaded gas costs more, but Assistant NAPCA Commissioner for Standards and Compliance William H. Megonnell has pointed out that Amoco ads have long stressed that "leaded gasoline shortens the life of spark plugs, and . . . halogens added to scavenge the lead, shorten the life of tailpipes and mufflers." Also, lead destroys the very sensitive catalytic devices on which hinge Detroit's present hopes to clean up the ICE.

Perhaps the most misleading advertisements of all are those by several major oil companies implying that, as a response to newly emerging environmental demands, they are not only taking the lead out, but adding detergents. They are supposed to keep the crank case "anti-pollution valve" from sticking, thus helping to decrease carbon monoxide and hydrocarbon emissions. It is true that detergents are beneficial, and NAPCA, for instance, thinks that all fuels should contain them. However, the implication that this is a reflection of their new environmental conscience is misleading. They have all had detergents for some time. Most misleading of all is Chevron's ad for F-310, which compares a clear balloon full of exhaust from an engine using Chevron gasoline with a dirty balloon containing exhaust supposedly generated by a competitive brand of fuel. The dirty black balloon didn't get that way from the exhaust of a car in which any standard brand of competitive gasoline was used, because virtually all the popular gasolines contain similar detergents. Under contrived conditions, the company ran a car without any detergents in the gasoline at all until it was thoroughly fouled, and then performed the "comparison" with what the consumer is persuaded to believe is a popular competitive gasoline. The Federal Trade Commission has cited Chevron for deceptive advertising.

Liquid gasolines refined from petroleum are not the only fuels which may be used by automobiles with internal combustion engines. Several forms of natural and manufactured gas also work, and work better: they burn cleaner, cost less and do less damage to engine parts. Gases are chemically simpler hydrocarbons than those found in gasoline; therefore, they create less smog. Gaseous fuels were the choice of most ICE-driving entrants in the industry-supported 1970 Clean Air Car Race.

Natural gas is usually found with petroleum (oil) deposits. The largest component of natural gas is methane. It is available as a fuel in two forms—Liquid Natural Gas (LNG) and Compressed Natural Gas (CNG). The most common method of handling natural gas is to compress it. Liquefaction is more difficult. Natural gas liquefies at very low temperatures (minus 259 degrees Fahrenheit). The liquefaction process must be carried out in special plants, and less than 20 centers are currently in operation. The system is gaining popularity for use in shipping natural gas overseas, since it is cheaper to refrigerate a ship than to pressurize it. As an automotive fuel, however, LNG is handicapped by the fact that each tank provides only enough fuel to travel about 50 miles.

Methane is also produced during the decomposition of organic materials. Some landfills require networks of pipes to channel off the gas before it concentrates enough to explode. Gas from garbage is a potential source of transportation-generating power.

Propane is found both with natural gas deposits and in petroleum. Because it is easily liquefied, it is "bottled" into cylinders and sold as Liquid Petroleum Gas (LPG). LPG is widely distributed as a household fuel, and for years some taxi and delivery truck fleets have used it.

The process of converting automobiles to use either LPG or CNG costs $300 to $400, and it frequently can be performed by propane dealers in a few hours. LNG requires specially insulated tanks to maintain its very low storage temperatures; conversion costs therefore are double those of the other two types of gas.

Because gaseous fuels sell for less than gasolines, producers have not been motivated to explore for new sources—hence there are inflated predictions about the imminent depletion of natural gas reserves. Such claims are unnecessarily alarmist, especially since it is possible to manufacture gas from coal, and there are coal reserves for over 500 years remaining.

Variations on the standard internal combustion engine are also available in the American car markets. Some of the alternatives produce more pollutants, but others promise significant reductions.

Diesel engines burn fuel which is less completely refined than ordinary gasoline, has a lower octane rating and is lead-free. Because the combustion temperature is hotter, combustion is more complete and emissions of hydrocarbons and carbon monoxide are lowered. At the same time nitrogen oxides are increased.

In fall, 1970, General Motors purchased U. S. patent rights to the German-developed Wankel engine. This engine has certain advantages over the standard ICE of comparable horsepower: it is smaller, lighter, has fewer moving parts, runs without vibrating and costs less to produce. Emissions of carbon monoxide and nitrogen oxides are similar in Wankel and standard engines, but the Wankel throws out more unburned hydrocarbons. A Japanese model of the Wankel, the Mazda Rotary, has been able to meet federal 1971 standards by installing a thermal exhaust reactor. Car makers may consider the small size of the engine a boon when pollution control devices must be tacked on. Large American cars with standard engines have little room left for such mechanisms.

General Motors and Ford have said that by 1972 they will introduce trucks with gas turbine engines. Chrysler developed a handful of prototype turbine cars several years ago. The turbine principle is essentially the same as the one which operates jet planes. In its adaptation to vehicles, the turbine is less noisy, although its steady high-pitched hum is not especially pleasant. The major drawback of the turbine engine, according to a government engineer, is that its nitrogen oxide emissions are excessive and difficult to control. Mileage is relatively poor, and the temperature of the exhaust is hotter than that from the ICE. Also, production costs are high. The turbine system is promising, but from the perspective of the present it does not look like the best replacement for the standard ICE.

If the ICE can't be made to run clean, then the public and the government must persuade the industry to produce new engine systems. The most promising of these have been available since the very beginning of the auto age, though they are farther than ever from public acceptance. Between 1900 and

1930 both steam and electric propulsion were overtaken and then virtually eliminated as challengers to the ICE.

The original drawbacks to the electric vehicle were its short driving range after charging, its heavy weight and its need for special recharging equipment. Range and weight are still problems, though recharging is now easier. Modern electric vehicles offer a few pluses: they are quiet, and they emit no pollutants. However, until fuel cell technology is developed (car-sized fuel cells are still in the conceptual stage), electric cars will consume electricity generated at power stations, which do pollute. The National Economic Research Associates reports that the energy consumption of all motor vehicles operating in 1968, had they been powered by electricity, would have increased the power plant load by 43 percent. It is impossible to compare directly sulfur dioxide (produced by coal-burning generating plants) or radiation (from nuclear power plants) to the HC, CO and NO_x emitted by standard ICE-equipped cars. However, some general comparisons do place electric vehicles in a favorable light. One source estimates that a typical electric car uses enough electricity to cause a power plant to produce only 85 percent as much pollution per mile as a gasoline car that meets 1975 standards. And in terms of efficiency of energy use, the electric vehicle is significantly ahead of the ICE.

The dark horse of the auto engine race is the old-fashioned steam engine. Although in 1900 there were more steam-driven cars than any other type, by 1908 they were on the way out. The last commercial steam car was built in 1930. Since then the steamer has been disregarded for being too expensive, freezing up easily, demanding too much water too frequently, and threatening to explode. By the middle of the 1960s practically all these early technical problems were engineered out. Starting time was quickened by using smaller quantities of vapor. A process was developed to recycle vapors, permitting the original supply of water to be used over and over, rather than blown off. Only a small amount of fluid at a time becomes steam, eliminating the danger of explosion.

The Senate Commerce Committee in 1969 carried out an extensive study of alternatives to the ICE. Out of this effort came a very readable report which concludes that the steam engine "is a satisfactory alternative to the present internal combustion engine in terms of performance, and . . . it is dramatically superior in terms of emissions."

Rankine cycle is the generic term for the class of engines, including steam, in which a fluid produces the energy. The Rankine cycle engine is a simpler machine than the ICE. It has no transmission and no clutch—thus, fewer parts which must be replaced when worn. It runs quietly on inexpensive low-grade fuel like kerosene and betters the mileage achieved by ICEs. The cars grow old gracefully; antiques have been reported still running after several hundred thousand miles. And the Rankine Cycle Engine creates almost no pollution.

With the exception of American Motors, U. S. auto makers have denied any interest in the steam car. However, Nissan Motors of Japan, producers of the Datsun, have already contracted with American inventor Walter Minto to develop a prototype Rankine cycle car adaptable to mass-production by the end of 1972. Minto's demonstration model is already complete, and work on the prototype continues on schedule. He is likely to use freon or another chemical which will work like water in a steam engine without freezing or evaporating.

William Lear, famous for his work with the Lear jet, entered and rapidly withdrew from an experiment to develop a steam car entry in the 1969 Indianapolis 500. All along he has been working to design a mass marketable steam car. His latest scheme employs a fluid called Learium.

One tactic to speed acceptance of the steam car is to encourage local, state and federal agencies to experiment with Rankine-cycle vehicles in their motor pools. President Nixon set an example with his October, 1970, order to all federal agencies to use low-leaded or lead-free gas whenever possible. The California State Highway Patrol, under the direction of the state legislature, has already contracted with two steam engine companies to convert a conventional car to steam. The results of this test will be especially interesting since highway patrol cars must meet extra performance requirements. San Francisco and Dallas are testing steam-powered buses as part of a project financed by the Department of Transportation.

The problems encountered by steam advocates, like those faced by pollution control boards in the 1960s, illustrate the stranglehold auto companies have on American transportation. General Motors, largest U. S. manufacturer of automobiles for decades and the largest corporation in the world, claims it is fighting air pollution with a $40 million annual research budget in pollution control. The authors of *Vanishing Air* effectively decimate GM's claim by providing some figures for comparison:

GM's "official" figure of 40 million annually (albeit only since 1967) sounds like a good deal of money. However, when measured against other aspects of the corporation's operations, the figure withers to inconsequentiality. Forty million dollars is about 16 hours of gross revenue for the corporation. (GM grosses about $2.5 million an hour, 24 hours a day, 365 days a year.) The GM funds allegedly budgeted for pollution research equal about 0.17 percent of the company's gross annual sales of $23 billion. The research figure is one-sixth the annual advertising budget of $240 million, and it is only about $13 million more than the $27 million GM is spending annually in a 10-year program to change the signs at company dealerships.

Obviously, there is more to GM's rhetoric than meets the eye. Large corporations have tried hard to arouse sympathy among the general public, while simultaneously raking them for profits and injuring them with pollution. The automobile may be the mainstay of this country's economy, but air pollution and highway-gutted neighborhoods are not. There is no excusable reason why General Motors, Ford, Chrysler and the other automobile manufacturers should not be forced to dip into their rich coffers to solve problems created by their products.

airports

• *The motorist driving past Chicago's O'Hare Field on Inter-state 294 is confronted by a startling sight: two jets hurtle down parallel runways a quarter of a mile apart, leap simul-taneously into the air, and bank sharply away from each other toward their separate destinations. Such maneuvers are necessary at O'Hare which handles as much traffic as the ten largest airports in Europe combined.*

• *If the city of Los Angeles has its way, it will build the world's busiest jetport beside the sleepy community of Palm-dale, California. Nearly half the present population of the United States—100 million people—may pass through its gates every year. This is seven times the number of passen-gers at O'Hare.*

• *According to Richard L. Garwin, chairman of the Presi-dent's Science Advisory Committee Panel on the SST, the noise of a supersonic plane at take-off will equal the noise of 50 subsonic jets taking off simultaneously.*

In the 1950's, airports ceased to be the almost exclusive domain of the rich. Affluence has created a nation of vacation-ers and tourists, and airborne ones as well. Corporations have growing numbers of executives and managers for whom a trek across the country by air is as routine as a trip to the super-market.

When the numbers of flying businessmen and tourists are totalled a clear image of the rapid rise of air travel material-izes. There were 6,403 airports in the United States in 1950; now we have almost twice as many. In 1955, less than 1 out of 3 intercity passengers traveled by air; now the number has risen to 6 out of 10. During the same period, airlines added

128

400 new planes, all of them jets with radically increased passenger capacity. Since then, the 737s and the 747s have been added. Altogether, the domestic commercial fleet flies the equivalent of 43 return trips to the sun each year. Meanwhile, the volume of air freight also expanded 400 percent between 1955 and 1965.

But the really astronomical growth in air travel is yet to come, if officials at the Federal Aviation Administration (FAA) are correct. John Goodwin, chief of its Environmental Planning division, forecasts another 300 percent increase by 1980. "To handle that kind of traffic, every major city in the country will have to have at least two airports by then," he said. But, he adds, the opposition generated by each proposal for a new or enlarged airport may make this an unrealistic expectation.

Indeed, two-airport cities are probably wishful thinking on the part of the FAA, the federal agency created in 1958 with a mandate to "promote" aviation. (Not to be confused with the Civil Aeronautics Board, the sole function of which is to regulate rates.) Over the past few years a number of bitter airport battles have been fought across the nation. Today, a major controversy is raging in New York over the proposed expansion of Kennedy airport into Jamaica Bay. On the other side of the country, outraged citizens in Palmdale, California, are trying to stop the city of Los Angeles from sending a plane over their homes every half-minute or so. In New Orleans, a storm center is forming because of a proposal to build an airport in Lake Pontchartrain. And in Florida's Everglades an uneasy peace was declared after construction of what was to be the world's largest jetport was stopped—at least for a while.

These protestations suggest that the presence of an airport is much more disruptive than it used to be. And it is, for reasons which are rather obvious but sometimes forgotten.

First, most existing airports were built in the 1920's and 1930's, when jetliners were still science fiction and suburbs were in their infant stages. Most of these airports are now surrounded by houses, and the residents have to live with enormous passenger jets thundering overhead. The drone of the old DC-7s is not to be compared with the roar of the newer generation of jets. And the new supersonic planes will be far noisier yet. Although residents near airports will not be subjected to sonic booms from planes heading for that particular airport (since the planes will have slowed down to land) the general rise in airport noise from the monsters will certainly outweigh that consideration. As it is now being projected, the French supersonic Concordes will bank steeply upward as they land and turn on their engines at full power to slow themselves.

Meanwhile, finding suitable locations for new airports is becoming virtually impossible. Today there is considerably less open land than there was 30 years ago. Yet our traffic bottlenecks and poorly developed rapid transit systems militate against moving airports too far away from cities. Even when they are located far away, there is the danger that they will encroach upon a smaller community or degrade a much-needed scenic area.

A third reason for the unpopularity of airports is simply the development they foster. Every new airport brings along with it a flock of speculators and developers, eager to cover the surrounding areas with motels, restaurants, rent-a-car agencies, and industrial parks. Aside from the aesthetic impact of such development, it can do serious ecological damage to an area. It was the anticipated new city—not necessarily the proposed jetport itself—that would have spelled the ruin of the Florida Everglades.

While airports are unpopular with the people who suffer their adverse effects, they are highly regarded by those who stand to gain from them. The airlines have had significant buying power over the past 15 years, and they will continue in this role at least until 1975. Between 1955 and 1965, U. S. airlines invested $5.5 billion in new equipment; the projection for the 10 years between 1965 and 1975 is over $10 billion. Their role in the U. S. economy has been compared to that of the railroads in the last century. Furthermore, virtually every sizable business or industry is dependent on air travel. Thus, inadequate airport facilities mean less business, and less business means a "stagnating" local economy.

In a sense, then, airport promoters are damned if they do and damned if they don't. The public wants a prosperous community and the speed and convenience of air travel. It doesn't want noise, pollution, rampant development, and despoiled scenic areas. Rarely can both wishes be granted.

To most, the costs of more planes and airports, in social

and aesthetic terms, outweigh the economic benefits. But airport proponents usually dismiss their opponents who value such considerations as "emotional," because their reasoning is based upon such uneconomic factors as peace and beauty. However, there are arguments that can be made against the proliferation of airports, and there are legitimate ways to oppose them. The Airport and Airways Development Act of 1970 establishes the guidelines for all airport construction that is partially financed by the federal government. Since virtually every airport is built with federal aid, a brief examination of this act is a good place to begin.

The new Airport and Airways Development Act is the first to give more than token consideration to environmental deterioration. This assertion, expressed more euphemistically, was made by an official at the Federal Aviation Administration. Nevertheless, the act declares from the outset that "the nation's airport and airway system is inadequate to meet the current and expected growth in aviation," and decrees that "substantial expansion and improvement of the airway system is required." With this as a declaration of policy, it seems wise to make full use of the stipulations pertaining to the environment that come later.

For anyone trying to oppose a new airport, section 16 is the most important part of the act. "It is declared to be national policy," it begins, "that airport development projects . . . shall provide for the protection and *enhancement* [emphasis added] of natural resources and the quality of environment of the nation." No project having an adverse effect is to be authorized by the Secretary of Transportation, it continues, unless "no feasible and prudent alternative exists and . . . all possible steps have been taken to minimize such adverse effect."

Under this same section, a provision is made for public hearings "for the purpose of considering the economic, social, and environmental effects of the airport location and its consistency with the goals and objectives of such urban planning as has been carried out by the community." Although "hearings" is clearly in the plural form, John Goodwin at the FAA says that only one hearing is actually required. Whatever the case, the FAA will refuse to provide financial aid for the construction of the airport (it pays a flat 50 percent of every project) until the public has been offered the opportunity to make heard its views and present testimony. Nor will the allocation of funds be considered unless the public agency assigned to airport development has filed a written report establishing the suitability of the site. Theoretically, a locality with sufficient funds can build an airport regardless of what the FAA says—as long as federal safety requirements are met. That this should happen, however, is quite unlikely.

There are other sections of the act designed to safeguard environmental quality and the interests of communities. Any group undertaking to oppose an airport project should obtain a copy (formally designated Public Law 91-258) from a Congressman or from the House Appropriation or Senate Finance committees and become familiar with the pertinent sections.

It should be obvious to anyone who has followed the airport disputes that have arisen over the past few years that no airport was blocked by a public hearing alone. Unless a solid body of support can be mustered and a convincing argument formulated, the chances of success are slim. Some groups can muster little support, but can develop a strong case against airport construction; others may manage to raise a citizen furor without being able to build a powerful case. A group which can do both is a definite force to be reckoned with.

Alan Stewart, director of the Dade County Port Authority, would have to agree. Stewart's agency had been quietly buying large tracts of land some 50 miles from Miami before it announced plans to build a gigantic jetport there. The land happened to be immediately to the north of Everglades National Park—directly in the path of the drainage system that is the life sustenance of the park during the dry winter season. Surprisingly, the site was approved by the FAA and Secretary Volpe, with no objection from Interior Secretary Hickel.

This, however, did not placate conservationists—in fact, they were incensed. Appealing to Stewart was a futile gesture; he characterized them as "butterfly-chasers," and displayed his appreciation of the Everglades by lumping all the wildlife into a single category—"yellow-bellied sapsuckers." Sometimes he even dispatched assistants to speak religiously of man's responsibility to "exercise dominion over land, sea, and air," or to reassure the worried conservationists that the Port Authority would preserve "a Seminole poling a dugout."

Such off-handed arrogance won Stewart a number of determined enemies, who decided that the best strategy was to make a national issue of the controversy. Working expeditiously in a climate of growing environmental concern, they soon assembled an impressive coalition of interests. In addition to every major conservation group in the country, it included the United Steel Workers, the American Fisheries Society, the United Auto Workers, the American Forest Institute, and the Garden Clubs of America.

If Stewart wasn't shaken by this formidable opposition, the Departments of Interior and Transportation were. Both dispatched study teams to the area, and in separate reports they reached almost identical conclusions. Development of the jetport, they said, would "inexorably destroy" the park. The Port Authority, becoming anxious for the first time, contracted Stewart Udall's environmental consulting firm, Overview, to find a location for the airport. For their $75,000, though, they weren't satisfied with his answer. Udall suggested moving the site away from the Everglades and prohibiting private development around the jetport.

The controversy had reached such national dimensions that it now looked as if a verdict would be delivered by the President himself. The groups in the coalition appealed for a massive outpouring of public concern. Letters began to flood the White House. Before long a decision was made to halt construction and a search for an alternative site was begun.

The fate of the Everglades is still very much in question. There are stipulations written into the agreement which might fan the ashes of the controversy and cause it to ignite again. Now, however, environmental groups are well prepared and watching their opposition's every move.

The Everglades controversy was uncommon among airport disputes in that it became a national issue transcending local politics in many respects. Opponents of the jetport won because they made an effective appeal to America's pride in an irreplaceable national resource. In New York, opponents of a proposed runway expansion into Jamaica Bay have also employed the same argument. By convincing New Yorkers of the value of a wildlife refuge on the edge of the city (a rare blessing indeed) they hope to arouse them to take action.

The efforts of the Committee to Save Jamaica Bay have been imaginative and enterprising. Unsatisfied with Interior

Secretary Hickel's pronouncement that building the runways would enhance the area (by displacing polluted water with a landfill), they cooperated with the city's Parks Department in making a study of the Bay. After consulting with hundreds of ecologists, biologists, wildlife specialists, and other experts, they released an impressive report which held that an expansion of such proportions would destroy Jamaica Bay's intricate web of life. They didn't stop there. After investigating airport operations, they discovered, among other things, that: (1) most of the flights to and from Kennedy are less than half full; (2) many of the planes fly distances so short that high-speed trains could reach the same destinations almost as fast; (3) updated instrumentation in the control tower could greatly ease the pressure felt by the airport; (4) rescheduling away from peak hours would further dissipate much of the overload.

After this act of pre-emption, the New York Port Authority had no choice but to conduct a similarly painstaking investigation. They commissioned the National Academy of Sciences—an historical first for a local agency. Meanwhile, the Committee to Save Jamaica Bay was circulating petitions all over the city, holding demonstrations, recruiting influential people to join the cause, conducting pray-ins at the Kennedy airport chapel, and urging politicians to support their cause. One of the most attention-getting demonstrations was staged by a flotilla of private fishing boats. All of this took place before a public hearing had even been called. As of this writing, the future of the Bay is still uncertain.

An airport is obviously a rather awesome creation to find oneself pitted against. If the airfield already exists, the citizen often feels helpless to stop the construction of "just one more" runway. If it is a proposed airport, he may feel that he is fighting counter to the vast wave of public support for a more convenient landing spot. In actual fact, this is rarely the case. Airports are usually built by airport authorities or companies to make money—and if they hit stumbling blocks, they then raise the cry of "in the public interest."

As has been shown, an airport can be stopped if the conditions are right and if citizens are willing to fight hard enough. Just like any building project, airport construction is an essentially political decision, and, like all political decisions, can be countered.

The first rule that should be followed is to form a broad coalition of people and groups. An individual may pester and annoy officials, but it is unlikely that one voice will change minds or exert pressure.

After getting together at least the beginnings of a coalition, conduct careful investigations to bring forth all possible evidence against the site (and, if possible, the need). Express it dramatically—the citizens of Palmdale had simply another large figure representing the expected amount of traffic until they reinterpreted it as a plane passing overhead every 28 seconds, which is clearly an untenable situation. Also determine whether new instrumentation, rescheduling, etc. at an older airport might make a new or expanded one unnecessary.

To be effective, groups should assess and, if possible, challenge the study submitted by the promoters of the airport. Citizens should insist that the matter be left to the ecologists and not the economists.

It is essential that citizens find out where and when each public hearing is held. A hard-pressed airport authority may make it very difficult to discover such facts, but even if it means scanning every local newspaper closely and calling the proper authorities daily, it must be done. A stormy hearing session is one of the most effective tools a group has, and a missed chance might mean the difference between victory and defeat. Once a hearing is announced, make certain that it is well attended. Also try to secure expert testimony on as wide a range of problems as possible. Noise, land use, traffic flow, prevailing wind patterns, proximity of nationally protected areas and a host of others are applicable to the testimony.

Groups should not hesitate to use a variety of tactics, including demonstrations, rallies, picketing, leafleting, petitioning and using the media. All local elected officials should be bombarded with protests, queries and various bits of information, as should congressmen.

Write letters and send telegrams to all decision-makers involved. The first organization one should exert pressure on is, obviously, the airport company or authority. They originate the plans, make the fiscal request, and glean the profits. If they are obstinate, and if federal funds have been requested (as is usually the case), contact the Federal Aviation Agency's office in the appropriate region. In the continental United States they are:

Eastern Region
Federal Building
John F. Kennedy International Airport
Jamaica, New York 11430
Tel. 995-3333

Area: Connecticut, Delaware, District of
Columbia, Kentucky, Maine, Maryland,
Massachusetts, New Hampshire, New
Jersey, New York, Ohio, Pennsylvania,
Rhode Island, Vermont, Virginia, West
Virginia

Southwest Region
P. O. Box 1689
4400 Blue Mound Rd.
Fort Worth, Texas 76101
Tel. MA 4-4911

Area: Arkansas, Louisiana, New Mexico,
Oklahoma, Texas

Central Region
601 East 12th Street
Kansas City, Missouri 64106
Tel. FR 4-5626

Area: Illinois, Indiana, Iowa, Kansas,
Michigan, Minnesota, Missouri, Montana,
Nebraska, North Dakota, South Dakota,
Wisconsin

Western Region
5651 West Manchester Avenue
P. O. Box 90007, Airport Station
Los Angeles, California 90009
Tel. 670-7030

Area: Arizona, California, Colorado, Idaho,
Nevada, Oregon, Utah, Washington,
Wyoming

V

Southern Region
   3400 Whipple St.
   East Point, Georgia
   Tel. 526-7222
      Mail: P. O. Box 20636
         Atlanta, Georgia 30320

   Area: Alabama, Florida, Georgia,
   Mississippi, North Carolina, South Carolina,
   Tennessee

If the FAA is not impressed with the urgency of the situation, a strong protest should be lodged, along with a demand that the Agency initiate a study of the region by an impartial organization, such as the National Academy of Sciences. Attempts should be made to secure a stated promise that the FAA will not approve any federal money if the analysis of the situation indicates possible irreparable harm to an area.

If that tactic fails, another possible recourse is with the congressman from the district in which the airport will be built. If he is convinced by his constituency that there is widespread opposition to an airport, he may be in a position to request the House Appropriations Committee not to allot money for the project, or even to specifically prohibit the FAA from funding an airport. Since most representatives come to the Appropriations Committee begging for money for their particular districts, a statement from a congressman that the district does not want the money is extremely forceful.

A group should concentrate on opposing the airport site, not on proposing an alternative. Objections can be raised about any site no matter where it is. People who have felt obliged to suggest that an airport could be built at another location were sometimes surprised by the flurry of objections they encountered, and some were tempted to concede that the original location was really the best after all. Finding places where airports can be constructed is the job of public agencies and the Federal Aviation Administration, not private citizens.

Along with highways, airports symbolize America's "progress" and greatness to a generation of U. S. planners. If real progress and greatness are ever to be achieved in this country and elsewhere, such massive building programs should be stopped everywhere they are proposed. The decision rests in the hands of every harassed citizen.

factory vs. worker

• *One out of every four asbestos workers in New York City dies of a rare lung cancer called asbestosis. At least one out of four textile workers in carding and spinning rooms has contracted byssinosis, a fatal lung disease.*

• *Five times as many man-days are lost from job-related disabilities as from strikes. During the last four years, more Americans have been killed at their jobs than in Vietnam.*

• *The government's limit for a worker exposed to sulfur dioxide is five parts per million despite the fact that a recent report by the National Air Pollution Control Administration indicates that "most individuals will show a response to sulfur dioxide when exposed for 30 minutes" to such a level. When sulfur dioxide concentrations in London reached only .25 parts per million, a rise in the daily death rate was noted.*

Most environmentalists and other members of the "reading class" have never been inside a factory. They do not regard the factory environment as a serious ecological problem. However, the facts clearly show that industries contain the most polluted, most destructive environments in our society. The situation inside the plant is an intensified version of the pollution that is infiltrating the total environment.

Not all contemporary factories resemble the infamous sweatshops of the nineteenth century. Not all plants are iron foundaries where men work amidst thick black dust while giant machines constantly shake, pound and vibrate huge metal carts filled with red molten iron. Not all plants are like automobile factories where the noise is always so loud that no man can hear the man next to him on the fast-moving, nerve-straining assembly line. Many factories today have adopted "enlightened" managerial techniques like proper lighting, ventilation, and even air conditioning. However, modern workplaces expose men and women to dangers more lethal than anything known in the past—the dangers of modern chemicals.

In recent years the public has become alarmed by chemical substances in the environment such as lead, mercury, pesticides and carbon monoxide. These substances, and literally thousands more, are to be found inside every factory in this country in concentrations far beyond what the outside population will ever experience. An estimated 6,000 chemicals are now in common industrial use, with 600 being added every year. Very little is known about these chemicals except that they kill and disease people. They cause premature aging and mental retardation. They cause cancer, skin diseases, emphysema, heart diseases, liver diseases, respiratory diseases. Today's American work force consists of 80 million weak, sick men and women whose lives are prematurely shortened because of the intense pollution of their working environments.

The story of in-plant pollution is best told by the workers themselves. They may not always know which chemicals are the ones that are killing them or what they should do about them, but a growing sense of malaise is creeping into the factories as more and more are fainting and coughing and dropping dead at their jobs. Two men who work in chemical plants tell the story this way:

> Now we're using all kinds of products from polyethylene, polystyrene. We get this product that is all coming from crude oil. Half of our people don't know—even the scientists don't have time to take all the samples of all the new things that are being manufactured now. I see these guys going in in the afternoon, they get three or four shots and they come up all lively. Yea, but after the guys are out, they're not lively. They come home just about walking, and I see this every day and it hurts me; it hurts all of our people.

> Joseph Demski, Local 8-406, Oil, Chemical
> and Atomic Workers Union

And well, my father worked in a chemical plant right next door to the one I work for; about twenty years. He's dead now. I had an uncle; he also worked in a chemical plant; the same plant right next door to me. He died of cancer, this cancer in the throat. He had a tube in his throat and it was the result of working in this chemical plant; he didn't have it before he went there. But a certain chemical that he inhaled got in his throat and his throat was a mess and he died. I mean, I don't like the expression—but he died like a dog.

Harold Smith, Local 8-447, Oil,
Chemical and Atomic Workers Union

Statistics are always misleading, and statistics on occupational health are particularly incomplete and inadequate. 14,500 workers die every year from an accident suffered on the job. That is, more men are now dying in the course of earning their livings than are being killed in Vietnam. Statistics also indicate there are about 2.2 million serious industrial accidents every year—the exact figure will never be known. But more troubling than that is that nobody has even tried to measure the extent of industrial disease—the millions of men and women whose lives are crippled by heart troubles, lung diseases, hearing loss, cancer, nerve paralysis, and other such fringe benefits of their jobs.

American factories have never been pleasant places to spend eight hours a day, but now they are becoming more deadly as new mysterious chemicals and esoteric processes are introduced. What figures there are indicate that the conditions of the workplace have been deteriorating over the past ten years. In 1958 the number of workers who died from work accidents was 13,300—or 8 percent less than today. Also in 1958, the accident frequency rate was 11.4 accidents per million man-hours worked, as compared to a rate of 12.8 for 1968. Workmen's compensation insurance rates and fire and explosion insurance rates have been sharply rising. By all indices, the industrial accident rate, which had been declining in the years after World War II, took an upward turn in 1958 and reached a new high in 1966. More recent statistics indicate that it has not yet begun to fall.

The statistics concerning job accidents are not entirely believable. They are collected by polling one or two states and then projecting that figure onto the entire nation. Furthermore, company management often conceals on-the-job accidents with tricks like bringing injured workers into the plant and assigning them work in the parking lot to prevent the payroll from showing "time lost." A recent Department of Labor study by Jerome Gordon shows that the true on-the-job accident rate may be 10 times the time-lost figures—bringing industrial accidents to possibly 25 million each year. The study by the Department of Labor, which cost $58,000, was in danger of being suppressed until pressure for its release had built up among the United Auto Workers and other organizations.

The term "industrial accident" is not an accurate description of the cause of on-the-job injuries. "Accidents" are the product of the total in-plant environment, and are not merely freak and random happenings. When factory environments are experienced as constant noise, heat, dust and foul smells, accidents will tend to occur. Tired and tense workers cannot always take meticulous care in their every action. The one who misses a split second in his timing might have his hand crushed by a moving machine. These mischances cannot be termed "accidents," because the designers of plants fail to consider and compensate for natural traits of the human beings who will work there.

At the present time, workers are practically defenseless against the invisible perils of their jobs. Of the 6,000 chemicals in industrial use, recommended maximum exposure levels have been established for only about 450. That leaves about 5,600 chemicals in common use, about which practically nothing is known. And no one has even attempted to study "synergistic effects," or the results of chemical combinations.

One problem workers often face is that they simply do not know what chemicals they are working with. Substances will arrive in boxes or tanks which are labeled only with a code or brand name. As one worker says,

> Most of us are using things that we don't even know the types of effects they have on the people that work on them. I know that some of these materials that I mentioned, at one time or another, used to come in with warning signs on the drums or on the bags, and now they no longer have them.

> Nick Kostandaras, Local 7-148, Oil,
> Chemical and Atomic Workers Union

Information is systematically kept from the workers about the health hazards of their jobs. When a safety inspector is called in to inspect a plant, the workers never see the report he files. When a company doctor makes a medical examination of a worker, the man is never shown the diagnosis. Ignorant of the nature of the perils they face, workers are left with an uneasy feeling that all is not well.

Even when workers do know what chemicals and gases are in the plant, they receive no help in identifying or monitoring their effects. Plant monitoring devices, when they exist, are often faulty or incorrectly calibrated. Toxicity tables are never posted for the workers to see. And when people become sick they are taken to the company doctors who are not anxious to acknowledge job-related disease. Company doctors will usually ask a sick man about his hygiene habits and his diet before they ask what substances he has been inhaling and handling on his job. As one worker in a chemical plant in Bayonne, New Jersey, says:

> Anyone who's involved in a health problem, particularly in our industry, has to be submitted to the doctors that the companies choose and, whether they're killing us or curing us, we have no recourse until they bury us, or discharge us, and then we have to go to another doctor, or process through compensation.

> Tom O'Leary, Local 8-623, Oil,
> Chemical and Atomic Workers Union

When a worker is injured or made ill by the conditions of his work, legally, he does not have the right to sue the company. His only legal recourse is to file for Workmen's Compensation. Workmen's compensation laws vary enormously from state to state. If a worker loses his hand in Texas, he receives $5,250 in payments; if he loses his hand in Arizona, he receives $27,500.

Another failing of workmen's compensation is that the laws seldom provide compensation for industrial disease. Although the widely known diseases, like pneumoconiosis (black lung), silicosis and asbestosis are covered in some states, these represent exceptions to a general rule. Few other diseases are covered, and 12 states do not recognize compensation claims for any diseases at all.

In terms of preventative approaches to the problems, there

are very few legal avenues for help. The only federal legislation that now exists is the Walsh-Healey Act, and the recent Construction and Mine Safety Acts. The Walsh-Healey Act, applying only to plants which contract with the federal government, provides for less than 20 federal safety inspectors to cover the 75,000 plants with 27 million workers who come under the Act. These inspectors actually inspect less than 3 percent of the Walsh-Healey plants every year—and of those, an average of 90 percent are found to be in violation of the standards. The only enforcement provision of the Act is that the government may threaten to cancel its contracts with violators.

Legislation at the state level is equally unsatisfactory. In the 50 states there are a total of 1,600 safety inspectors—less than the total number of game wardens. Average state expenditures for safety standards, inspections and enforcement are 40 cents per worker, with some states as low as 2 cents per worker. Unlike water pollution laws, state safety laws vary so much that companies can play states off against each other when they choose plant locations. For example, when Pennsylvania recently passed a law forbidding the use of beta-naphthalamine, an agent that causes bladder cancer, the plant in the state that used beta-naphthalamine closed down and moved to Georgia.

Strong federal legislation is desperately needed in the realm of occupational safety and health. In order for any legislation to begin to solve the problems of occupational health, it must provide for accurate testing and standard-setting for all industrial chemicals and materials; it must provide for regular inspections and monitoring of workplaces by outside inspectors as well as workers in the plant; and it must provide for strict enforcement measures which allow for immediate closing of imminently dangerous situations. Heavy fines should be levied on companies that fail to comply with the standards. Legislation to this effect would provide a first step toward cleaning up the polluted workplaces.

Factory workers are paid by their bosses to risk their lives and health in the polluted environment of the factory. Management has not been willing to accept responsibility for the health and safety of their employees. Workers, on the other hand, are only beginning to demand that their bosses install monitoring devices and pollution control equipment.

Management usually claims that the problems of the in-plant environment are unfortunate, but necessary conditions of economic progress. The bosses say that 80 percent of industrial accidents are caused by worker carelessness, and that the larger environmental problems of noise, heat and fumes cannot be helped. These claims are not true. There are ways of monitoring plants and even redesigning factories to minimize the health hazards to the workers. Even with the present dearth of knowledge about industrial substances, measuring and monitoring devices can be an effective way of keeping gas, noise and dust levels under control. And modern engineering ingenuity, if it were applied to factory design, could virtually eliminate some of the worst offenses.

Measuring devices are used to find out the amount of pollutants present in a given environment. For in-plant pollution, the most useful devices are those which monitor fumes and gases, dust and particulate matter in the air, and noise levels. There are many of these devices on the market. The most useful testing device for in-plant gas is the "M-S-A Universal Tester" which can detect substantial concentrations of about 140 different gases, vapors, dusts, fumes and mists—including common killers like carbon monoxide, chlorine, sulfur dioxide, toluene and phosgene gas. The M-S-A Universal Tester works on the same principle as a bicycle pump. A piston-type pump draws air into a tube and through specially treated filter paper which changes color when a particular pollutant is present. Different filters are used to test for different substances. The M-S-A Universal Tester has the additional advantages of being lightweight, easy to use, and inexpensive. The tester itself costs $82, and the accessories for each type of pollutant cost about $8 apiece. The entire M-S-A Universal Testing Kit, complete with all accessories and detectors for about 140 substances, costs $460. Further information can be obtained from the Mine Safety Appliances Company, 201 North Braddock Avenue, Pittsburgh, Pennsylvania 15208.

Monitoring devices, or indicators, are like measuring devices except they take continuous measurements and have an alarm unit to signal when concentrations of specific substances reach danger levels. Monitoring devices are sometimes found inside plants, but they are often broken or set to go off at concentration levels far above the recommended exposures. Therefore, workers are encouraged to use their own monitors. M-S-A makes portable monitoring devices for several contaminants, including carbon monoxide, combustible gas, and oxygen.

Several easy-to-use and relatively inexpensive noise meters are on the market. The simplest is the "General Radio Type 1565-A Sound-Level Meter" which runs on a flashlight battery and is small enough to be operated with one hand. It makes accurate measures of sound levels, and is particularly useful for periodic spot-checks. The Type 1565-A Sound-Level Meter costs $365. For more information, write General Radio, West Concord, Massachusetts 01781. (GR has several handbooks for laymen on basic techniques of sound measurement which they will send free of charge.)

Several complicated measuring and monitoring devices exist to detect the presence of lead, boron hydrides, arsine, hydrogen floride, combustible gases, and other potentially harmful substances. Some other companies which should be contacted for information are:

> Foxboro Company
> 367 Neponset Avenue
> Foxboro, Mass. 02035

> Mast Development Company
> 2212 East 12th Street
> Davenport, Iowa 52803

> Technicon Industrial Systems
> Dept. 104
> Tarrytown, New York 10591

> Analytic Instrument Development, Inc.
> 250 South Franklin Street
> West Chester, Pennsylvania 19380

In terms of plant engineering, it is impossible to propose specific plant designs that would be applicable to every factory. Each has a unique set of hazards, and the plant design must be tailored to them. However, a few principles can suffice to show that it is possible to engineer health.

Ventilation systems can be designed to capture dusts,

fumes, vapors, and mists in the air and to carry them out of the work area. Proper placement of hoods, ducts, air cleaners, and fans can create an exhaust system that will minimize the amount of contaminants in the air. Ventilation systems must be designed to meet the specific needs of the plant and to allow for air currents and sources of air pollutants.

Dust can be controlled by general ventilation as well as by enclosing the dust source or moistening the particulate matter. Noise can be controlled by different techniques of machine insulation, noise absorption or substitution of less noisy machines. Techniques of noise control, dust control, and fume and gas management have already been developed and are being employed widely in consumer commodities—but rarely in factories. There is no reason why these same techniques could not be adapted for factories when they have been used successfully elsewhere.

For example, in 1969 the Ford Motor Company (whose cars have been advertised as quieter than a Rolls Royce) was challenged by the United Auto Workers. Ford's Buffalo, New York, plant was so noisy that an employee asked that changes in plant design be made based on the noise-control techniques Ford used in its cars. The request was denied. A wildcat strike ensued, and Ford finally agreed to make some improvements.

If companies could be required to design their plants with workers' needs in mind, many occupational health and safety problems could be solved.

Despite all the technical and technological possibilities that industry has well within its grasp, little is being done to implement the changes, even when control devices are being produced by the company that so badly needs them. If workers are not going to accept the management ploy that "the technology doesn't exist," they certainly won't accept an answer that "we don't have the money," or "the problem doesn't really exist." To save their own lives and the lives of others, workers must demand these changes be effected immediately.

Federal legislation can make it possible for workers to begin to protect themselves. But even the best health and safety legislation will not clean up the workplace unless workers use their initiative to call in inspectors, insist on monitors, demand regular medical checkups, and understand the names and toxicity of chemicals in the plant. The problems of the workplace ultimately must be solved there.

Several international labor unions have begun programs to inform their members about the dangers of their jobs and to encourage them to act in self-defense at the plant level. The Oil, Chemical, and Atomic Workers Union (OCAW) has been at the forefront of the fight, devoting a lot of union money, time and energy to finding out what the problems of their members are and helping locals get the technical assistance they need for constructive action. The most interesting program of the OCAW is a series of conferences the union has been holding for local members. At each conference, people from locals are asked to tell about the problems they are confronting in their plants. A panel of scientists and medical doctors is present to answer specific questions the men and women ask about their contact with chemicals or their health problems. The conferences are taped, transcribed, printed, and sent out to other locals so that the information contained in the questions and answers can be shared. These conferences provide a forum for educating local members about the problems in their own plants and for educating union officials about the problems of their membership. After the conferences, the international union continues to help the locals by getting the technical assistance they need to meet specific crises, encouraging them to use monitoring equipment, and developing specific contract language directed at the issue of working conditions. The 1970 Bargaining Policy Program of the union made health and safety the first priority.

In the last two years, several other international unions have begun to raise the issues of health and safety. More and more, union newspapers are publishing information about factory conditions. The United Auto Workers, the United Steel Workers and the Industrial Unions Department of the AFL-CIO held conferences about the problems of in-plant pollution.

In 1971, ten international unions will sponsor a course in industrial hygiene in conjunction with New York's Mount Sinai School of Medicine. One hundred local union members will be invited to attend a week-long series of lectures, seminars and demonstrations given by top scientists and medical doctors on topics in the field of occupational health. The

sponsors of the course hope that it will serve as a model for
similar courses to be held at the regional level.

In addition to educating their members and providing
monitoring equipment, there is much that local unions can do
in this field with existing state and federal legislation, inadequate as it may be. The Walsh-Healey Public Contracts Law
does contain health and safety standards applying to many
toxic materials. The Act applies to all employees working on
federal contracts of more than $10,000. Workers should find
out if they are covered by the Act and familiarize themselves
with its provisions. Anyone covered by the Act can request an
inspector or an investigation if he feels that his plant is vio-
lating the standards set by the Act. Inquiries about the Act
will be answered by the Wage and Hour and Public Contracts Division, U. S. Department of Labor, Washington,
D. C.

More recent legislation such as the Construction Safety
Act, the Longshoremen's and Warehousemen's Safety Act,
and the Coal Mine Safety Act, should also be studied by
workers in those industries.

There are also ways that workers can find out what is already known about industrial chemicals. Two publications
that every local union should have are:

Sax, N. Irving, *Dangerous Properties of Industrial Materials,*
3rd edition, published by Reinhold Book Corporation, 430
Park Avenue, New York, N.Y. 10022. Price $35.

Committee on Threshold Limit Values, *Documentation of
Threshold Limit Values*—1970, published by University Mi-
crofilms, P. O. Box 1346, Ann Arbor, Michigan 48106. Price
$10.

Sax's book is the most complete index of industrial chemicals, and includes toxicity ratings and descriptions of the deleterious effects of about 12,000 chemicals. The second book
contains the 450 Threshold Limit Values that have been established by the American Conference of Governmental Industrial Hygienists. A condensation of that book, "Threshold
Limit Values of Airborne Contaminants," is available at a
price of 50 cents per copy from the American Conference of

Governmental Industrial Hygienists, 1014 Broadway, Cincinnati, Ohio 45202.

But pamphlets can't provide solutions to situations such as this:

> We do have quite an air pollution problem in our area. On top of sodium peroxide, chlorine gas, phosgene, TDI, metallic sodium, right across the street from us there's a diamond research development plant, and I don't know what they're making over there—nobody can find out.
>
> But something got loose over there and drifted over into our plant and put fourteen of our guys into first aid, wondering why they couldn't breathe. And we had two of our guys lose their sight for a few hours due to the effects of this stuff, and we can't even find out what's going on over there.
>
> Now as long as the wind is from the east, it's not going to bother us, but the wind doesn't stay that way all the time and we do get some pretty noxious fumes from that place every now and then. It got to the point where our parking lot is just north of the research plant, and it's even changing the colors of the paint on our cars. So you know it isn't doing our lungs any good.
>
> Albert Nist, OCAW,
> Local 7-509, Ashtabula, Ohio.

Ultimately the issue of in-plant pollution must be made a primary concern in collective bargaining. Specific health and safety standards can be incorporated into collective agreements. Also, the question of who should finance monitoring devices and industrial hygiene courses can become subject to negotiations. Some unions are already developing innovative health and safety demands. For example, the United Rubber Workers, in their 1970 contract negotiations, won a provision for management to pay one-half cent per man-hour of work into a fund to finance research in the field of occupational health. Similarly, the 1970 Bargaining Policy Program of the OCAW calls for one-tenth of one percent of the revenue per barrel of crude oil refined to go into a Health and Safety Fund.

Collective bargaining will never be a complete solution to

the problems of in-plant environments for the simple reason that more than 75 percent of the work force is not unionized. Furthermore, even the most powerful unions find it difficult to force management to negotiate on the issue of health and safety. Management regards this area as its domain. The collective bargaining approach and the legislative approach to the problem are both necessary first steps toward cleaning up the workplace, but lasting changes will only occur when workers are sufficiently informed and aware of the problems to take direct action at the local level.

Obviously, "in-plant pollution" is only a literary convention, for as Albert Nist's story points out, pollution does not respect such barriers as doors or windows. If the air is bad inside a factory, it will be bad outside, too. Workers are exposed to more dangers and discomforts than any other group of citizens, but their situation is not such that they must fight for gains single-handedly. The community group which helps workers wage a successful battle also benefits by having a cleaner, healthier community.

Students, scientists, doctors and environmentalists all have skills which are valuable to workers in their struggle against the unknown dangers that confront them. Outside expertise can provide the technical knowledge and laboratory facilities to help workers identify the chemicals in their plants and learn about their toxicities. The conferences held by the OCAW demonstrate how successfully medical skills can be put to the service of the workers.

In return for the services that doctors, scientists, and environmental groups can render, workers have a lot to teach these groups about the ways their plants are contaminating the community. In one breath the workers can tell about the substances used in the plant, and in the next breath they can tell exactly which substances the plant is dumping into the water supply and the atmosphere. Because the environmental problems inside the plant and outside the plant are intimately connected, much can be gained by a coalition with the workers.

There have been some instances in which community people and workers have joined forces to fight polluting factories, but these instances are as yet very rare. Occasionally a local union will invite the community to their meetings or an environmental group will talk to a union to get information on a

factory's pollutants. There is room for much more cooperation—not for the purpose of closing down the factory, but
for the purpose of forcing the factory to treat its workers and
the community with a healthy respect.

factory vs. neighbor

• Union Carbide Corporation's Ferro Alloy Division plant at Alloy, West Virginia spews out so much corrosive smoke that the sun is blotted out much of the time and the town's church has enclosed its statue of St. Anthony in a protective clear plastic case. Described as "a 24-hour pall of black, yellow and orange smoke and soot," the estimated 28,000 tons of grit emitted annually by the plant are equal to one-third the total of New York City's particulate pollution.

• On the evening of June 22, 1969, Ohio's Cuyahoga River caught on fire. A massive oil slick, apparently from upstream industries, was unaccountably ignited and flowed with the river, burning two bridges. Firemen reported five-story-high flames and estimated damage from the half-hour blaze at $50,000.

• In a demonstration of how potent polluted water can get, a Japanese newspaper, the Mainchi Shimbun, successfully developed film using river water. The newspaper collected water from 13 spots along streams, ditches and canals polluted by paper mills, and used the raw water as if it were developer chemical in its photo laboratory. The developing took from 20 to 43 hours, and produced fuzzy but recognizable pictures.

In bygone days, when an industrialist proclaimed that "the factory has made America everything it is," he did so with pride. Recently, however, this contention, expressed as exuberantly as ever by big business, is falling on somewhat less receptive ears. America, the modern land of milk and honey, is also the land of dirty air, fouled water and shattering noise.

153

Industrialists, despite their loud disclaimers, have made America everything it is in these ways, too.

Generally speaking, the person who lives near a factory finds himself subjected to one or more of three major annoyances—air pollution (smoke, soot, invisible chemicals, smells), water pollution (garbage, chemicals, bubbles, proliferation of algae, dead fish) or noise. All three are waste products and represent an unwillingness on the part of the management to spend the money to control them. Although it is a rare industry that can utilize air or water and return them completely unchanged to the outside world, there are many processes and devices that will keep these precious resources as uncorrupted as possible. Air and water pollution will be discussed in this section; noise pollution, since it is so common and widespread, will be dealt with under its own heading.

Of our dozen or so major environmental crises, air pollution stands in the foreground. The National Wildlife Federation, in evaluating six indices (air, water, soil, forest, wildlife and mineral) gave air quality the lowest rating—"very bad and getting worse." Partially offsetting this is the fact that Americans are more aware of and concerned about our bad air. On the other hand, air standards are particularly difficult to legislate and to enforce.

Air pollution is extremely serious. It is ugly and unpleasant. It corrodes metal and stone, buildings and monuments. It forces repeated and expensive cleaning of rugs, clothes, walls and drapes, sometimes totalling an estimated $200 extra per person per year. It diminishes visibility, posing hazards to airplane pilots and automobile drivers. It injures vegetation, stunts plant growth and damages crops. It is very likely responsible for certain regional weather changes and may be causing other more widespread climatic alterations. Worst of all—thus far—air pollution is a known killer.

In December, 1930, the Meuse River Valley in Belgium became host area to the first major recorded air pollution disaster. Struck by a week-long inversion—a weather phenomenon caused by a layer of warm air which traps colder stagnating air beneath it—thousands of residents of the region became ill. Before winds dispersed the accumulation of pollution, 60 persons died from the poisoned air. Temperature inversions are common throughout the world and are not inherently dangerous unless they cause concentrations of pollutants.

Similar tragedies struck the small town of Donora, Pennsylvania in 1948 where 6,000 of the town's 14,000 residents fell ill and 20 died, and London in 1952, where 4,000 died.

In the past, factories and the household burning of coal were the primary causes of air pollution. Over the last two decades the automobile has moved to the forefront of the crisis and coal use has shifted from the homeowner to the electric utility, but in the United States utilities and factories still account for 45 million tons of airborne pollutants yearly, or about 32 percent of the total.

The substances which primarily contribute to and make up our air problem are diverse and include solid particles, liquid droplets and gases. They are:

Coarse dust particles and fly ash. These are larger than 10 microns in diameter (a micron is 1/125,000 of an inch and anything larger than 10 microns is visible to the naked eye). They are principally produced by the incomplete burning of coal, and settle out of the air quickly, posing problems only in the vicinity of a factory. They tend to make an area very "dirty," but they rarely cause respiratory problems since they are large enough to be screened out before they reach the lungs.

Mists. These are liquid particles up to 100 microns in diameter (about one-fourth the size of a small raindrop). They are released industrially from spraying or impregnating operations, and often evaporate to form gases or even smaller particles called aerosols.

Aerosols. This is a general term which refers to solids or liquids less than one micron in diameter. Principally they include fumes (solids) and smoke (solids or liquids), both of which are formed as vapors condense or as chemical reactions take place. Smoke in addition is a byproduct of all forms of combustion. Aerosols are emitted by a wide range of manufacturing processes.

Dust. These particles, ranging from 1 to 10 microns, can arise naturally or from many industrial processes. Dusts and aerosols are small enough to penetrate deep into the lungs. If they carry dangerous chemicals on them, they are harmful because the lungs have no mucous protection deep inside them.

Sulfur oxides. Sulfur is a basic impurity in coal and fuel oil, and is released by cars and any coal fire, as well as by chemical plants, metal processing plants and burning trash. With oxygen it forms sulfur dioxide and sulfur trioxide, both of which corrode stone, paper, metal, fabrics and leather, and harm people and vegetation. With water, the very dangerous sulfuric acid is formed which can pollute streams and kill wildlife. Other sulfur compounds, like hydrogen sulfide gas, which smells like rotten eggs, are products of oil refineries and paper and chemical processes.

Carbon monoxide. This odorless, tasteless and invisible gas results from incompletely burned fossil fuel (coal and gas) and is primarily emitted from cars and factories. It is a deadly poison which the body readily substitutes for oxygen. In less than fatal doses it causes dizziness, heart strain and headaches.

Carbon dioxide. This is not a dangerous gas and is, in fact, necessary to the survival of vegetation. In recent decades, however, it has been produced in tremendous quantities as a result of burning fuel, and scientists are questioning whether it might trap heat in the atmosphere and heat up the earth, causing the polar ice caps to melt. The question is frightening to contemplate, although few conclusive answers have emerged.

Hydrocarbons, nitrogen oxides and photochemical oxidants. These are simple, common substances which apparently have the potential to combine into powerful pollutants. The complexity of the chemical processes involved is far beyond the scope of this book, but authorities in Los Angeles and other cities "blessed" with lots of bright sunlight find photochemical oxidants and the resulting "smog" among their biggest headaches.

Lead. Lead is a cumulative metallic poison which is released from smelters, fuel combustion, dust and sprays, as well as from automobiles which use leaded gasoline. Environmental and human damage from lead is still under investigation.

Others. These include beryllium (a component of alloys), arsenic (metal smelting), asbestos (brake linings and insulation), and cadmium, mercury, vanadium, nickel, chromium and manganese—all are part of the air we breathe and all have been shown, or are suspected, to be poisonous or harmful. Nearly all of them are byproducts of factories.

The factory poses a very severe problem to the environmentalist. In some other areas he can attempt to alter his style of life to ease his conscience: he can buy a small car or use a bicycle, or refrain from using pesticides, or cut down on electricity consumption. Against an industrial polluter in his community, however, he has only two options—he must ignore the annoyance and the danger, or he has to exert pressure for change.

Pressure against an industrial polluter can come from many quarters and can take different forms, but it is advisable to check first where the federal government has already led the way, before becoming enmeshed in a situation which bypasses legal processes. As Hazel Henderson, former chairman of New York City's Citizens for Clean Air, remarked, "We are promised from the President on down a now-or-never fight to restore our air, water and land. The politicians, government and business officials—our leaders, in fact—have finally caught up with the people!"

The first federal air pollution control act was passed in 1955. It was weak and ineffective, yet it remained on the books, unchanged for 12 years due to industrial pressure and lack of coherent citizen involvement. Finally, in 1967, the Air Quality Act was passed, and this (with various amendments) represents major governmental action on air pollution.

The Act authorizes the Department of Health, Education and Welfare (HEW) to designate air quality control regions based on various factors affecting pollution, such as climate, topography and urbanization, for nearly 100 metropolitan areas.

HEW then develops air quality criteria for each major pollutant in the region. These criteria detail levels at which the pollutants, whether alone or in combinations, show harmful effects on public health or welfare. At the same time the department provides information on control techniques for each pollutant, including technological data, emission control costs and economic feasibility.

After receiving the HEW criteria and control data, each state must formulate standards or goals which are to be met. These standards, which refer to a state's air quality control regions, set maximums on the total amounts of specific pollutants permitted in the ambient air. (Ambient air quality standards have been defined as "pollutant levels that cannot legally be exceeded during a specific time in a specific geographic area.") Before adopting standards, the state must hold a public hearing. After adoption, the standards are subject to federal review and approval.

Once standards are approved by HEW, each state must produce a plan for implementation, maintenance and enforcement of its air quality standards. If HEW finds either the standards or the implementation plan inadequate, the Act empowers it to refuse approval and formulate its own standards or plans for the air quality region in question. These then must be adopted.

This procedure has already been completed for many but not all of the air quality regions. The plan for implementation and the procedures involved is what concerns the eco-activist now. How is the law converted into action?

After standards and plans are in effect, the federal government continues to monitor air quality in a region. If the control measures are ineffective, HEW notifies the state which must then take "reasonable" enforcement action within 180 days. If the state does not do so, and if the pollution problem is an interstate one, HEW (through the Department of Justice) can take a polluter to court. If the problem is purely an intrastate one, then HEW can act only by request from the governor of the state.

The Air Quality Act of 1967 is a comprehensive act, but it is a cumbersome one. Because of its vast increase in potential effectiveness over earlier legislation, Congress permitted states and industries considerable amounts of time to "gear up" and tighten standards.

As citizens became more and more concerned about air pollution in the late sixties, they began to notice the built-in delays of the 1967 act. Setting up ambient air quality standards and establishing emission standards is a very roundabout way of getting some control measures, especially since engineers and mathematicians ran into major problems trying to correlate the two. When the act was being debated in Congress, it was proposed that national emissions standards be set up, and many environmentalists later felt that this would have been a much simpler, quicker approach. Most air quality regions do not correspond to any existing unit of government so that enforcement is likely to be fairly weak. Furthermore, the act requires the states to go through the process of setting standards and writing implementation plans for some 30 to 40 pollutants.

The administration of the act by the National Air Pollution Control Administration (NAPCA) has also come under fire, most notably in the Ralph Nader Task Force report, *Vanishing Air*. Between the time that the act was passed in late 1967, and the time that it was amended in late 1970, not one Air Quality Region had a working implementation plan. In fact, NAPCA's Commissioner had not even finished designating all the regions. Congress, realizing some of these shortcomings, speeded up the process in some ways when it amended the act in 1970.

Most large cities in the country now have laws governing air pollution, and they have agencies set up to enforce the laws, often adjuncts of the local health department. In smaller cities, the job is usually handled by the health department as it exists, or by a board of building standards. Rural areas usually have no provisions for control, and a citizen group will have to start from the bottom. Local agencies vary widely in the degree of their effectiveness and sincerity. In New York City, 13 out of 30 inspectors were recently suspended for perjury and for taking bribes. In many other cities officials sincerely interested in solving the air pollution problem are hampered by lack of support from the city council or administration.

It is the agency's duty to find out what companies are in violation of the city code, and to order these companies to comply. Most companies faced with an abatement order will ask for a variance, or a time extension for installing equipment, and this is a situation which citizens can use very well to their advantage. In Cleveland, Ohio, the control division cited Republic Steel, Cleveland's largest corporation, for its emission of red iron oxide dust. Republic first appealed the order, saying that it was not valid, and giving some fairly childish reasons. It claimed that the Ringelmann chart, which was the measure the city used to determine the company's illegality, was inaccurate.

A Ringelmann is a chart of five shades from black to light gray. An air pollution inspector holds the chart in front of him, at a distance and angle specified by the law, and compares the blackness of the smoke coming out of the stack to the shades on the chart. A Ringelmann can also be used for white smoke, by measuring opacity, or the degree to which the inspector cannot see through the smoke. If 90 percent of the sky behind the smoke is obscured from view, this smoke would be the equivalent of Ringelmann 5, no matter what the color is. The chart is open to a good deal of subjectivity and it has been challenged in court by a number of companies, but it has been declared valid.

Republic Steel claimed that iron oxide dust does not present a hazard to health, and therefore was not illegal, but the Cleveland code clearly states that companies can be cited on the basis of visible emissions alone, regardless of what the emissions contain. Luckily for the company's critics, the Cleveland code requires that a public hearing be held on a request for variance.

Within two weeks enough publicity had been circulated by the Air Conservation Committee and several local newspapers that Republic withdrew its request six days before the hearing date. The citizens were jubilant. Compliance, unfortunately, was another story. Republic was given 90 days to submit plans for the improvement of its facilities, although they had previously claimed that the plans already existed. After the time period was up, and no changes had come about, Clevelanders found that Republic had been granted an extension. "You can't expect a company to solve in 90 days something that's been a problem 20 years," was the comment.

Even though factories can take comfort from the fact that they contribute less to the air crisis than the automobile does, they do have a domain in which they are pre-eminent: water pollution.

The National Wildlife Federation's 1969 report gives our

water quality a "bad" rating and places it just behind the air as an ecological crisis situation. Lake Erie is termed "on the verge of death" by many authorities. The other Great Lakes and many of our major rivers are also in very serious trouble.

There are over 300,000 water-using factories in the United States. Industry is the largest user of water and industrial wastes account for by far the largest volume and most toxic of pollutants. In fact, major industries are believed to discharge approximately three times the amount of waste as is discharged by the 150 million sewered persons in this country.

Probably the most perplexing aspect of the industrial waste problem is that the discharges consist of an enormous variety of materials. The Federal Water Quality Administration (FWQA) in 1969 listed a total of 51 agents that are dumped into the nation's waterways, and immediately added that the list was known to be partial rather than complete. The FWQA is presently in the process of compiling a more comprehensive list by sending out 250 questionnaires to a random sample of industries across the country, asking them detailed questions about effluents, processes and materials used, as well as present and projected waste treatment facilities. The industries, however, are under no legal obligation to answer the questionnaires, and many environmentalists doubt that the survey will be helpful in combating pollution.

The areas hardest hit by industrial discharges into water are the Ohio River Basin, the Northeastern states, the Gulf states and the Great Lakes states. Not surprisingly, these areas have the highest concentration of factories. Most significant is the finding by FWQA that over half the volume of the wastes discharged by factories into water comes from four major groups of industries—paper manufacturing, petroleum refining, organic chemicals manufacturing, and blast furnaces and basic steel production.

Common industrial waste products can be reduced to two general classes of materials, settleable and suspended solids, and organic materials. Solids which settle on the bottom of a river or lake cause pollution by smothering the organisms which live there; these dead organisms then float to the surface and decay. Suspended solids are often highly poisonous to fish and other marine creatures which are not particularly discriminatory about what they eat.

Organic materials create water pollution in a unique way.

When an organic substance decays, it uses up considerable amounts of oxygen. (In fact, as an example, it is speculated that as a dead tree decays, it uses as much oxygen as it produced during its whole life span.) The average lake or river contains a great deal of dissolved oxygen, produced by algae in the water. This suspended oxygen is what the water utilizes to cleanse itself as well as maintain life. Therefore, if too much organic waste material is discharged, the water's oxygen supply is used up and the river or lake "dies."

There are other perils facing our waterways. Phosphorus compounds and nitrogen, both essential to underwater life in small quantities, have disastrous effects on a lake or river in high concentrations. Although these elements are needed to produce food for aquatic animals, excess amounts result in overfertilization and alteration of the aquatic system and rapidly lead to algae "blooms." The algae proliferate so rapidly that they deplete the water's oxygen supply, eventually killing all higher forms and asphyxiating themselves. This process, which is known as eutrophication, occurs continually in all life-sustaining waters. In recent decades, however, man has speeded up the process a thousandfold, and Lake Erie is literally dying centuries before its time.

Factories cannot be held completely responsible for the eutrophication problem—our burgeoning population also plays a large role—but many aspects of it are man-made, and industry (and its products like detergents and fertilizers) must be held accountable for its part.

The other major water pollutant is one which was not suspected by scientists until recently. It is heat (or thermal) pollution, and its effects are also pronounced and serious. The primary thermal polluters are electrical energy generators, but other industries contribute their share, too. As an example, it requires 14,000 gallons of water to make $10 worth of steel, and 97 percent of all the water utilized by industry is used in the cooling process. Clearly we are faced with a major problem in disposing of this waste heated water.

Thermal pollution has a marked effect on fish, killing them outright or disrupting their breeding habits. A factory which raises the water temperature even five degrees may effectively eliminate all fish life in that section of a stream. Furthermore, it may produce effects upstream as well as downstream for the warm water may act as a barrier to fish that spawn far upstream.

Heat disrupts a body of water in other ways, too. Warm water can hold less dissolved oxygen than cold water, and water which is already overloaded with oxygen-demanding organic wastes will be taxed further when it is heated. A river which is only mildly polluted will degenerate markedly downstream from a continual discharge of heated water.

The story of federal legislation concerning water pollution approximately parallels that concerning air pollution, although preceding it by several years. Water quality is somewhat easier to monitor than air quality because it tends to fluctuate less and because rivers and lakes are more easily defined and observed than the air.

Federal enforcement authority on interstate and navigable waterways has been strengthened over the years since initial enactment of the Federal Water Pollution Control Act of 1956, notably by the Water Quality Act of 1965. The act called upon the states to establish standards for their interstate waters. These standards were then accepted as federal standards by the Secretary of the Interior.

To set standards, the states had to make decisions concerning the uses of their water resources, the quality of water to support these uses and specific plans for achieving such levels of quality. Once the standards were accepted by the Interior Department (USDI), they became federal standards, subject to federal government enforcement.

Like the Air Quality Act, the Water Quality Act also calls for a fairly tedious, drawn-out three-part abatement procedure. Under it, the Secretary of USDI called a conference in which the state agencies involved and anyone they brought along had an opportunity to make a full statement of his views concerning the discharges. A summary of the proceedings was drawn up, and if the Secretary approved, the polluter was expected to comply with the plan. If the Secretary felt that the abatement plan was not sufficient, he gave the state six months to remedy the situation.

If, after six months, this had not been satisfactorily accomplished, a public hearing was held. Testimonies were given and the hearing board (comprised of five members selected by the Secretary of USDI but including members from the state and other relevant agencies) decided whether abatement to that point had been satisfactory. If it had not been, the board made recommendations which were sent to the polluters and the state. Another six months was allowed to clean up the discharge.

In the case of a failure to take the recommended action in the allotted time, USDI could request the Justice Department to file suit.

As mentioned, this cumbersome procedure is comparable to the one followed against air polluters. There is, however, another option open to the government in the case of direct violation of the water quality standards of a particular interstate body of water. In this specialized case, FWQA merely notifies the violator of his violation and gives a six-month time period to allow voluntary cooperation and abatement. If at the end of the six months nothing has been done, USDI can initiate court proceedings. This maneuver has been used successfully against at least six major polluters, including the Interlake, Republic and U. S. Steel companies and the City of Toledo, Ohio.

Interestingly, citizens fighting water pollution have one of their strongest allies in an act that was passed in 1899. This is the Rivers and Harbors Act, section 13 of which (commonly called the Refuse Act) prohibits the discharge of "any refuse matter of any kind or description whatever" into any inter- or intrastate navigable waterway in the United States unless a permit is issued by the Army Corps of Engineers. (The act is not very well adhered to; the Corps reports that no permits have been issued to date in 23 states and only 266 permits were in effect in 1970!)

The Refuse Act is a very powerful law—harkening back to the days when flotsam posed several physical hazards to wooden ships—and recent court decisions have given it even more clout. Refuse includes "all foreign substances and pollutants" as well as thermal pollution. Refuse that is dumped on the banks of waterways that can be washed into the water is also subject to the law. And a dumping need not be willful or negligent—an accidental dumping can also be prosecuted. Even more useful to the eco-activist is the legal definition of the word "navigable" in the Act, which includes all water sufficient to float a boat or a log at high water.

What is even more impressive about the Refuse Act is that it provides a monetary incentive for information obtained from private individuals. The Act entitles "the person or persons giving information which leads to the conviction" of a polluter, one-half of any fine levied. This is more than idle talk. In an Interlake Steel case in 1969, one of Interlake's employees noticed that the company was dumping iron oxide and oil into the Calumet River. After nearly 50 letters, he finally got the U. S. Attorney in Chicago to act, and he received one-half of the $500 fine. In a more spectacular instance, an employee of the Mobil Oil Company reported an oil leak into Maine's Kennebec River for which he was personally responsible. He received half of the $2500 fine.

There is, unfortunately, one obstacle to the stringent enforcement of the Refuse Act. For various political reasons, Attorney General John Mitchell has issued a statement that manufacturers who are discharging toxic materials as part of their manufacturing process, especially if they are on a schedule of abatement with the FWQA, will not be prosecuted under the Refuse Act. This apparently exempts major, continual polluters from penalties applicable to the small industry or occasional individual who discharges wastes. It also leaves the intrastate waterways vulnerable to persistent polluters unless the state has standards for those waters.

There is, however, a possible action called *qui tam* under the old federal statutes. Part of the provision is that people furnishing enough information to convict an offender will receive part of the fine. Whereas ordinarily only the government can act against a criminal offender, these informers have been allowed to bring their own suits in the name of the United States when the government fails to take action. *Qui tam* has only recently been applied to an environmental question. Marvin Durning, a Seattle attorney, is suing a pulp and paper mill, ITT Rayonier, for continually dumping wastes into Port Angeles Harbor for five years. He had asked the U. S. Attorney to prosecute, but no action was forthcoming.

Another action which is applicable to environmental issues is the writ of mandamus, a court order directing the defendant to act. Generally one obtains writs of mandamus to force elected or governmental officials to carry out their jobs when they appear not to be doing so.

The decision to take an industrial polluter to court is often a difficult one to make. On the one hand, judicial decisions can be extremely strong and forthright, providing large fines and even jailings or injunctions for non-compliance. On the other hand, environmental law is a very new area and many judges instinctively shy away from precedent-setting decisions of what they consider a radical nature. Furthermore, there are only a handful of attorneys and law offices at present which are competent or even interested in the field and most of them are on the east and west coasts.

To this point, the thrust of most environmental legal actions against factories have been nuisance suits, trespass suits and negligence suits. Depending on the type of case, these may result in an injunction or the payment of damages or both. The pattern of these cases, originally highly favorable to industry, is gradually evolving toward a more favorable interpretation of the sanctity of the environment.

The success of a law suit often depends a great deal upon what are apparently lucky circumstances, and this fact works against major, sweeping victories. Courts are of necessity conservative bodies and rely only upon absolutely conclusive evidence. It is therefore easier to nail a small isolated factory in a rural or residential area than it is to win against a massive plant in the midst of an industrial park or a manufacturing area, even if that one company is an obvious source of environmental damage.

One environmentalist says his rule of thumb is not to take a water polluter to court if there are more than two factories on a particular stream. Ecologically, of course, this makes no sense, since it means, for instance, that an oil refinery in New Jersey can hide behind the safety in numbers of the state's many refineries. One spectacular *qui tam* action was begun in 1970 when the Bass Anglers Sportsman's Society of Alabama filed suit against 175 industries in the state, the Army Corps of Engineers, the Secretary of the Army, and the Alabama Water Improvement Commission for dumping wastes and allowing wastes to be dumped into state waterways without permits. The complaint was later amended, but it remains a sweeping attempt to force compliance with the Refuse Act.

Law suits can be and have been successfully waged on a variety of environmental conflicts and issues. They tend to be very expensive, however, and a corporation is certain to have greater financial resources than a citizens group. For this reason they are considered by most eco-activists to be a last resort after all other avenues of attack have failed.

Regardless of whether a law suit is planned, contemplated or even feasible, a certain amount of information is necessary before launching a campaign against a corporation. Not only should the citizen group be aware of the factory's products, methods and interrelationships with other components or products, it should have a good idea of the types of pollutants the factory discharges or emits. There are various methods of monitoring and studying the waste products of a factory, and in most cases the law provides that a state pollution control board must be allowed to enter the factory to measure these by-products. Of course, it is often necessary to convince the state agency to exercise its responsibilities.

Even without equipment, the average citizen can do his own evidence-gathering. Streams should be checked on either side of a factory to see if they degenerate on the downstream side. Bubbles, discoloration, foam, smells and dead fish are all indications of pollution. Water temperature on both sides of the plant should be measured at various times of the day. A factory's sewage pipes are often some distance away from the factory, and one should attempt to trace any pipe that is mysteriously discharging sewage (or even water) from what seems to be nowhere. If there are fishermen in the area, find out what they know about the particular stream or river, including unexplained fish kills or periods when catches were unusually small. The hard-working investigator might even gather past information about a stream from a local historical society.

Air pollution leaves similar clues. Structures downwind from a smokestack should be closely investigated. Even if they are not dirty with black soot or fly ash, they may have other less obvious discolorations such as white, chalky dust or orange residues. Glass and exposed metal should be checked for corrosion and pock marks. As mentioned in the preceding section, automobile exteriors often show the first signs of corrosion. Trees and other vegetation are also very susceptible to atmospheric emissions, and can be used as preliminary detectors of unhealthful conditions. Sulfur dioxide, for instance, turns evergreen leaves and needles brown, and smog will cause petunia leaves to glaze. Most pollutants also stunt a plant's growth significantly.

Of course, one of the best sources of information is the worker in the factory. In all likelihood he will know even more than the public relations department, even if they are helpful. If the worker is not antagonized, threatened or linked with the plant's management, it may turn out that he is as disturbed about the pollution as the factory's neighbors. And while he may be unable or unwilling to speak out publicly or even give his name, he may reveal facts and observations that would otherwise be unobtainable. It is important to form such alliances, possibly by stressing the public health aspects of pollution rather than its aesthetic or exploitative aspects.

Most groups, after determining exactly what the problem is and who is responsible, start at the very beginning—by talking to a company official, usually in the public relations department. In virtually every case this marks the fruitless beginning of a long campaign. Public relations men are not paid (or trained) to solve problems; they are there to intercept complaints and smooth over hostilities. Even in the rare instances when a public relations office is more than superficially sympathetic to a citizen group, it is never involved in a company's decision-making process.

Almost invariably the first meeting between a company and concerned citizens will accomplish nothing. As Eileen Kohl of the Council on Economic Priorities put it, "You can't go to a company and tell them they're doing bad things because they'll tell you they're doing the best they can. The best advice is not to take anything a corporation has said at face value. Be equipped to properly evaluate everything they say."

After the first disappointments, a concerned group must get down to some hard work. Whether the problem is air or water pollution, the first step is to exert pressure on the local and state authorities to monitor, measure and examine the emissions or discharges. This is an important step, for a regulatory agency's evidence stands up in court much more authoritatively than that of a collection of laymen. Also, it is particularly difficult to monitor a large smokestack by physical (rather than observational) means.

As previously mentioned, the Ringelmann chart does hold up in court, however it has a major drawback. The Ringelmann can only be used to monitor black smoke and other visible emissions, whereas some of the most dangerous chemical byproducts of a factory cannot be seen or smelled.

Factories have an easier time cutting down on the visible emissions than on the others, and often they will run their machinery at half speed or less during the time the management knows they are being monitored. This is a serious problem for any group which has demanded professional monitoring, for it is an expensive, time-consuming task. Often daily photographs of a smoke stack will document a factory's "slack period" if a local agency suspects trickery.

In the case of air pollution, most authorities recommend that citizen groups not attempt to monitor by themselves, as readings can easily be misunderstood and challenged in court. In the case of water pollution, this is not quite as true, and a sealed, dated bottle of stream water may be accepted as evidence. In a town with a university it is often possible to find chemistry students and professors who are willing to help with technical matters. In a larger city it may be possible to find one or two environmentally concerned members of a chemical society who would help, although most tend to have vested interests in companies which, themselves, may be substantial polluters.

If local authorities are adequately performing their duties, these studies can be submitted as additional evidence. If the authorities are ineffective or unhelpful, the studies may convince them to monitor—or the facts may convince a judge to issue a writ of mandamus, ordering the agency to act.

In either case, once the nature of the danger is established, the next step is to publicize it. Aside from the normal publicity measures discussed elsewhere in this book, there are some tactics which are particularly suited to an obstinate industry. One is to get a copy of the board of directors of the firm and determine their other holdings and businesses. Whereas a picket line around a factory is fairly ineffective, a picket line (with detailed literature) around a bank or a food store is apt to stir a great deal of interest. If one of the board members does happen to be president of a bank, it may be possible to persuade some of the major non-industrial organizations which have accounts there, to withdraw them. In other cases, a boycott may be effective.

Of course, in many instances a large company like General Electric or Union Carbide is essentially "too big" to picket or boycott effectively, and its board members may be invulnerable to attack. In this case it is often possible to ridicule and expose its national advertising policy. One instance of such exposure ocurred early in 1970 in Lewiston, Idaho. Potlatch Forest, Inc., a large lumber manufacturer and processor, ran a full-page advertisement in *Time* magazine, stating "It costs us a bundle but the Clearwater River still runs clear," and depicting a breathtaking photograph of a wilderness river. Student journalists at a Lewiston college, however, knew better, and in their newspaper showed that the photograph had been taken 50 miles upstream of Potlatch's plant. The scene in Lewiston, with smog and smoke-filled air and frothy, dirty water was starkly different from the Potlatch "eco-pornography."

One of the best measures a group has as to whether its campaign is starting to be effective or not is to look for company reaction. As soon as the company begins to respond to criticism, even in the most general ways, citizens know that they have finally reached some nerves. And if a citizen group is ever mentioned in a company's statements by name, rejoice! That group has then become a full-fledged thorn in the company's side.

Corporation responses will range widely from threats to pledges and from disclaimers to pleas for compassion. Some of these will be backed up by convincing arguments and may be distributed via full-page newspaper ads or long television commercials. The environmental group has to present equally convincing rebuttals if it wants to counteract what may be a favorable public image toward the company among those not closely involved in the struggle. Hazel Henderson has compiled a list of common company claims and the environmental responses. In a speech before the Citizens Workshop on Air Quality for Metropolitan San Antonio, this is how she put it:

Now a list of put-downs to the most frequent arguments used by polluters:

1. *Pollution isn't really a health hazard. Answer:* Statistical evidence correlating air pollution with illness and death is readily available from the National Air Pollution Control Administration, your local Cancer Society

or Tuberculosis Association—so have pamphlets handy as ammunition.

2. *Pollution isn't a problem in this area. Answer:* Since we know pollution contributes to the development of many human diseases, and we know that it can be blown hundreds of miles and respects no political boundaries, the best protection for our citizens is setting standards to prevent further degradation.

3. *The company would like to control pollution but doesn't know how. Answer:* Many polluting companies will insist that no technology exists to rectify the situation. The best tactics for citizens faced with this problem is to obtain a list (from any stock brokerage house) of all the major companies who manufacture and sell air pollution control systems . . . you may want to buy stock in them, too. Then your group can offer your assistance to the polluter in locating the right company to call in and design the control equipment. Tell them very sweetly that without any fee, your group will arrange for a salesman or engineer to call and give them a free estimate! If the company drags its feet, your group can buy a share of stock and bring the subject up at the next annual meeting.

4. *The company would like to install control equipment but can't afford it. Answer:* Not only is the equipment available, but there are federal tax incentives; and in many cases, they will save enough valuable materials from going up in smoke to pay for the equipment. Add that the company is going to have to spend the money sooner or later, and with current inflation they might as well do it now and get a public relations benefit. If a company official still argues about cost, say you are writing an item for your organization newsletter and you want to quote his answer to this question, "You say pollution control equipment is too expensive; well, don't you think people are worth it?" Incidentally, a good general rule for citizens is never to become too friendly with those *nice* public relations men or even sometimes with your own control officials, or you will become so sympathetic to their problems that you lose sight of the

larger, public interest. . . . Another good technique is to
recruit the wives of local company officials to join your
group. There's nothing like the Trojan Horse strategy!

On the question of using low-sulfur fuels, the company
may advance two common arguments. The first is that low-
sulfur fuels reduce the amount of sulfur oxides, but may increase photochemical reactions and smog—to which the
reply is that this is an unproven theory, and the company
must be very callous indeed to stick with a known killer in
order to avoid what may be only a wild hypothesis. Its other
contention may be that there is not enough low-sulfur oil or
coal to meet the standards. This argument was advanced in
New York City, along with threats of power blackouts.
When the Clean Air Law was passed there, the biggest oil
supplier merely built a $50 million de-sulfurizing plant in
Venezuela and now removes the sulfur there and sells it.

The most serious threat a company can advance is that if it
is forced to clean up its emissions, it will shut down the plant
or move it elsewhere. When this statement is advanced, the
citizens at least know that they are well on their way to hum-
bling the once-proud corporation. Any threat to shut down a
factory should get the widest publicity with clear, cogent citizen arguments, because the company will attempt to split the
community, pitting workers against environmentalists.

If the issue at stake is water pollution, the answer is an
easy one. All states with the exception of Maine have approximately the same laws concerning water quality. These
laws are also more stringently applied to new factories than
old ones, and it will not do the company any good to move
the plant to a new state. It may also be helpful to try and
ascertain exactly where the company plans to move, and
warn citizen groups in the new area to be on the alert.

If the issue is air pollution, the citizens' only real answer is
that eventually there will be national standards applying to all
the states, and the company will have to clean up at its new
location.

Most industrial shutdown threats are presented to scare
and divide a community. If a company is making a decent
profit from the plant, it is unlikely that it will close it down
to avoid what are essentially small capital improvements. If
the plant is only marginally productive, the management may

be looking for an excuse to close it down anyway. Shutting a factory is not something that can be done capriciously by an annoyed president, since it involves a major justification to stockholders and a loss of a considerable investment.

Slowly, almost imperceptibly, the American corporation is beginning to change. While company presidents might not worry about the effects of their plants' pollution on nature, they are beginning to worry about its effects on community relations. While few court decisions have closed down large factories, pressure is increasing from citizens who feel that we have exploited nature almost to the breaking point and must now let the system regenerate.

Although some changes are already apparent, most of them are not very significant. Corporations are trying many of their old tricks to see how serious their critics really are. They have studied some of the problems, shelved the studies and turned to their advertising agencies for help. The gratuitous nod of ecology is apparent everywhere, though few sources of pollution are being cleaned up. The factory is as dirty as ever, and the advertisements are merely adding to the hidden costs of pollution to the consumer.

The first step—forcing industry to admit the existence of a problem—is well under way. Now citizen groups must begin the second step in earnest—put an end to corporate domination of our lives, from the air we breathe to the kinds of death many of us will face.

water treatment

• *Several years ago, the residents of Amarillo, Texas, had their very own blues song, "Where has all the Flour Gone?" One of the town's bakeries dumped 1800 pounds of flour into the sewers, killing all the bacteria and destroying the whole sewage system.*
• *In New York, the sewer system overloads and pours raw sewage into the city's rivers and ocean area an average of 50 times a year. In Boston the same thing happens about every five days.*
• *A 1970 government study of water purification plants showed that 77 percent of the operators of the plants nationwide were inadequately trained in fundamental water microbiology, and 46 percent were deficient in chemistry relating to their plant operation.*

There are more than 150 million sewered persons in this country. Approximately the same number are served by public water supply systems. Relieved of the trek to the well and to the outhouse, most Americans take clean, plentiful tap water and functioning waste disposal systems for granted. Few persons think twice about what happens after a toilet is flushed. A sanitary kitchen and bathroom, according to the implicit assumption, obviously indicates a sanitary system throughout.

Unfortunately, the facts do not bear this out. The water in the United States is not only dirty, but is also, in many instances, dangerous. Furthermore, it is rapidly deteriorating. It is not an exaggeration to say that a national water crisis is looming directly ahead of us.

The problems that the United States will soon be facing

are the result of a combination of circumstances. On the one hand we have a large population which is growing rapidly and reaching extremely dense concentrations in a number of regions. In precisely these regions, too, the number of factories has proliferated greatly; their discharges are increasingly dangerous and unpredictable, as new chemicals are developed and used. In contrast to these growths, relatively few new sewage systems have been constructed and even fewer old ones have been modernized. In effect, many U. S. communities are making do with systems that were barely adequate 20 years ago.

Despite the advances that have been made in medical technology, the water in this country is not uniformly safe. It is true that the classic communicable waterborne diseases of the past—typhoid fever and dysentery—were brought under control by the 1930's, but Americans are still subjected to outbreaks of communicable disease from inadequate sewage treatment. The Bureau of Water Hygiene of the U. S. Public Health Service in 1970 found evidence of bacterially contaminated water being served to consumers in communities ranging in size from under 500 to over 100,000. And actual cases of illness are not hard to find.

In 1965, Riverside, California (population 85,000) was hit by a waterborne epidemic which affected 18,000 residents.

In 1968, Angola, New York's water disinfection system failed, resulting in a 30 percent rate of gastroenteritis. The town uses the same lake for sewage disposal and drinking water.

In 1969, more than half of the Holy Cross (Massachusetts) football team was stricken with infectious hepatitis because of the failure of a control procedure system.

In 1970, residents of Fall River, Massachusetts (population over 100,000) were instructed to boil all their drinking, cooking and washing water for a two-week period because of massive bacterial pollution. Only this action prevented the outbreak of disease.

Although these isolated, but serious cases, would give cause enough to worry, it is likely that they represent the tip of the iceberg. Not only are many cases not so easily solved or so severe as to warrant special attention, but there are numerous inorganic chemicals and trace elements which abound in our water in tiny but significant doses. These are neither detectable nor filterable, but they are being shown to cause marked human and animal damage.

In the past, when the pressure of population and industry was less, man lived in an essentially "open system" whereby certain waters were marked for consumption and others for expulsion. Now, we are increasingly being forced to use water as a "closed system"—reusing it where the need arises.

Hydrologists estimate the total usable surface water supply from rainfall at 700 billion gallons per day. According to one calculation, we used 270 billion gallons daily for industrial, agricultural and domestic purposes in 1965. A more recent estimate rates our current daily demand at about 440 billion gallons. Both estimates agree that we will enter the 21st century needing about 1000 billion gallons daily. Needless to say, the total usable supply will remain approximately constant.

Multiple reuse of water means just that—utilizing water twice, or more, before it is allowed to flow out into the larger ecosystem and purify itself naturally. Unfortunately, we simply do not possess the technological capability to purify water so as to make it fit beyond a doubt for human consumption. Some water is presently being reused by industry, but at this point that represents the limits of our present skill. To understand the seriousness of the problem it is necessary to understand how both a sewage system and a water purification system work.

A municipality has a choice of four degrees of sewage treatment. It can provide either one or two stages of treatment (primary or primary coupled with secondary) and it can decide whether or not to combine the wastes of dwellings and factories (sanitary sewage) with street runoff (storm sewage). The best system is one which separates the wastes and provides both primary and secondary treatment for each. Unfortunately, such a comprehensive system is a rarity in the United States although anything less is unsatisfactory.

Raw human sewage is not a poison, but it does pollute water. This occurs because bacteria are required to break down the wastes, and to do this they need oxygen. Although there is some dissolved oxygen in all waterways, masses of sewage have a high biochemical oxygen demand (BOD) and rapidly deplete the waterway's supply, eventually "killing" it. Sewage treatment reduces the BOD of the wastes.

Of the 7500 communities which have sewers, 1300 dump their wastes untreated into lakes, streams and rivers. Not only does this include human waste with its massive BOD as well as the frequently poisonous effluents from industry, but also such blatantly obvious objects as sticks, rags and containers from the streets.

All the remaining sewered communities have primary treatment. In this process, larger objects are screened out and the waste water is then fed into settling tanks. In these tanks, solids either rise to the surface or settle to the bottom; the liquid is then poured out and the solids are carted away. The process removes street debris and approximately 35 percent of the organic pollutants (and their resulting BOD). If a community provides no further treatment, chlorine is added as a disinfectant.

Five out of eight municipalities which have primary sewage treatment also have secondary treatment. There are two methods this treatment can use; both remove 80 to 90 percent of the organic pollutants from sewage water. The more satisfactory method is the "trickling filter," whereby the sewage is trickled slowly over rocks. These rocks are coated with bacteria which digest the organic wastes. Communities which cannot afford the space such a plant takes up use the "activated sludge" method, which consists of churning the sewage with oxygen- and bacteria-filled sludge. Often the final effluent is chlorinated before being discharged into a stream or lake or the ocean. (Chlorine disinfects the effluent, but it also kills the beneficial bacteria.)

In certain very rare cases, communities subject their wastes to yet another process, tertiary treatment. This involves sending the twice-treated effluent into "sitting ponds," where the remaining 10 percent of the BOD is removed by action of fish and other organisms in what is, in reality, a minute ecosystem. Water remains in the pond for about four days, and the phosphorous-stimulated algae are continually removed to combat eutrophication. Another tertiary treatment is known as "polishing." Here the water is run through activated carbon. Both methods are quite expensive to set up and to maintain, and they use a great deal of land. Without strong federal incentives and support, it is unlikely that communities will decide to employ this final step in the treatment of their wastes.

Sewage treatment technology has not progressed very far or very fast. These methods were developed 70 years ago at the Lawrence Experiment Station in Massachusetts, and are still considered the best techniques available. Under optimal conditions, the procedure works—but under stress most systems collapse.

One of the sewage system's main points of vulnerability is the bacteria, or "bugs," which are integral to the operation. Chrome, grease and many other substances can easily kill the bacteria, either by poisoning or by smothering, and the system must then be bypassed until a new crop of bacteria is grown or shipped in. One small factory is capable of knocking out a huge plant.

Factories are the bane of the sanitary engineer, but he has another foe, too—the weather.

Most cities, for reasons of economy, have sewer systems which indiscriminately mix street runoff with human and industrial waste. In dry weather, this makes little or no difference. In a rainstorm or after a snowstorm, however, the system in addition to its usual load must be able to cope with millions of gallons of extra water. Without special storage tanks, the system overloads and automatic valves open up, discharging raw sewage into the nearest waterway. In this way man has actually succeeded in turning Nature's traditional purifier—rain—into one of the villains of water pollution.

In the separated sewer system, or the system which employs huge subsidiary holding tanks, the overload phenomenon does not occur, but estimates as to the cost of providing such service to communities across the nation range up to $50 billion. Even if the money were available, citizen concern is so slight that the sewerage issue is a politically "dead" one in Congress and the state capitals. Little is likely to change without citizen pressure.

In each watershed, the town farthest upland is free to receive relatively unpolluted drinking water. What of the communities, however, farther downstream which are forced to rely upon a stream whose waters already have traces or quantities of sewage in them? What, for instance, of Washington near the end of the Potomac, or Baltimore which uses the Susquehanna River for part of its drinking supply? It is precisely because sewage treatment is often so inadequate

that many water purification plants have to maintain stringent standards. The results of laxity, as has been shown, can
be disastrous.

The general procedure used to purify water in communities across the country is as follows.

Water is taken from a reservoir or river, metered to record
the rate of flow, and chlorinated to keep it sterile. It is then
fed in large pipes to the city. In some cases this distance may
be dozens or even hundreds of miles. If the reservoir or river
is at a higher elevation than the city, the water merely flows
the whole way; if not, it must be pumped.

When the water reaches the filtration plant, alum is added
at the rate of approximately one grain per gallon of water.
Alum is a coagulating agent which collects mud and suspended material and precipitates it out as "floc," a sticky, gelati-
nous solid. The alum is stirred into the water in flocculating
tanks, and the suspended materials settle out in large settling
tanks, through which the water flows very slowly.

After the coagulation, the water in most communities is
slowly filtered through about 20 inches of sand. As the water
passes through the sand, the remaining particles of suspended
matter in the water adhere to the grains of sand. Several
times a week the process is reversed and the sand is washed
clean.

After filtering, water either enters holding reservoirs or the
town's distribution system. Often other chemicals are also
added—hydrofluosilicic acid ("fluoride") to inhibit tooth
decay, lime and soda ash to decrease acidity, activated carbon to remove tastes and odors, copper sulfate to destroy
algae in reservoirs. The addition of these substances depends
on the community, the season and the necessity.

As is apparent, water purification concentrates primarily
on eliminating suspended solids in the water and waterborne,
bacterially-induced disease. Most systems are relatively or totally ineffective in dealing with such substances as pesticides,
mercury, selenium, lead, arsenic and some of the other trace
poisons which are not easily detected or excluded. Not coincidentally, it is precisely these materials which pass unchanged through the sewage plant, too. The fact is, virtually
nothing can screen out mercury, lead, DDT and arsenic once
they are released into the eco-system—except living organisms which trap and hold the poisons in their bodies.

Communities which pollute streams, lakes, rivers or ocean areas with organic wastes must be held responsible for this action no matter how hard they plead for extra time and compassion. Even with the relatively unsophisticated sewage methods we are using today, there is no excuse for pollution from human waste. Only the very smallest streams are unable to handle the BOD left after secondary sewage treatment, and it is unlikely that large cities would discharge volumes of waste into small streams.

Industries which pollute the water are to be condemned even more strongly. Industrial wastes are often so unpredictable and hard to detect that no savings to a company is worth the risk of dumping them into the waters. Mercury pollution, in particular, is now believed to be extensive in this country and pleasure fishing has been banned in several states. Yet, the Justice Department has negotiated deals with mercury polluters along the lower Mississippi tributary system, cutting their disposal allowances from five pounds to one pound per day. In terms of human health requirements, the action of the Department verges on criminal.

Because of the power of many companies and the relative weakness of various town and city agencies, a "deal" is often likely to be made behind the citizens' backs. This "deal" is that the town provide sewage service for the company in return for the company not moving elsewhere. If the town is lucky, the plant will consent to provide its own primary treatment before dumping the waste into the town's system. In most cases, the town's system cannot handle so much extra sewage, and it begins to consistently release partially-treated or untreated sewage into the water. Even if it can handle the volume, it can rarely detoxify the contents and it then becomes morally and legally responsible for any contamination. (If the company is very powerful, it will convince the town that it is a "citizen" and shouldn't have to pay extra for sewage service.)

What can the citizen do about his drinking water and sewage treatment? In most cases, until a situation becomes severe, not very much. Health authorities probably will not step in unless there is a threat of communicable disease, and this probably will not happen unless the whole system breaks down. Sewer authorities will very likely be quite hostile.

This is no reason not to become involved, however. The

entire environmental scene is so much in the spotlight these days that situations change very fast. The first thing to do is to visit your local sewage and water purification plants. In a large city probably less than one in a thousand residents even knows where these are—and this is one reason that the situation is so bad. Agencies out of the public eye are apt to be less careful, less well staffed and underfinanced. Citizens should find out where their drinking water comes from and what kinds of sewage systems and treatment facilities their city has.

If the answers to questions about water are troublesome (drinking water comes from a polluted river, combined sewage system with no treatment, no analysis of mercury or DDT content, etc.) a group should raise a fuss. It should demand that samples of tap water be analyzed by the health department. If they are found dangerous, the media should be called, and politicians contacted. There are few areas as sensitive as the safety of a water supply.

Citizens concerned about the sewage system should raise a fuss about that, too. Residents downstream from an inadequate sewage facility should be informed of what kind of water they are receiving, and urged to complain—particularly to congressmen. The federal government has paid lip service to the need for sewage systems and it should be held liable for its rhetoric.

If their sewer system is giving "free rides" to factories, groups should find out about it and then protest. As described in an earlier chapter, it is unlikely that factories will close down because of sewer charges. The BOD of their effluents is often hundreds of times greater than that of an entire town, and they cannot be classified as ordinary "citizens."

Lastly, citizens should go easy on their water supply and be kind to their sewer system. The more water we use, the less is available and the more will have to be reused. The more that is reused, the worse quality we will have. Water should not be left running unnecessarily, wasted on a lawn that gets enough rain, and dishwashers and clotheswashers should not be used unless they are full, since they always use the identical amount of water.

As for the sewers, too many Americans use the toilet and kitchen sink like garbage cans. Recent reports indicate that cigarette filters are hard on the system. Even too great a quantity of toilet paper can cause problems. Chemicals must not be put down the drain.

Garbage disposals increase the load one imposes on the sewage system by 25 percent. Rural residents should compost their garbage—it will be a service to them and to the sewers. In a city, the decision is a difficult one, but experts recommend that one find out which is in better shape—the town's sewers or its sanitary landfill. The one that is hurting most should be spared the "hard work."

Like so many of our environmental problems, water supply and sewer service have been subjected to a minimum of public consciousness and inquiry. We take our plumbing for granted. To realize how important these facts of modern life really are, consider for a moment what it would be like if, simultaneously, all our toilets backed up and all our faucets spewed only mud—or nothing at all.

solid wastes

- *The amount of solid waste collected annually includes 30 million tons of paper, 4 million tons of plastics, 100 million tires, 30 billion bottles, 60 billion cans, 7 million discarded automobiles, and uncounted millions of major appliances.*
- *The amount of electricity needed to produce one ton of aluminum out of recycled cans is 187 kilowatt-hours, while it requires over 16,000 kilowatt-hours to make a ton of aluminum from raw material.*
- *The cost of collecting and disposing of solid waste amounts to $4.5 billion annually.*

Solid waste has long been an overlooked environmental problem. Once thrown in a trash can and carted off in a garbage truck, it tends not only to be forgotten by the average citizen, but by federal, state, and municipal governments, as well. Because it blights only an immediate area, unlike air and water pollution, it is not of primary concern. Solutions in this area follow an inadequate piecemeal approach. What has only recently been recognized is the desperate need for a total view of the problems related to solid waste.

The most complete legislation on the solid waste problem came with the passage of the Solid Waste Disposal Act of 1965 which defined solid wastes as "garbage, refuse and other discarded materials, including solid waste materials resulting from industrial, commercial, and agricultural operations, and from community activities."

The per capita generation of solid waste increases as population continues to expand. Figures based on New York area projections indicate that the amount of solid waste generated in the metropolitan regions can be expected to triple by the year 2000. Moreover, projections for the Washington, D. C. area indicate that solid waste will quadruple by the end of the century.

Unfortunately, the 1965 act turns its attention to the "disposal" of solid waste, paying only minor attention to the other alternatives of recycling and reuse. The major thrust of the bill is towards development of new technology for disposal and towards the development of interstate and regional cooperation for sanitary land fills. Previously, responsibility for solid waste disposal, collection and processing was at a local level. The federal government now assumes the responsibility for research, training demonstrations of new technology, technical assistance and grants for state and interstate solid waste planning programs.

The act has two major purposes: to start and accelerate a national research, development and demonstration program on solid wastes and to give technical and financial support to interstate, state and local agencies in planning, developing and conducting solid waste disposal programs. It authorized appropriations ranging from not more than $10 million in fiscal 1966 to not more than $32.5 million in fiscal 1969. The money is divided between what is now the Bureau of Solid Waste Management in the Department of Health, Education and Welfare (HEW) and the Solid Waste Research and Economic Resource Evaluation Studies Programs of the Bureau of Mines in the Department of Interior. The Bureau of Solid Waste Management then receives 60–70 percent of the total when both agencies receive the maximum allowable appropriations.

Even with the First Annual Report of the Council on Environmental Quality (August, 1970) concern with anything more than disposal technology is minimal. Under the concluding section titled "What Needs to Be Done," several points for research and demonstration projects in the Bureau of Solid Waste Management and Bureau of Mines are listed in this order: collection procedures, household sorting, sorting from mixed refuse, removal of litter, and finally recycling. Two other points are then listed: available federal funding should be directed to selective, large-scale demonstrations and innovations in solid waste management; and maximum recycling and reuse of materials are necessary to reduce the growing volume of solid waste. This is noted only as a final and last concern, whereas it should have been first.

So wealthy is the United States that it can afford to spend $4.5 billion on solid waste. So misguided is solid waste management in the United States that, though almost all the money spent is for only 13 percent of the problem, that 13 percent still has a detrimental effect on our environment. Over 3.5 billion tons of material are annually wasted which has some economic value. The solid waste problem in this country is malignant. As Roger Starr wrote in *Horizon*, "A famous Soviet leader once promised to bury us, but we are achieving it without his help."

Solid waste is everything solid which we choose to waste rather than use, reuse, salvage, or recycle. It is good scraps, packaging, household goods, litter, cars, tires, scraps and slags of industry, agricultural and animal residues, and mineral tailings. It is solid material for which the costs of retaining are shortsightedly outweighed by the immediately obvious benefits of discarding it.

For handling purposes solid waste can be divided into four categories with the following breakdown:

Agricultural Waste . . . . .550 million tons
Animal waste . . . . .1.5 billion tons
Industrial waste . . . . .110 million tons
Mineral waste . . . . .1.1 billion tons
Collected waste (residential,
    commercial and municipal) . . . . .250 million tons

Of the collected waste, the only major subdivision with which waste disposal is concerned, 146 million tons were disposed in open dumps, 25 million tons were placed in sanitary land fills, 15 million tons were disposed in incinerators, 4 million tons were composted, salvaged or dumped at sea, and 60 million tons went uncollected.

The present solution to take care of this heterogeneous mass is simply to dispose of it. Of the several disposal methods which have been developed, the most common is the landfill. Ninety percent of the nation's solid wastes are disposed of at landfill sites. In order to be considered sanitary, the Bureau of Solid Waste Management requires that there be no open burning, that the refuse is covered daily, and that it not pollute the ground water. Ninety-four percent of the nation's landfill sites do not meet this criteria. Failure to meet any of these criteria results in environmental degradation. Exposed sites pollute surface waters by run-off from rain and snow, harbor disease vectors, and emit foul odors; improper burning pollutes the air; and improperly located sites pollute ground waters. Other possible problems not considered by the Bureau are visual pollution from exposed sites, and damage to eco-systems by the poor choice of site locations, particularly those that are used to fill in tidelands and estuaries. Estuaries and tidelands are particularly critical for the nurseries of the sea. Another major problem is that much of the waste used in a sanitary landfill never decomposes and establishing the ecological balance by bacterial action is almost impossible. In Elyria, Ohio, a landfill was dug up and 10-year-old newspapers were found to be still readable.

Another side effect is the creation of methane gas which is a byproduct of decomposing garbage. If proper ventilation is not allowed for the methane to escape into the atmosphere, the concentration of the gas will kill surrounding vegetation and it may even explode. This was a problem with one sanitary landfill in New York City where, according to consulting engineer Leonard S. Wegman, the cost of venting the methane gas problem was approximately $30,000. Wegman called the smell itself, "utterly unbelievable." While proper engineering can deal with this byproduct of decomposition, it must be done carefully.

Sea disposal of waste by present methods is a water pollutant. It is either dumped directly or containerized in corrodible containers, and in either case may end up returning to shores and tidelands. It may even take on international ramifications by drifting to other country's shores.

One important concept in the subject of waste disposal is that of volume reduction. Obviously the less space that refuse takes up, the less impact it will have upon the environment. The two possibilities are incineration and compaction. Of these, however, only incineration is acceptable. Once materials are compacted, at thousands of pounds per square inch, and buried, which is the destiny of all compacted wastes, the costs of recovery and separation are so high that, barring some dramatic breakthrough in technology, recycling becomes economically unfeasible.

Incineration, theoretically, is a simple answer. Yet the obvious connotation of an incinerator is the typical, run down, smelly unit that constantly pollutes the air. Modern incinerators with prohibitive air pollution control devices are available, but the cost per pound of incinerating juxtaposed with land filling is considerable. Few incinerators in use today work efficiently. Pittsburgh has been using an incinerator for 30 years, but it will be closed down this year because it violates the new particulate emission standards in that state's air pollution laws. Even newer incinerators like the one used in Philadelphia installed in 1965 cause considerable air pollution.

It is possible to build incinerators that are 100 percent free of air pollution, but the cost is high. In Dallas, for example, officials considered installation of such an incinerator three or four years ago but chose instead the sanitary landfill when they discovered the cost to be about one-third less. Well-designed incinerators, like many that have been used in Europe for years, will always cost more, but they can reduce solid waste up to 95 percent, leaving a residue that will not smell, smoke, produce gas, harbor rats or flies, or settle when built upon.

There are various other methods of disposal which should be considered: composting is one. There is the process of producing a soil conditioner and fertilizer. Yet experiments in the U. S. have been largely unsuccessful. Of nine composting plants built between 1951 and 1966, six were shut down because of the lack of a market for the compost. However, composting is still a competent way to recycle minerals and other resources in solid wastes. The problem is largely one of economics. Much research is being conducted in this area. In Houston, Texas, one composting plant has been operating since 1967. It treats 360 tons of solid waste per day (of the 200 tons per day generated by the city), and the compost is then resold in bags. Salvaged material such as paper, rags and metal are also sold.

Another disposal method recently investigated is that of shipping solid wastes away from metropolitan areas. This was proposed for Philadelphia where refuse would be shipped by rail to strip mines in Schuylkill County, some 80 miles away. The residents of Schuylkill are resisting the plan, however, because of the possibilities and problems of water pollution.

At present it is at a standstill. The concept is a good one if adequate disposal areas—such as empty mines—exist. If however, the method is used merely to replace one eyesore and health menace with another, then complaints on the part of the residents of an outlying region are well justified.

Research continues, and attention recently has been drawn to ideas of disposing of solid waste in not such conventional terms. Many of the plans seem feasible but have drawbacks that must be seriously considered. Proposals include devising systems to shoot solid wastes into outer space where they will remain in orbit indefinitely. One needs to consider this only briefly to discover the proposal highly unecological. The vision of the earth surrounded by its own waste and filth as it moves through the universe may be only a logical extension to our present attitude for dealing with solid wastes.

Much attention has been given recently to home trash compacters. While the idea seems good, it is at best only a temporary measure. The cost notwithstanding, the compacters do only what they say . . . compact the volume. They do nothing toward helping to actually dispose of the waste. Furthermore, their methods—wrapping the trash in non-degradable plastic and spraying it with deodorant—only increase the detrimental effects upon the environment.

Many other projects have been suggested to perhaps alleviate the solid waste disposal problem: building incinerators fueled by nuclear energy; grinding up solid waste and disposing of it through sewage treatment plants; squeezing the waste into hard blocks for building roads or incinerating it to the point that it can be used for paving material; creating garbage farms where it can be worked into topsoil. All of the proposals have potential but not for the immediate future; it is a sure fact that even these programs, if they are deemed feasible, will soon be overloaded.

Industrial solid waste poses an even more complex problem than does municipal waste. The nature of factory production creates wastes more varied and more likely to contain toxic substances. It includes processing, general plant, packaging, shipping, office and cafeteria wastes. A distinction should be made between solid waste and scrap which are solid materials that can be recycled at a profit.

Because industrial solid waste is as varied as industry itself, a different attitude has developed toward its disposal. This waste is less obvious since it is often stored in warehouses and back lots of industrial properties in piles of sludges, slags, and waste plastics. Then, too, industrial waste is largely disposed of in private dumps, hauled away by private contractors. Divided up, some is disposed of by land fills on the plant site; some is incinerated and then the residue hauled away. But the cost of such processes is rising because of increased hauling costs, the unavailability of land, and stricter regulation of dumping practices.

Industry as a whole has usually only considered solving its solid waste problems when it is economically feasible. But industry is quickly learning that this attitude cannot continue. Consequently, attempts at recycling as part of the manufacturing process must be developed.

In general, waste materials are rarely reintroduced into the industrial process which generates them. While some industries do recycle parts of their own waste, the disposal problem has led to an entirely new industry—that of secondary materials. The secondary waste industry includes roughly 9,000 recognized establishments with total annual sales of more than $5 billion. Copper, iron and steel, rubber, paper and textiles are all recycled into secondary materials for reuse. New attention must be given on a federal and local level to support these types of industries. Markets must be generated for use of secondary materials, because production is not feasible unless the products are purchased.

For instance, the problems inherent in generating markets for secondary materials may be seen in the example of the fate of junked automobiles. Contrary to popular belief, automation is now capable of separating the ferrous and nonferrous materials of cars. Furthermore, a high grade of iron and steel can be produced from junked cars. However, because scrap metal is harder to move than iron ore, railroads often give priority to new material over the secondary materials. Since railroads are integral to the business, the markets are stifled before they can begin.

Ultimately, disposal of industrial wastes becomes a complex problem because such factors influence it. But with a growing regard for the secondary materials industry, new technology will be developed for recycling and reusing industrial waste.

As both the citizen and the industrial giants find that significant roadblocks to recycling develop, more and more effort should be expended on what is called "source reduction." This philosophy, of course, revolves around the idea that if less waste is built into a product, less will remain after the product is used. This concept, however, is a two-way street. Industry may be the prime offender, and complaints that the environmentally aware purchaser in effect has no choice in what he buys are definitely true. It must be also realized that it is to the public that industry caters, and there have been many products which have failed in the open market because the packaging was not glamorous enough.

The first step in source reduction is to limit all forms of planned obsolescence. Planned obsolescence comes in two forms. The first is style change, as with the automobile, and the second is poor or faulty workmanship and material. If goods did not undergo a style change every year, the demand for them would drop, and therefore, their production would also drop. If goods were built to be repaired instead of replaced, the market for new ones would be reduced and production would be reduced with it. In either case, the demand for raw materials would decrease, the economic cost of disposing of obsolete items would drop, and the negative effects on the environment would be reduced.

Salvage, utilization, recycling and reuse of waste materials could be greatly increased if society planned for salvage and recycling when making the merchandise and packages. If homogeneous metal containers could be used, many more of them could be recycled, and at a greatly reduced cost. If less plastics were used, the poisons of plastic combustion would be less prevalent, the life of incinerators would be increased, fossil fuels would not be depleted so rapidly, and the stability of landfill sites would not be threatened by the non-biodegradable plastics shifting and compacting slowly.

Present glass recycling plants require the glass to be separated by material and color. If glass containers were of a more uniform color and material, the cost of separation would not be so great, and the solution of crushing and remelting, as is being suggested by the Glass Container Manufacturers Institute, would be viable.

Robert Finch, Ex-Secretary of HEW, estimated that by 1980 the amount of solid waste generated will nearly triple. Somewhere, an attempt must be made to hold down the amount of solid waste generated or other attempts at disposal will simply be self-defeating. A prime example is paper. The American Paper Institute reports that the amount of paper being recycled is increasing, but not nearly as fast as the production of paper from wood pulp. A new experimental recycling project at National Steel faces the same problem. Six-hundred thousand new tin-free steel beer cans, donated by Continental Can Co., were remelted into new primary steel, but this figure becomes insignificant when compared to the five billion steel cans that were added to the market in 1970.

While the Resource Recovery Act is providing money for HEW to study tax structures that will finance a reclaiming system, industry is increasing the volume of solid waste in the expectation that the government, or even the consumer himself, will pay for these recycling systems. The percentage of paper recycled will continue to drop, says the American Paper Institute, until "strong [financial] motivations are present at every point in the recycling system." The steel industry dramatizes this point. Mr. William Stephenson, chairman of the Jones and Laughlin Steel Corporation, says, "The steel industry has demonstrated its ability to recycle, but it's not our job to collect the cans. Now it's up to the government and the people."

The Resource Recovery Act should attempt to stop the growth of municipal wastes at the same time that it is trying to find technological and economic solutions to the disposal problem. Granted, there is one section of this bill that will require an investigation into "changes in current product characteristics and production and packaging practices which would reduce the amount of solid waste." However, enough advance research has been done about solid waste for government to act in some areas. It seems obvious that the responsibility now rests with the government and the people to see that the necessary demands are made upon industry.

Recent legal battles over banning the non-returnable bottle proves this last point. The government is hesitant to initiate legislation to disturb the continuing growth of the industry. To the politicians, growth is a sign of a healthy economy. This is where the citizen must take action.

Glass is a very inexpensive product to produce. It is much cheaper to produce new glass products than to recycle old ones. But it's also very difficult to dispose of old glass. When glass bottles get into disposal systems, many problems ensue. When incinerated, glass melts, causing a solid, hard-to-dispose-of residue. When put into a sanitary land fill, bottles, even if broken, never decompose and take up available land space. Research is being conducted to find new uses for old glass. One example is the development of "glasphalt" where glass is used as an aggregate for paving materials. But even new technology and new uses for glass cannot compete with the rate of growth of production of glass bottles.

The nonreturnable bottle has been the biggest boom the glass container industry has ever experienced. According to the Glass Manufacturers Institute (the same people that sponsor rock group anti-littering ads on television and radio), the sale of beverage bottles has tripled since 1959, when the nonreturnable bottle was introduced on a large public basis. The average returnable bottle is used 14 times before it is discarded; the nonreturnable bottle, therefore, increases the number of bottles sold. This causes the number of bottles in municipal waste and litter to grow dramatically. With the introduction of the nonreturnable bottle also came the large increase of glass in the composition of solid waste.

Municipal and state governments, only at the constant prodding of citizens, have slowly begun to take action, but never without a fight from the bottling interests. Washington state citizens after collecting over 100,000 petition signatures were able to get an initiative on the ballot of the 1970 election. If passed, it would have required a five-cent deposit on all beer and soft drink containers. Canners, beverage barons, and supermarket czars shelled out an estimated $500,000 to wage a strong media campaign which resulted in the defeat of the proposal. Glass industry supporters even produced a survey that charged passage of the amendment would cost the state (suffering with some of the highest unemployment in the nation) 1700 jobs.

Meanwhile, the beverage container industry, along with their trade association, Glass Containers Manufacturers Institute, has taken to dramatic advertising campaigns to wage a psychological war with consumers over the issues of nonreturnable bottles and litter. While they attempt to appease consumer demands, their practices go on.

A reputable industry source reports that in Pacifica, California, where a recycling program was instituted by citizens,

.things are not going well. While bottles are indeed being picked up and returned to the Owens-Corning Glass Company for recycling, Owens-Corning promptly hauls them at their own expense to a dump for disposal.

With industry opposition like the Pacifica dump-in and the Washington State anti-deposit drive, citizen efforts may appear futile. They are not, but it becomes clear that the solution will not come simply through fights for bans on nonreturnable containers or against using marshes for sanitary land fills. Such campaigns, while important, only treat the symptom, not the illness.

There are certain simple steps that the concerned citizen can take. Although such measures seem quite ineffective when one realizes the vastness of the problem, they may at least help to broaden the base of environmental awareness among those who are fortunate enough to live far from a dump or a town incinerator.

For those suburban and rural homeowners who have enough garden or land space, the most significant action they can take is to make a compost pile. To do this, put vegetable scraps, leaves and grass clippings in a heap in the backyard, and cover with some manure and lime and then with a layer of leaves. Virtually all leftover food, including meat and egg shells, can be added to the pile, and it should be turned over once a week or so. Lime should be included with every new addition. Within a month or two, the compost will make excellent, non-polluting fertilizer.

Milk, soft drinks, beer and other items should only be purchased in returnable bottles and these should be returned. If a supermarket has discontinued selling returnable bottles, demand that they be brought back. Meanwhile, shop elsewhere for these items.

Given the choice, buy vegetables and fruit loose. You can see what you are buying, and there is one less plastic wrapper to discard.

Check with local junk dealers to learn what items they will accept. Many of them accept (and pay for) paper, and some scrap iron processors accept cans and other non-ferrous metal. Where recycling programs exist, aluminum is worth about $200 a ton. Where they don't exist, demand that they be established.

Never use paper where there is an alternative. Use cloth

dishtowels, napkins, place mats, clothes, diapers, etc. Don't use paper plates, plastic silverware (unless you keep it!) or other disposable items. Furthermore, publicize each new development so that others will begin to think about them.

Instead of accepting junk mail as a price of modern living, write to the post office, demanding that they remove your name from the list on the grounds that the mail is "ecologically obscene."

One approach which fledgling ecology groups can use to stimulate interest and provide for more pleasant and healthful environments—especially in urban neighborhoods—is the community clean-up. Make arrangements with the Sanitation Department to have trucks and other equipment in a neighborhood on a Saturday morning from 9 A.M. to 2 P.M., and then publicize the event throughout the neighborhood. In many cases this could be the beginning of a community organization which can later combat the problem of solid waste at the local, regional and state level.

This is not an easy battle to wage. It means realizing that an individual can do little to solve the problem by "keeping his corner of the world clean." It means building a power-base of sheer numbers of people who will demand a new attitude and stand up to industry and politicians. It means realizing that the solid waste problem, like all environmental problems, will not just go away, but that it is also not unsolvable. It seems obvious that no one is going to solve the problem, neither the government nor industry, until it is demanded.

pesticides

• *The presence of DDT has been detected literally every-where on the earth's surface—in the water, in the soil, in human and animal tissues. Britons are accusing Americans (and the prevailing westerly winds) of dumping DDT on their nation by way of rainfall. Researchers, checking out a hypothesis, have found DDT residues in the fatty tissues of fish and penguins in Antarctica, although the chemical has never been used within thousands of miles of the continent.*

• *Tests have shown that two chemical compounds in combi-nation can be as much as 100 times as toxic as either one alone. This multiplying action is known as "synergistic ef-fect" and its potential for occurring—either intentionally or accidentally—increases with the invention of every new com-pound.*

• *DDT and related pesticides have been shown conclusively to affect the calcium-producing potential of birds. Birds with high residue levels of DDT lay eggs with appreciably thinner egg shells than the norm—so much so that the eggs often break during incubation. There is even one case of an eagle laying a shell-less egg. This phenomenon is partially responsi-ble for endangering the bald eagle, whose numbers are de-clining drastically.*

Pesticides, generally called "economic poisons" by govern-ment and industry, are a wide variety of poisonous chemicals devised to combat insects (insecticides), undesirable plants and weeds (herbicides), fungi (fungicides), rats, mice and other rodents (rodenticides), fish (piscicides), mites (miti-cides) and other pests.

Pesticides, by and large, are very dangerous. The better

they work against their targets, the more likely they are to cause significant damage to non-target organisms and to the environment in general. The worst aspect of the problem is that modern science knows almost nothing about the effects of these chemicals. Dr. Loren Jensen, researcher at Johns Hopkins University, did not understate the ominousness of the pesticide crisis when he explained, "Their presence depends on your ability to detect them."

Incredible as it seems, the implications of current research are that the entire world's environment might not be able to handle more than a few tons of pesticides per year. The enormity of the problem is such that the scientific community has not been abe to come to grips with any of the evidence or the implications for over three decades. It is also worthwhile to note that, while the controversy flares, the chemical industry is producing over one billion pounds of pesticides every year.

DDT is the best-known pesticide in existence today, having gained fame during and after World War II for its effectiveness against both insects and disease epidemics. For over a decade it was widely used despite a quietly growing criticism of some of its effects. In 1962, with the publication of Rachel Carson's *Silent Spring,* the opposition jelled and became more vociferous.

DDT is technically known as a chlorinated hydrocarbon. This class also includes dieldrin, aldrin, toxaphene, lindane, DDD, heptachlor, chlordane and endrin. Unlike such ancient poisons as pyrethrum (made from the chrysanthemum flower), the chlorinated hydrocarbons are complicated synthetic compounds. One of dieldrin's nine different chemical formulas, for instance, is 1,2,3,4,10,10-hexachloro-6,7-epoxy-1,4, 4a,5,6,7,8,8a-octahydro-1,4,*endo-exo*-5,8-dimethanonapthalene. Their characteristics, generally speaking, include low toxicity to man (they are relatively safe to handle), a broad spectrum of targets (they affect many organisms indiscriminately), and persistency (they remain in the ecosystem for long periods with little or no change). They are also highly soluble in fatty tissue, becoming an integral part of an animal's body.

The savage environmental effect of DDT's two prime attributes—persistency coupled with fat solubility—was not fully appreciated until several years after its initial use. Eventually, after millions of pounds of chlorinated hydrocarbons had been sprayed, dusted, poured and spread across America's landscape, the truth began to dawn on some scientists.

In Clear Lake, California, in 1957, the first recorded major disaster caused by chlorinated hydrocarbons occurred. In that year a large number of grebes (fish-eating birds) were found dead in and around the lake. Investigations showed the lake area had been sprayed three times with the chlorinated hydrocarbon DDD. The water contained .02 parts per million (ppm) of the pesticide. The dead grebes contained more than 100,000 times the lake's concentration. What had happened?

The explanation that emerged was that microscopic organisms in the lake had accumulated DDD concentrations of about 5 ppm. Fish feeding on these organisms had accumulated residues of 2000 ppm of the persistent chemical in their fatty tissues. The residues in the grebes after they ate the fish became so large they could not survive. Instead of dispersing, the DDD had magnified as it moved "up" the food chain. The implications for man, perched at the top of the chain, are ominous.

Persistence, in the case of the chlorinated hydrocarbons, is generally measured in years or even decades. Although they are not permanent, they are highly resistant to "breaking down" (that is, decomposing into their simpler and safer components in the environment). This attribute originally led to their wide acceptance since farmers found it necessary to spray their crops only occasionally each season. Later, when the evils of persistence were uncovered, a new type of pesticide, the organophosphate, was introduced.

Organophosphates, such as parathion, malathion, phosdrin, TEPP, schadran and chlorthion, are similar to the chlorinated hydrocarbons only in so far as they are broad spectrum pesticides. Unlike DDT, they are relatively non-persistent and highly toxic. In other words, the danger in using them shifts from the environment (where they last only for several weeks or months) to the consumer, applicator, packager and disposer. Whereas DDT is easy to use, the organophosphates —which are related to the nerve gases invented after World War II—pose severe immediate hazards to man. Parathion, for instance, was responsible for at least three deaths and over thirty illnesses in North Carolina in 1970. In 1967 it was also responsible for large-scale fatal poisonings in Tijuana, Mexico (600 stricken, 17 died) and Chiquinquira, Columbia (600 stricken, 80 died), when parathion containers leaked onto foodstuffs.

Organophosphates, which attack the nervous system and kill by asphyxiation, are equally dangerous when ingested, inhaled or absorbed through the skin. Many semi-literate or Spanish-speaking laborers become sick because they can't read the labels and aren't aware of the very real dangers to themselves. (In the United States, no labels are printed in Spanish and no symbols except the skull and crossbones are used). Most fatalities occur when small children drink from, lick or play with glass bottles which contain or did contain organophosphate pesticides.

A third class of pesticides are the carbamates, notably carbaryl (Sevin). These are quite recent additions to the field, and little analysis of them is available. They are similar to the organophosphates although not quite as toxic. Chemical companies consider them a "step in the right direction," although environmentalists believe that further research may reveal harmful effects.

The fourth class is actually the oldest. This includes the arsenicals (containing arsenic) and the pesticides based on heavy metals (lead and mercury). Although these pesticides are still in remarkably wide use, there is virtually no responsible group in this country which considers any of them "safe" under any conditions. Arsenic is a well known deadly poison and the metals are permanent, cumulative and quite toxic. That is, they are poisons which never leave the body and slowly cause complete debilitation and death. The best advice about pesticides containing these substances is to stay away from them—they are neither safe to handle (like DDT) nor are they safe in the environment (like malathion).

Arsenic and mercury compounds are often used as herbicides. Golf courses in particular have come under fire for using mercury herbicides. In an effort to avoid excessive contamination from arsenic and other metals, newer synthetic materials have been used to control weeds and unwanted plants. The most famous of these are 2,4-D and 2,4,5-T. These two products were originally thought the safest and most effective herbicides available. The Department of Defense (DOD) was so impressed with their powers that it used the two chemicals (with some variations) in the defoliation program in Vietnam. As is well documented, the DOD's modern "scorched earth policy" was so effective that Vietnam in all likelihood will take decades to recover. During the military build-up years of 1966-68, the needs of the Army were so great that 2,4-D and 2,4,5-T were all but impossible to procure in the United States.

The chemicals are now generally available in this country, and North America is now being treated to their benefits— and dangers. Scientific tests have shown that 2,4-D can cause birth defects in mammals, and certain restrictions have been placed on its use although it still accounts for 20 percent of the nation's herbicide production. As Shirley Briggs of the Rachel Carson Trust explained, "Any chemical so physiologically active with one form of protoplasm should have had more study than these received before being released widely into our environment." The Justice Department (with the apparent advice and consent of the Departments of Interior, Agriculture, and Defense) does not agree. In June, 1970, Attorney General John Mitchell announced a major new program of *cannabis* eradication using the herbicide 2,4-D. *Cannabis,* or marijuana, has been growing wild in this country since its cultivation as a substitute for Manila hemp during World War I. On the contention that wild *cannabis* is a health hazard, the government is pitting against it 2,4-D, another health hazard. Such diverse groups as the Litton Industry's Bionetics Research Laboratories and the Health, Education and Welfare Department's Mrak Commission have united in strong opposition to the use of 2,4-D, on the evidence of its teratogenic (defect-inducing) propensities.

The report of the Mrak Commission is, especially for the newcomer to the pesticide crisis, an excellent review of what has happened, a chilling prediction of what may be in store for us, and a scathing indictment of both industry and government for allowing the crisis to occur. The official title of the 667-page document is "Report of the Secretary's Commission on Pesticides and their Relation to Environmental Health, parts I and II, U. S. Department of Health, Education and Welfare, December, 1969,"* and few stones are left unturned by the committee.

---

* Price $4. Available from Superintendent of Documents, U. S. Government Printing Office, Washington D. C. 20025.

In many real respects it is the government and not industry which is responsible for the reckless proliferation of pesticides in the environment. Despite the fact that, in many cases, the chemical companies have used lies, smear tactics and behind-the-scenes maneuvers to discredit their opponents and promote their products, this is not a unique phenomenon among big business in the United States. When a government takes on itself the task of registering, regulating, approving and testing poisonous chemicals and keeping an eye on their labels and precautionary warnings, then that government shares responsibility for their ultimate harmful effects.

Defenders of the chemical companies have been quick to brand their critics as "against progress" and "anti-capitalists" and one, Louis McLean, General Counsel of the Velsicol Chemical Company, once wrote in the journal *BioScience,* "They [the critics] are actually preoccupied with the subject of sexual potency to such an extent that sex is never a subject of jest." Many attacks were directed against Rachel Carson as the prime "trouble-maker" including a quip, quoted in Frank Graham's excellent book, *Since Silent Spring,* such as, "I thought she was a spinster. What's she so worried about genetics for?"

Despite such despicable acts, industry can only be censured for its attitude and not blamed for its environmental callousness. It is against the government—and particularly the U. S. Department of Agriculture (USDA)—that the finger of responsibility points. Under the Federal Insecticide, Fungicide and Rodenticide Act of 1947 (FIFRA), the Pesticide Regulation Division was created and placed in USDA. The Pesticide Regulation Division was entrusted with approval, regulation and registration of pesticides and authorized to test new chemicals as they were produced and approve their recommended dosages and uses. Presently there are 900 to 1,000 chemical compounds combined into about 65,000 different formulations—and many of these formulations have several different uses.

Since its inception, the Pesticide Regulation Division has been, as one critic put it, "overly impressed with the necessity of pesticides and insufficiently concerned with their dangers." On the whole, pesticide registrations have been granted quickly and easily. Moreover, relations between the Pesticide Regulation Division and private industry have always been very close—closer than most environmentalists would like. A classic case of incestuousness occurred in 1965, with the Shell No-Pest Strip. This colorful innocuous-looking household insecticide contains an organophosphate which continually emits a vapor into its surroundings. Despite warnings from the Public Health Service and other scientists, and a general lack of sufficient information, John Leary, head of the Pesticide Regulation Division's pharmacology section, continually urged approval of the product. In 1966 Leary left USDA to join Shell. It was later determined that two USDA scientists connected with research on the No-Pest Strip were paid by Shell as well as by the Department. Only in the summer of 1970 did the U. S. Department of Agriculture agree with the Public Health Service that the strip should be banned from "kitchens, restaurants and other places where food is stored."

The most spectacular example of the Pesticide Regulation Division's less-than-vigilant approach toward registration may be gleaned from its use of the powers it has. The 1947 act states that a pesticide will be banned if the Pesticide Regulation Division sends out a notice to that effect and the notice is not responded to within 30 days. If the company that manufactures the specific chemical refuses to comply with the request, it responds to the Pesticide Regulation Division's notice with a request for an investigation by an independent scientific board. If the board finds against the USDA, the matter is dropped and the pesticide is vindicated; if the board finds against the pesticide, the manufacturer can then request an open hearing. In the 23 years of the Pesticide Regulation Division's existence, this procedure has never reached the third step, an open hearing. As Harrison Wellford of the Center for the Study of Law and Social Policy said, the three-stage cancellation procedure "provides industry a lot of time to exert pressure to change people's minds." Once again environmentalists find the regulatory agency too close to the group being regulated.

In August, 1970, President Nixon announced the formulation of the Environmental Protection Agency, an "umbrella organization" which will combine most of the environmentally-oriented divisions of USDA, Departments of Interior (USDI), Health, Education and Welfare (HEW) as well as other groups. It is not clear as yet how effective this new

Agency will be and how long it will take to get "off the ground." Most critics are happy to see USDA's power in the field diminished. Wellford, however, remains skeptical. "Until now," he said, "the chemical lobbies had to pressure Agriculture, Interior and HEW on many of these pesticide issues. Now there will be only one department to gain audience with." Ecologists, too, will find less bureaucracy in their way—it remains to be seen, however, which lobby will be more effective.

Generally speaking, pesticide foes have found stronger allies in the Departments of Interior and HEW. HEW, which includes the Public Health Service and the Food and Drug Administration, has always been concerned with the human health hazard of pesticide use and has attempted to make its recommendations on the subject final and conclusive. (If USDA, however, rejects the recommendations, HEW's only possible response is to have the FDA confiscate food whose pesticide content exceeds certain limits—wherever those limits are set). The U. S. Department of Interior, certainly the government's most environmentally aware department, has even less actual power. Its sole response to a USDA refusal of a recommendation is to place a pesticide on its own restricted list. This outlaws its use on USDI lands (the Department is the largest landholder in the country, with over 500 million acres), but exerts no other pressure on government or industry.

The complexities of the federal government are awesome—and are made more so in this case by the unpredictability of forthcoming actions and stances of the Environmental Protection Agency. Most politically-oriented ecologists advocate that the concerned citizen make his feelings known to his elected officials in the national and state capitals, particularly members of agricultural and environmentally concerned committees and subcommittees. Ecological issues have become politically weighty enough for these representatives to give consideration to letters and complaints from citizens and local groups. Another potentially receptive group is the state agriculture commission (the official name of such agencies varies from state to state). Although its members are generally appointed, they still feel some pressure to respond to local action. Often, in this case, petitions and demands for open hearings are more effective than individual letters. For more local issues such as town or community spraying programs (mosquito control, etc.) complaints are best registered with city or town councils or with the mayor's office.

To stem the tide of pesticide use, complaints are necessary but they are not sufficient. To be effective one needs a substitute for the chemicals, and this is the domain of the scientists, not the legislators. The questions then arise: What can modern science do to open up new directions of pest control? After all, it was science which unleashed these new forces. Can we afford to sit back and hope man will voluntarily control himself? Or have we again reached a level of complexity beyond the capabilities of our meager regulatory processes?

Nearly all researchers are quick to assert that far too little work has been done in the field and that, given time, the basic dilemmas of the pesticide will be worked out. The general feeling is that the chemical pesticide was such a spectacular breakthrough that few people realized what a simplistic and crude method it really was. The "honeymoon" with such products as DDT and parathion appears to be turning sour. Scientists are beginning to look into far more sophisticated techniques such as biological, radiological, cultural and integrated controls. These alternative methods—some very new ones hold promise, some ancient ones are being reinvestigated—are focusing away from the "extreme" method of poisoning toward a more "natural" approach.

Biological control, for instance, relies upon Nature's own methods of selection in a stable environment. Studies are made to determine the most effective and specific predators of a pest species. These predators are then raised in huge quantities and released in particular areas. In the case of imported pests, researchers attempt to find the predators which controlled them in the original area, and these are then also imported. Predators are not the only natural controls; for instance, viruses and other disease organisms have been used. These methods have been extremely successful in New Zealand, Java, Fiji and Hawaii, and moderately successful in some parts of California and Kenya. For reasons which are as yet not well understood, biological control has been far more successful on islands than in large continental areas. Research is continuing, however, and it is likely that breakthroughs will eventually point the way to biological control in this country of such persistent imported pests as the gypsy moth, the European corn borer and the Japanese beetle.

Scientists are also pursuing irradiation of male insects. The males, which are sterilized by the process, are released in huge quantities to seek out and mate with normal females. Such a union produces no offspring, and if all the conditions are right, an insect population can be decimated in a few generations. The screwworm, a cattle pest of the Southwest, has been controlled by this method, and the continuing release of sterilized males along the U. S.–Mexico border has checked the migration of the screwworm northward. The approach has the obvious advantage that the species cannot develop resistance to sterility; on the other hand, there are cases where sterilized males cannot compete effectively against the sexually more aggressive normal males.

At the University of Wisconsin, a novel approach to the termite problem is being investigated. Termites secrete a trail-marking chemical which is utilized to pass on certain directional information to other termites, generally the location of the food. Researchers have been able to synthesize a similar chemical, and are testing the possibility of tricking termites into following a false trail to a trap where they can be destroyed.

Another important approach to the control of insects involves what are broadly termed cultural methods. Some of these methods, like crop rotation and crop residue destruction, have been practiced since ancient times and are considered the basis of good farming techniques. Others, including development of hardy and healthy crop strains, involve the most recent and sophisticated scientific study and experimentation. It has been found, for instance, that plant tolerance of, or resistance to, a pest in some instances is an inherited characteristic. The selection of such characteristics is a long, tedious process but it has paid off in such areas as south and east Africa where hairy varieties of cotton have been found resistant to attack by leaf hoppers.

If enough research is done on the habits and needs of pests, other less technologically sophisticated remedies are sometimes highly successful. In Europe, early and late plantings of cereals have been utilized to avoid losses to the Hessian fly, whose greatest numbers occur in the middle of the season. In Asia, the flooding of rice stubbles has helped to control the rice borer by drowning the insect while it is in its resting stages. A similar philosophy has even been proposed for human pests—the Massachusetts Audubon Society has recommended that strict zoning laws be enacted to prevent families from moving to mosquito-infested areas and then clamoring for a DDT eradication program!

Obviously the problem of insect and agricultural pests is an extremely complex one, and one which becomes more complex the deeper one digs. Dr. Loren Jensen explains, "It is a misnomer to term the present era 'the age of man.' Technically and objectively it is 'the age of the insect.' Insects are our chief competitors for the world's food supply, and it is with insects that we must reckon."

As is usually the case with seemingly insurmountable problems which appear to respond to overly-simplistic breakthroughs, the pesticide crisis is not one which will disappear by itself. After the environmental panic and the industrial paranoia subside, it will be up to the scientists to bridge the gap between the farmer's needs and the doctor's fears.

Almost certainly the ultimate answers will be found in integrated control methods, such as sexual attractants which lure insects to a poisonous trap, and other schemes which diversify man's attack on pests. Since present evidence indicates that insects very likely are ultimately less vulnerable to poisons than man is, it is up to the human species to use its intelligence and flexibility to combat the insect species' numbers and voracity.

The big question we must all face is, what can the average citizen do? Scientific breakthroughs, no matter how spectacular or how likely, may be years away. Cultural and integrated controls take time to develop and even longer to implement. In the meantime, the environment is suffering terrible degradation, species are being wiped out and the health of mankind is being affected. Starting in the home and the immediate neighborhood, what ecologically sound steps can be taken?

• Sanitation is of prime importance in the fight against insects. Dirty kitchens provide ideal homes for roaches and ants; messy backyards are ideal for many insects and rodents; city dumps are hosts for a wide variety of insects, rodents, and other scavengers. Studies have shown that such an innocuous item as a child's pail can provide an excellent breeding ground for mosquitoes if it collects rainwater.

• Polluted streams provide excellent havens for mosquitoes because fish, their natural predators, are killed off and the mosquito eggs mature in safety. A chemical control program will only insure the continuing murder of fish and the continuing proliferation of the mosquito nuisance. The Audubon Society recommends cleaning up the streams and then stocking them with minnows, bluegills or bass. In ornamental ponds, goldfish are successful in curbing mosquito populations.

• Backyard gardners often contribute to the pesticide crisis. Insecticides and herbicides are rarely needed to "protect" ornamental gardens from the relatively minor insect damage they suffer. When an emergency arises only the safest pesticides should be used and only in sparing, specific amounts. If a herbicide nozzle attachment is used on a water hose, get an attachment which will prevent the chemical from seeping back into the water supply.

• The use of beneficial insects often yields far better results than the use of chemicals. Lady bugs, aphid lions, vadalia, ant lions, lacewings, praying mantises, fireflies, dragonflies and trichogramma wasps are all beneficial insects and prey on, among others, aphids, mealybugs, spider mites, moth eggs, caterpillars, plant lice, crickets, locusts, beetles, cutworms, cankerworms, mosquitoes, armyworms, bagworms, cotton bollworms, corn-borers, and luna moths. For instance, in one test the release of 200,000 aphid lions per acre proved as successful in controlling the cotton bollworm as the heavy use of DDT.

• A garden's own natural fortitude will often save it from severe damage. Most gardens, if they are well-fed, well-watered and maintained will grow with sufficient vigor that pest attacks won't be very harmful. As Shirley Briggs put it, "Never spray on principle before you know that an actual problem exists. Do not apply a persistent poison for a temporary problem."

• Pesticides are often used professionally on products that one would suspect least. Some wax papers and shelf papers are impregnated with hard pesticides. These are always to be avoided, as it is likely they will be in contact with food or utensils. If there is a bad indoor insect problem, it is far better to apply a safe product such as Silica Gel after plain shelf paper is installed.

• Dry cleaners and cloth manufacturers also use powerful chemicals (lindane and dieldrin) in a process usually referred to as "permanent moth-proofing." These chemicals are chlorinated hydrocarbons and they are absorbed through the skin. In the long run they will cause more damage than the moths.

• Pesticide disposal is the most serious problem facing chemists in the field today. It is such an awesome dilemma that most environmentalists refrain from making any unequivocal recommendations at all. If small pesticide surpluses remain, the best rule is to leave them, sealed, on a shelf away from food, children and pets, until satisfactory disposal methods are developed. If your county or community has a high temperature incinerator, call those in charge to find out the best procedures to use in bringing in pesticides, and the best time to come (often the incinerator will be hottest in midweek). Be sure to mark the name and ingredients of any chemical which was transferred to an unmarked container. Certain herbicides, for instance, explode at high temperatures.

• The burial of pesticides is not recommended unless one is sure of such facts as the depth of the water table, the type of soil, the existence and location of wells in the area, etc. Organophosphates should be mixed with at least ten times their weight of lime. Pesticides, including aerosols, should never be poured down the drain, the toilet or on the open ground. Nor should they ever be thrown in with the trash. It is best to notify sanitation authorities to find out what is recommended.

• Be skeptical of any claim, whether by advertisement or word-of-mouth, that a certain product is a "cure-all" for any problem. Pesticide manufacturers delight in a homeowner's panic at the sight of bugs or weeds, and many persons have been conditioned to reach for a chemical before analyzing a problem. A neighbor will enthusiastically tell of a product that is "just the greatest" while simultaneously mentioning that his pet has been acting strangely or his child has a new rash, without connecting the two. If a real "cure-all" is developed, it will certainly be reported in the news before a company's advertisers even get word of its existence.

• Keep a sharp eye on local, state and federal pesticide programs, either through the local media or through one of the many environmental publications. The enlightened actions of thousands of concerned individuals can be wiped out with one disastrous decision by a governmental agency. In the Southeast, for instance, the USDA is about to embark on a massive chemical eradication program against the fire ant, a pest of cattle and man. The $200 million effort calls for the spraying of 450 million pounds of mirex bait (mirex is a chlorinated hydrocarbon) over 120 million acres in nine states. Only the concerted actions of environmentally aware citizen groups have held the program up this far, and it is doubtful whether it can be halted. Keep in mind that the government is not necessarily a leader in the fight against chemical pesticides.

• Modern fertilizers now often include some pesticidal chemicals right in the mixture, "to help," as one gardener put it, "nurture and kill your garden at the same time." These are generally promoted with the fertilizer name and "plus" or "plus 2." These should be avoided, for the pest problem may not even exist in your region, and in any event, it can be attacked later with a variety of methods. The ingredients of all fertilizers should be checked before purchase.

• Home and garden pest control companies should be used only in the last resort and then only after thoroughly checking on the products they use and the methods they employ. Many of these companies, which after all rely on word-of-mouth recommendations, are unaware of their contributions to environmental destruction. If a company refuses to divulge its chemicals, do not hire it.

• There is a growing trend around the country toward organic farming, even on a large scale. If there is a roadside fruit or vegetable stand which sells pesticide-free produce, patronize it. Many farmers use pesticides unthinkingly and unnecessarily, and if they find an economic reason for abstaining, they will. Consumers can help the cause by being less finicky about imperfect produce and more conscious of good taste and good health.

• Education is important. One should know which chemicals should and should not be used. Labels should always be read and all pesticides should be handled with care. A comprehensive list of environmentally damaging pesticides is available from Northern Virginia Conservation Council, Box 304, Annandale, Virginia 22003. Here is a list of harmful and relatively harmless common pesticides.

NEVER USE	DO USE
DDT	Rotenone
DDD (TDE)	Ryania
aldrin	Silica Gel
chlordane	Pyrethrum
dieldrin	(pyrethrins)
endrin	Allethrin
heptachlor	Sulphur and
kelthane	sulphur-lime
kepone	Bordeaux mixture
lindane	UNLESS fortified
methoxyclor	with lead or arsenic
perthane	Nicotine sulphate
thiodan (endosulfan)	(handle with care)
toxaphene	Copper-lime
BHC (benzene	mixtures
hexachloride)	Sabadilla
strobane	Diatomaceous earth
arsenic	Dri-Die
lead	Drione
mercury }—compounds	Warfarin
thallium	Red Squill
Baygon	
Zectram	
Sevin (carbaryl)	
methyl carbamate	
Baytex (fenthion)	
Azodrin	
Bidrin	
carbophenothion	
Clorthion	
Coumaphos (Co-Ral)	
Dibrom	
Diazinon	
DDVP	
Dimethoate	
Dursban	
EPN	
Ethion	
Guthion	
methyl parathion	
Parathion	
Phosdrin	

NEVER USE

Schradan
Thimet
TEPP
Malathion,
  unless necessary
Dinitro or DN
  compounds
Captan
Folpet (phaltan)
1080
picloram
Amitrol
2,4-D, except small
  specific doses
2,4,5-T
Thiram
Weed Bars

power generation

• *Of the nation's combined amount of raw power available from all sources—work animals, motors, turbines, etc.—electrical energy represents only about one-fiftieth. But it produces one-fourth the nation's air pollution.*

• *"Suppose, for instance, that all electric power is to be produced by modern 1,000 megawatt power plants and that each requires an area of only 1,000 feet on a side. If all the country's power needs were presently being met by 300 such large power plants, in less than 20 doublings—that is, in less than two centuries—all of the available land space in the U. S. would be taken up by such plants."—Dr. Malcolm Peterson, Committee on Environmental Information.*

• *By the year 2000 the population of the United States is expected to double. If current patterns continue, each of the 320 million Americans alive then will consume as much electrical power as 12½ 1950 Americans.*

Contemporary Americans indulge in a style of living that is inextricably plugged into electric power plants. Electricity is produced today by an antiquated process based on the steam engine which James Watt introduced in 1776. Newer and better technologies exist for producing more electricity with less pollution, but U. S. power companies and the federal government trenchantly refuse to invest in them. Unless they do, the nation will soon—within a few decades—face an energy crisis situation characterized by (1) exhaustion of certain fuel supplies, (2) shortage of land on which to site generating stations, and (3) a population whose health is seriously endangered by environmental pollution.

Three basic facilities are used to generate electricity: fossil-fueled power plants (oil, coal, natural gas); nuclear-fueled power plants (uranium fission), and hydroelectric stations (dams and pumped storage plants). In the first two types, fuels are burned to heat water to steam, which is used to turn the huge turbines that generate electricity. Hydroelectric plants use the power of falling water to turn the turbines.

One facet of the "energy crisis" is the inability of the electric power industry to keep up with increasing demand for more power (estimated to be 9 percent every 10 years). Demand is directly linked to consumption, so as more Americans buy more manufactured products, energy needs are increased. Industry uses 65 percent of the total electricity generated, according to 1968 figures. Average domestic customers use only about 31 percent. Therefore, the bulk of electricity is used to turn the wheels of industry and keep buildings and billboards well lit at night. As our Gross National Product rises, so does the level of power consumption.

As a result of America's growing appetite for electricity, there has been a realization that the supply of fuels to generate electrical power is not infinite. Dr. M. King Hubbert, a research geophysicist for the U. S. Geological Survey, estimates that most of the world's consumption of fossil fuels has occurred in the last 25 years. He figures that the time required to produce and consume the middle 80 percent of the ultimate amount of crude oil which can be produced in the United States is only 65 years, or less than a single lifetime. Estimates made by Dr. Hubbert and other energy forecasters reveal that all petroleum reserves may be exhausted within 100 years (at current levels of use). Of all the fossil fuels, only coal exists in sufficient quantity to hold out for several centuries, if used at current consumption levels.

Even atomic energy, which at one time was promoted as the energy source of the future, has definite limitations. Conventional atomic reactors, which produce electricity by splitting the atoms of heavy elements such as uranium, may run out of fuel within the next two decades.

Another contributor to the crisis in energy supply is the failure of existing technology to deliver the goods as promised. The utilities industry has pinned its hopes on atomic energy. Although $2.3 billion has been spent to develop this source, the effort has fallen flat on its face. Of the 22 electrical power plants fueled with uranium that have gone into operation in the U. S. in the last few years, at least half are now either dismantled, shut down, inoperable, or running at partial capacity.

Construction deadlines for new plants have been set back by failures in equipment production and delivery. Approximately four years is required to construct a modern fossil-fueled power plant and five years for an atomic plant. A report prepared by the trade association of the private electric utility industry, the Edison Electric Institute, indicates that construction of over two-thirds of the power plants ordered between 1966–1968 was delayed. The longest delays—up to a year—occurred in construction of nuclear power plants.

Funds for development of electric power generation have also been misallocated. In the past 25 years, research designed to implement nuclear production of electricity has taken the lion's share of federal and private funds for the advancement of all energy conversion methods. Of the $2.3 billion spent since the mid-1950s by the Atomic Energy Commission (AEC) to get the civilian reactor program rolling, a good portion of it has been used to subsidize the development of reactors by utilities.

The atomic oversell has had severe repercussions on the coal industry. AEC's promotion of atomic plants during the 1950s and 1960s virtually promised that use of coal for the production of electricity would soon be outmoded. "During the early 1960s," according to a *Wall Street Journal* report, "[coal] production dwindled to 403 million tons a year, and electric utilities were rushing toward nuclear power plants. Fearing a sizable loss of utility business and the resulting over-capacity, coal operators almost stopped opening new mines."

To improve the power industry's shoddy record in the key areas of energy production, new research and development calls for vast expenditures, not only by government, but by industry as well. The industry's record in this area is despicable. Particularly obvious is the practice of overselling electricity through advertisement. According to Senator Lee Metcalf, this utility advertising "increases consumer costs, decreases competition and supplants expenditures which should be made on research and development." Metcalf figures that private utilities "spend more money polluting air waves than cleaning air. . . . 51 percent of the 212 major electric utilities, according to the Federal Power Commission, did not spend a cent on research and development in 1968. . . . Advertising and other sales expenses by investor-owned utilities amount to eight times as much as the industry's expenditure on research and development."

This view is echoed by top Presidential scientific advisors. An August, 1970, report called "Electric Power and the Environment," prepared by the Office of Science and Technology, asserted that: "The general level of research and development expenditures by electric utilities, and particularly in respect to environmental matters, is far below an appropriate level for an industry of this size. . . . In 1968, for example, total direct research and development expenditures by electric utilities amounted to *less than one-fourth of one percent of operating revenues. . . .*" [Emphasis added].

Even if the fuel supply were inexhaustible, and if technology for generating power was working perfectly, the problem of environmental destruction remains. Each of the present systems for generating power does harm to the environment.

The burning of fossil fuels (coal, oil, natural gas) represents the third largest source of air pollution in the United States. Air pollution from fossil-fueled electric plants comes from three major sources—sulfur oxides, nitrogen oxides, and particulate matter (flyash). According to the National Air Pollution Control Administration (NAPCA), these contaminants are dumped on the U. S. at a rate of more than 45 million tons a year, a figure which, at the current rate of increase, is expected to reach 130 million tons by the year 2000.

About 90 percent of the electric industry's sulfur oxide pollution comes from the burning of coal; the rest is from the combustion of residual fuel oil with a high sulfur content. As a result of the chemical processes connected with the release of sulfur, sulfuric acid is often present in the air. This causes the severe corrosion of metals, deleterious health effects and destruction of plant life.

NAPCA studies indicate that adverse health effects occur when sulfur oxide concentrations in the air reach 0.11 parts per million (ppm) for 24-hour periods, or when mean annual levels reach 0.04 ppm. In New York City, such levels have been exceeded three or four fold. In July, 1970, New York City's Environmental Protection Administration argued against the expansion of Consolidated Edison's Astoria fossil fuel electric plant on the basis that it would cause ground level concentrations of sulfur oxides about 50 percent above the maximum permitted by the federal government. The argument was partially successful in that the city only permitted partial expansion of the Astoria plant.

Some methods to reduce the sulfur content of fossil fuels are being implemented, but only minimally. They include the use of fuels with a low-sulfur content (one percent or less); the removal of sulfur from stack gases of the plants; and the removal of sulfur from the fuel before combustion.

In addition to sulfur pollution, nitrogen oxide is released in large quantities by fossil-fired power plants. Almost half of the some 10 million tons of nitrogen oxides fouling the U. S. yearly comes from power plants. Current estimates indicate that in the year 2000, more than 25 million tons of nitrogen oxides will be released. Nitrogen oxides are implicated in the production of photochemical smog. Control techniques are virtually unknown, and at current spending levels will never be developed.

The third major air pollution problem from burning fossil fuels is the creation of particulate matter (flyash), more commonly referred to as just plain dirt. To control the creation of flyash, smokestack devices known as electrostatic precipitators are used. The latest model precipitators can collect 97 to 99 percent of the particulate matter created during combustion. Even with this efficiency, huge amounts of flyash are released from the big, new plants. A new coal-fired plant in Nevada releases about one ton of flyash per hour, even though it is equipped with a 97 percent efficient electrostatic precipitator. The ash that gets away is in the form of very fine particles which may pose a serious health hazard. They lodge in the tiny air sacs of the lung, where they may be especially harmful. Complicating the study of the effects of this hazard is the suspicion that sulfur dioxide absorbed on the particles may also invade the lungs this way.

The primary response of the electric power industry to the problems involved in fossil fuel combustion has been to build higher smoke stacks. These are designed to disperse the pollutants at high altitudes, preventing the contamination of areas immediately adjacent to the plant. Stacks over 1000 feet high are not an uncommon sight; however, the fallacy of simply raising the level at which pollution is dumped into the air is obvious.

Natural gas combustion does not contribute any significant quantities of particulates or sulfur oxides to the environment, and its combustion releases only half as much nitrogen oxides as an equivalent amount of coal. Unfortunately, natural gas is in very short supply, and its widespread use is consequently unwise. Some speculate that if natural gas were higher priced, oil companies would have the incentive to carry on more substantial explorations for new sources.

Nuclear power is widely advertised by electric utilities as "clean energy" (Consolidated Edison, New York), "the keystone of our clean air program" (Commonwealth Edison, Chicago) or other similar phrases. In fact, it's not so clean. Big commercial reactors routinely release radioactive substances into air and water. Safe transportation, processing and disposal of lethal radioactive materials, and especially radioactive wastes created by the reactors are other problem areas. A special concern is the question of accidental releases of radioactivity resulting from abnormal reactor operations.

Nuclear plants operate very much like fossil-fueled plants—except that the uranium is "burned" (fissioned) instead of coal or oil to heat water for steam to turn the electric power turbines in the plant. The principle of the reactor differs from that of the atomic bomb, since the fission process is carefully controlled to prevent an explosion.

Small amounts of ionizing radiation are spread into air and water by the emissions of nuclear power plants. Not a great deal is known about the effects of this radiation dose, but there is a risk of genetic damage. Two scientists from the Lawrence Radiation Laboratory (an AEC-financed facility at Livermore, California), Drs. John Gofman and Arthur Tamplin, have led the public outcry against careless use of nuclear energy. They conclude that if the public were exposed to the legally allowable radiation dose from atomic energy programs, 32,000 extra cancer and leukemia deaths would occur in the U. S. population. In addition, they find that the genetic toll (in a future U. S. population of 300 million) from environmental radiation would be far worse—somewhere between 150,000 and 1,500,000 deaths—not including a heightened infant mortality rate. Drs. Gofman and Tamplin want a downward revision of the allowable radiation dosage by at least a factor of tenfold.

After a nuclear reactor has been operating for approximately a year (or until the completion of its fuel cycle), its fuel load—uranium—is used up, leaving tons of radioactive byproducts sealed in its core. This radioactive poison (including strontium 90, iodine-131, plutonium, and a host of other deadly materials), must be shipped to a nuclear reprocessing plant, where any usable fuel is chemically removed. The radioactive leftovers must be stored indefinitely, since they will remain the most poisonous substances on earth—for periods ranging up to hundreds of thousands of years.

To date the AEC, empowered to oversee the handling of these wastes, has found no effective way to store them. At present, more than 80 million gallons of the most lethal wastes (high-level wastes) are stored in 194 underground tanks at various AEC disposal sites in the U. S. The nuclear industry will soon be adding up to 4 million gallons a year to that total.

Since the high-level poisons boil constantly in the tanks (from intense radioactive "decay"), ruptures and other problems result. The AEC is attempting to perfect a method of solidifying them for burial in abandoned salt mines. In the interim, it is spending $1.3 million to explore the possibilities of dumping some of the troublesome wastes into a bedrock formation beneath the Savannah River along the Georgia–South Carolina border. According to a report by the National Academy of Sciences, which the AEC has effectively ignored, the deadly radioactive liquids might escape into the river through unforeseen routes, which would sufficiently contaminate the southeastern United States to the extent that human life there would be impossible.

Whereas waste products are dumped, the fuel cores from nuclear reactors are sent to reprocessing plants, where some of the material is saved for reuse. Like power reactors, reprocessing stations have trouble operating within the standard radiation limits. A reprocessing plant in West Valley, New York, and owned by the Getty Oil Company, has been found with radiation levels in water nearby that are 10 times the current federal radiation safety levels. Dr. Ernest Sternglass, a radiation specialist at the University of Pittsburgh, reports that infant mortality rates in Cattaraugus County (where the plant is located) went up over 50 percent between 1966–1967, initial years of the plant's operation. Sternglass' figures for New York as a whole show a decline in the rate of infant mortality. Many have called for the plant to be shut down, but it still remains open. The reason may be that it is the only one now operating in the country.

Apart from the problem of atmospheric contamination from the allowable nuclear plant radioactive emissions is the possibility of accidents involving massive contamination. A report commissioned by the AEC in 1957 to study the worst possible consequences of a reactor accident showed that in an accident which released 50 percent of the plant's radioactivity, up to 3400 people would be killed, 43,000 injured from radiation, and up to 150,000 square miles contaminated by radioactive particles. This was estimated when all reactors were much smaller than presently built ones. The hazards from present-day accidents are significantly greater.

To contend with the shortage of uranium, a new type of reactor is in the development stages. The "breeder reactor" (so named because it is supposed to generate as much or more usable fuel than it burns) will produce a new type of nuclear fuel—plutonium. Radiation scientists are worried about the breeder because of the particularly hazardous nature of plutonium, whose toxicity is measured in billionths of a gram. An accident in a plutonium-bearing reactor would be far worse than an accident with the current type of reactor. It is widely recognized that breeder reactors are much more complex and, consequently, more accident prone than conventional reactors. They are the albatrosses of the AEC. Who wants to live near one?

A key problem in all power plants is the technological inefficiency of the steam-turbine method of generating electricity. This is expressed in "thermal pollution." Both fossil and nuclear-fueled steam-electric plants need cooling water for condensers, which wastes most of the energy produced by the plant.

Since electric power plants account for over four-fifths of all uses of cooling water in the U. S., thermal pollution (or thermal inefficiency) can be seen as the nearly unique problem of this technology. Thermal pollution has a number of bad effects. The addition of large amounts of hot water into lakes, ponds, rivers and waterways which serve as the "cooling ponds" of the power plants intensifies the effects of other pollutants already in the water. The hot water lowers the amount of dissolved oxygen in the water, which is also responsible for killing a number of heat-sensitive aquatic species (including such prized sport fish as trout and salmon). The added heat encourages the growth of heat-resistant organisms, such as algae—when these tiny plants thrive, they form thick mats of blue-green slime which clogs rivers, causes odors and radically deteriorates water quality.

New nuclear power plants are even less efficient than new fossil-fired plants—32 percent efficiency compared to 40 percent efficiency. This means that for each 1,000 watts of electricity produced, the nuclear plant will lose 7,285,000 British Thermal Units (BTU) of waste heat into water, and the fossil plant will lose 3,845,000 BTU of waste heat.

In 1970, the U. S. Department of the Interior published a report speculating on the future of Lake Michigan, particularly susceptible to environmental damage from the thermal pollution of scores of power plants being constructed on its shores. The report concluded that the "heat addition is essentially a cumulative problem that would contribute to assure eutrophication and be intolerable from the fish and wildlife standpoint by the year 2000."

The only known way to control thermal pollution is to add enormous water cooling towers to the power plants. These recirculate the process water in the plant from electric power condensers to a cooling element, then release it to the waterway. A problem arises from the use of the most common sort of cooling tower, the "wet" cooling tower—this tower releases great clouds of steam into the air around the plant (among other effects, the steam contributes to the icing of local roads and highways in winter).

Use of the power of moving water to drive the turbines of power plants eliminates the problems of "conventional" air, water and thermal pollution from central station electric power plants, but hydro power has unique problems of its own, not the least of which is the drowning of large land areas. One of the most tragic engineering boondoggles in history, for example, is the Aswan Dam in northern Egypt. Completion of the dam has severely interrupted the passage of silt down the Nile River. Before construction of the dam, this silt, bearing assorted biological nutrients, had nourished crops all along the river. The interruption of its flow now threatens to destroy more agricultural production than was created by intricate irrigation systems built near the dam.

The silt had also nourished various aquatic species near the mouth of the Nile, in the Mediterranean Sea. These species, including the important food-fish, sardines, are no longer found congregating in their former habitats. The Mediterranean sardine catch in the general region of the Nile delta declined from 18,000 tons in 1965 to 500 tons in 1968, the post-dam era.

Due to other changes in the natural cycles of the river, a host of new diseases plague the area. Some changes threaten the hydroelectric potential of the dam itself. According to Dr. Dean Abrahamson, "Water weeds have become so numerous behind the dam that they may increase water loss through transpiration to the point where the lake lacks enough water to drive the power generators."

Such incredible—and quite unforeseen—developments may make the damming of rivers to produce electric power an obsolete technique.

Hydroelectric power supplies only 4 percent of energy in the U. S. with the big dams concentrated in the Pacific Northwest. Very few areas of the world are suitable for hydroelectric installations, and now the international production of electricity by this method is only 2 percent of the total.

Not to be outdone by nature, engineers devised an artificial hydro method that is swiftly gaining in popularity in the U. S. This method is called pumped-storage generation. This novel means of producing power requires two pools of water, one on a hill or mountainside, and the other in a valley; a generator unit, situated midway between the two bodies of water, produces electricity when water is released from the upper pool to the lower reservoir. It is pumped back up the mountainside at night or when power needs are very low, and released again during daytime peak demand periods.

Prior to 1961, only four pumped-storage projects existed in the United States; today, over 100 are being planned or built. Environmental damage is related to changes in land use. Entire valleys which are flooded to serve as the lower reservoirs of pumped-storage projects become, in the words of one critic, "yo-yoing mudflats." In an optimistic booklet published by a West Virginia coalition of private power companies planning a joint pumped-storage project, the claim is made that the proposed project will create an interesting new ecological feature—"a fresh-water tidal zone."

When rivers are used as the lower reservoirs of pumped-storage projects, environmental damage is somewhat lessened. One of the longest fights in the history of the Federal Power Commission has been over the licensing of one such project proposed by Consolidated Edison Company in New York. The FPC approved the Cornwall project (Storm King Mountain) in 1970, over the objections of numerous New York conservation groups, led by the Scenic Hudson Preservation Conference. The FPC claims that construction of this project will make the "best use of available resources . . . with the minimum impact on our environment."

Solutions to the key environmental problems related to conventional power plants may come from the development and utilization of advanced techniques of energy conversion. Revolutionary new power stations are now feasible. They would bypass the steam cycle altogether and replace existing steam electric plants with power stations that would convert the energy of fuels directly to electricity.

Three energy conversion systems that offer great potential involve the use of solar power, advanced power conversion from fossil fuels, and conversion of power from the nuclear fusion reaction. To date, none of these methods have been implemented on a large production scale, with the exception of solar units, which have been developed by NASA for the space program.

Solar power offers a new future for the conversion of energy to electricity, particularly because of technological advances made in the space program. The use of solar power would be pollution-free. Until recently, however, it has not been thought of as an alternative to fossil and nuclear-fueled central station plants.

Extensive amounts of land would be required for solar collectors, and at present, the collectors are very expensive. Solar energy engineers, however, point out that desolate areas (such as Death Valley) could be used for the solar power plants. In addition, with the expanded development of solar power, collectors would be mass-produced, bringing costs down to competitive levels.

Dr. Peter Glaser, head of the engineering department of the consulting firm, Arthur D. Little, Inc., advocates the development of space-satellite solar power stations which would transmit solar energy to earth via microwaves. The microwave power would be converted directly to electricity and transmitted along established transmission lines.

Dr. Glaser is optimistic about the future prospects for solar power, even if the space system is not developed. He believes that rising fuel costs in the U. S. will make solar heating and cooling units for houses economically successful, as well as affording fuel savings nationally by as much as 30 percent (assuming, of course, the widespread implementation of solar units in houses). Besides the exciting potential for the national use of solar units in houses and the possibility of the space system, which would provide New York City's electricity needs in the year 2000, Dr. Glaser adds that solar energy "is the only energy source that can qualify for an important new social criteria—the absence of environmental pollution."

Nuclear fusion, the source of the sun's heat as well as the hydrogen bomb's explosive force, may soon be controlled in a special type of reactor containing the hydrogen atoms of ordinary sea-water as fuel. The atoms, contained in a magnetic field, would be heated to temperatures over 100 million degrees (Kelvin), at which point they would fuse together. The tremendous energy released by the fusion of the atoms would be directly converted to electricity.

Among scientists there is guarded optimism over the chances for speedy development of fusion technology. Dr. Richard F. Post of the Lawrence Radiation Laboratory expects this power source to be "in hand" within a decade. In fact, the excitement over the possibility of controlling the fusion reaction has interested at least one electric utility to put money in fusion research.

Another promising energy conversion technology is called magnetohydrodynamics, or MHD. An MHD generator converts electricity directly from high-temperature, ionized gases passed through a magnetic field. The process has already been successfully demonstrated in a number of countries, including the U. S., Russia and Japan. MHD generators would use only two-thirds as much coal to produce the same amount of electricity currently gotten from the combustion of coal in steam-electric plants.

In addition to conserving our fossil-fuel resources by using the MHD process, the MHD plants can be built with carefully-engineered pollution control devices capable of economically recovering sulfuric and nitric acids for commercial sale from the common pollutants, nitrogen and sulfur oxides. Since the MHD generator operates at hotter temperatures than conventional fossil-fueled power plants, the sulfur and nitrogen oxides are more concentrated in the smokestack gases.

To develop any one of the new and promising energy conversion technologies will require a tremendous amount of research and years of engineering development. *Fortune* magazine says that the problem of getting the necessary research programs financed in the U. S. "is becoming more obdurate than any of the problems facing underdeveloped countries. . . . The country that built the world's first central power station is now in danger of losing its leadership in the new level of technologies the times require."

To get a workable fusion reactor program, a good deal more money than has been invested in the past must be immediately put in the research effort. The Office of Science and Technology estimates that up to $200 million annually must be invested. In 1970, only $31 million (private and federal funds) was spent to develop fusion; by comparison, over $125 million was spent to develop breeder reactors.

A Russian MHD plant was started up in 1970; engineers in the U. S. believe that its cost is somewhere between $25 and $100 million. In this country, only $500,000 was spent last year to develop MHD for general use. Such an absurdly small funding level cannot hope to facilitate the introduction of this promising technology in the U. S.

As might be expected, no significant funding in any area of solar cell or transmission research is evident today in the U. S.

Only one technology which offers new promise is receiving substantial funding in the U. S.—fuel cell research and development. Fuel cells have been described as batteries with a continuous supply of fuel; a typical fuel cell, the hydrogen-oxygen cell, burns hydrogen and oxygen to form power. Its only by-product is water. In the past, the major difficulty has been designing fuel cells to burn fossil fuels. This seems to have been overcome, however, and a coalition of natural gas companies and electric utilities are planning to market large fuel cells for home and commercial use within the next five years. The coalition, TARGET (Team to Advance Research for Gas Energy Transformation) has spent $20 million (with Pratt & Whitney) to develop the system.

Successful development and marketing of the fuel cells might "at one stroke make central electric power generation for home use obsolete," says Dr. Bruce Netschert, a Washington, D. C. energy economist.

Although it is the scientists' job to develop new sources of power, they will not find the money to carry on research unless the public demands it. At the federal level, citizen pressure groups must wean control of energy development away from the AEC, an agency which many people believe functions as a trade association for the nuclear industry. Considerable pressure must be placed on legislators at all levels, and on all levels—national, state, local—of power regulating agencies.

The general public must also learn that more is involved in the power question than aesthetics. Power companies must stop advertising their monopoly product, which only increases and hurries a shortage of fuel. The rate structure, which presently favors industrial users over residential consumers, must be changed. Since rates are so much cheaper when large amounts of power are consumed, they are geared so that it actually pays to pollute.

The Federal Power Commission regulates interstate, wholesale (from power company to power company) sales of electricity. Intrastate and all retail rates are controlled by state agencies. Challenges to the rate structure, therefore, must be made through the state agencies—although it may be that a policy switch of this magnitude will come only through an act of Congress.

Power plants which threaten harm to human health and the environment should be cleaned up or closed down until adequate technology is developed. The most obvious point at which to challenge a power plant is before construction is begun, during hearings held by some of the several power regulatory agencies.

To intervene in formal hearings, legal assistance is a prerequisite. Be careful when choosing a lawyer, since in many states powerful power companies annually "retain" large numbers of lawyers "in case" they're needed to represent the companies in litigation. Check the *Lawyer's Directory* or the

Martindale-Hubbell Law Directory in your local library for background information on lawyers in your area.

Hydroelectric plants not owned by the government are subject to regulation by the FPC. A company that wishes to construct a hydro plant must file an application with the FPC, which then publishes the notice of application in the Federal Register and in the legal notices section of local papers, along with a deadline for filing petitions to intervene. If a citizen or group files a petition objecting to the planned facility, hearings are scheduled. An FPC-appointed examiner presides over the hearings and afterwards issues a ruling. FPC reviews his judgement before deciding to grant a license. After the license is awarded, anyone who participated in the hearings (but no other party) may file suit in federal court against the FPC to challenge the ruling.

The Atomic Energy Commission conducts hearings on nuclear power plants according to the same general procedure. A statement of the AEC hearing procedures which outlines how citizens can intervene—Part 2 of the Commission's Rules and Regulations—is available at a small cost to the public from the AEC's public information office, 1717 H St., N. W., Washington, D. C. If inquiries to the AEC about this publication yield no response, ask your congressman to get it for you.

Prior to December, 1970, the AEC judged only safety features of proposed reactors. Environmental groups have challenged this stand, claiming that the National Environmental Policy Act obliges the AEC to consider the environmental effects of each proposed reactor. At this writing a suit brought by environmentalists against the AEC is pending in the U. S. Court of Appeals in Washington, D. C.

Fossil fuel plants are not regulated by the federal government. Most states have public service commissions, electric power agencies or some such body which licenses them. Hearing procedures vary according to the state. In some instances, municipalities also exercise some control. Several states—Texas and Nebraska are two—have no regulatory agency that oversees power companies. In these cases, the utility has the same right to build as a steel company or any other industry.

Even though the federal government is not directly involved in regulating fossil fuel plants, some part of almost every electric generating facility requires federal approval. The 1899 Refuse Act requires the Army Corps of Engineers to issue a permit for heated water to be dumped back into its source. The Corps must also approve the construction of diversionary facilities like conduits which carry water into and away from the plant. Most local and state regulatory agencies are under the control of the industry they are supposed to regulate. Except where there is an especially progressive state agency, environmental groups can most successfully fight fossil fuel plants by interfering in the federal process. The National Environmental Policy Act can be used to challenge the Army Corps permits; either hearings will be set on the issue, or the matter can be taken to court.

Federally-owned power facilities like the Tennessee Valley Authority are not subject to the FPC, but they must clear nuclear plants with the AEC. Other types of government-owned electric utilities are subject to the requirements of the National Environmental Policy Act, which gives environmental groups the right to demand a statement of the environmental impact of the proposed project. Raising a controversy will probably persuade utility officials to hold hearings.

Polluting electric utilities already on the scene require different tactics. Vital background information on such companies is available from the FPC. Utilities must file advertising, political and other expenses each year; write to the FPC in Washington, D. C. and ask for a copy of Form 1 filed by your local electric utility.

Publicly controlled (cooperative) utilities are known for cheaper rates and greater public involvement, though the public utility systems are far less widespread than private utilities in the U. S. Information on the advantages of publicly-owned utilities vs. investor-owned utilities can be gleaned from Senator Lee Metcalf's excellent book on the subject, *Overcharge*, published in 1965, or by writing Senator Metcalf, U. S. Senate, Washington, D. C. Most information on municipal and public utilities is available from the American Public Power Association, Watergate Building, Washington, D. C.

An excellent example of a locally-based and controlled environmental organization with a great track record against a dirty utility is Campaign Against Pollution (CAP) in Chicago. CAP grew out of a loose coalition of Chicago-area citizens who decided to do battle with Commonwealth Edison Co., Chicago's huge private power company. The coalition was formed in late fall, 1969, with two goals in mind: (1) stop the massive sulfur oxide pollution of Chicago air by Com Ed, (2) deny any new rate increases to Com Ed unless their environmental policies changed.

Com Ed was an easy target for the environmentalists to pick. For years, it had been the biggest sulfur polluter in the area, dumping an average of 1.1 million tons per year on the city, while steadfastly insisting that it could not economically purchase low-sulfur coal. (Com Ed has also been the third largest particulate polluter in Chicago, dumping about 12,000 tons of dirt per year on the city.)

The broad-based environmental coalition (which became known as CAP in January, 1970) grew up as a community campaign. From the beginning of the group, action tactics were chosen spontaneously, and a strictly legal course of action was deliberately avoided. The community organizing was initiated by volunteers from Saul Alinsky's Industrial Areas Foundation (also in Chicago), a nationally known training center for labor and urban organizers.

The actual campaign against Com Ed's pollution policies ran from fall, 1969 to April, 1970, when CAP organized a stock proxy fight at Com Ed's annual stockholders meeting. According to Peter Martinez, one of the original organizers (and the current director) of CAP, the movement "had only one tangible goal to relate to—Com Ed. There was one organizing issue—forcing Com Ed to use low-sulfur coal. There was never an attempt to structure the fight in political language; we only tried to relate to tangible issues."

CAP started by publicizing rate hearings, gradually brought more members into the fray, and wound up holding meetings with Com Ed's top executives, shaking Mayor Daly's political machine, and getting a substantial commitment from the utility to switch to low-sulfur fuels. By the end of the campaign, CAP had over 1,000 active members, 400,000 Com Ed shares for use at the stockholders meeting (from individuals, churches, colleges, seminaries, and other community groups), and the active attention of the press, local and state officials, and national politicians.

CAP made a number of demands to Com Ed at the April

28, 1970, stockholders meeting, including a call for installation of cooling towers on a nuclear plant the utility is constructing on Lake Michigan. By the day of the meeting, the utility's public image had faded under CAP's constant barrage of facts backed by people. The *Wall Street Journal* noted at the time that CAP's contingent at the meeting included "banner-carrying high school and college students . . . mothers with small children, priests, elderly men and women along with well-dressed business and professional men. . . ."

By all accounts, the Edison campaign succeeded, not only in forcing the utility to reduce the use of high-sulfur fuels, but in setting an important precedent for the environmental movement. For the first time, a broad-based environmental coalition had successfully tackled a major electric utility and won. In fact, in July, 1970, long after CAP's public campaign, Com Ed was given a 4.5 percent rate increase by the Illinois Commerce Commission, contingent on strong pollution controls on its power plants. The utility had asked for a 6.1 percent increase. Paul Booth, a CAP co-chairman, said of the commission action: "It took us 11 months and thousands of hours of work. . . . I see it as tangible evidence of what the organized anger of thousands of consumers from northern Illinois has been able to do."

Citizen action against environmental destruction is most effective in groups, but even on their own, individuals can participate in efforts to avert energy shortages and environmental pollution due to overproduction of electricity. All it requires is sensitivity to the problem. Use as little electricity as possible.

The household's largest consumers of electric power are the essential items—refrigerator, stove, water heater, electric heating system. Choosing natural gas-fueled appliances may be a cleaner alternative, but natural gas supplies are limited. Select models which are not oversized for the job they will perform. The smaller the model (say, an electric refrigerator), the smaller the amount of electricity it needs to operate. Generally speaking, extra conveniences (like "frostless" mechanisms on refrigerators, self-cleaning devices on stoves) use extra power.

Measured according to average rates of use, the least guilty plug-in conveniences are the carving knife, electric mixer, shaver, and toothbrush. They are low wattage, and are not ordinarily used for long periods of time.

The residential consumer, it should be remembered, uses only 31 percent of the power produced in this country. Industry uses 65 percent. The wattage number of an appliance is not the only measure of the electric energy it uses. Some amount of power was used in its manufacture. Excessive luxuries and unnecessary appliances should be avoided, therefore, even if they do not require much electricity for operation.

The table below lists the average wattage of common household appliances as calculated by the Edison Electric Institute for 1969. To figure out how many kilowatt hours each appliance consumes annually, this formula was used:

$$\frac{\text{(Wattage of appliance x number of hours in use daily x 365)}}{1000}$$

Appliance	Average Wattage	Estimated Kilowatt Hours Consumed Annually
Air Conditioner (window)	1,566	1,389
Broiler	1,436	100
Carving Knife	92	8
Clock	2	17
Clothes Dryer	4,856	993
Coffee Maker	894	106
Deep Fat Fryer	1,448	83
Dehumidifier	257	377
Dishwasher	1,201	363
Egg Cooker	516	14
Electric Blanket	177	147
Fan (attic)	370	291
Fan (circulating)	88	43
Fan (furnace)	292	394
Floor Polisher	305	15
Food Blender	386	15
Food Freezer (15 cu ft)	341	1,195

Appliance	Average Wattage	Estimated Kilowatt Hours Consumed Annually
Food Freezer (Frostless 15 cu ft)	440	1,761
Food Mixer	127	13
Food Waste Disposer	445	30
Frying Pan	1,196	186
Hair Dryer	381	14
Heat Lamp (infrared)	250	13
Heat Pump (electric heating system)	11,848	16,003
Heater (radiant)	1,322	176
Heating Pad	65	10
Hot Plate	1,257	90
Humidifier	117	163
Iron	1,088	144
Oil Burner or Stoker	266	410
Radio	71	86
Radio-Phonograph	109	109
Range	12,207	1,175
Refrigerator (12 cu ft)	241	728
Refrigerator (Frostless 12 cu ft)	321	1,217
Refrigerator-Freezer (14 cu ft)	326	1,137
Refrigerator-Freezer (Frostless 14 cu ft)	615	1,829
Roaster	1,333	205
Sewing Machine	75	11
Shaver	14	18
Sun Lamp	279	16
Television (B & W)	237	362
Television (Color)	332	502
Toaster	1,146	39
Tooth Brush	7	5

Appliance	Average Wattage	Estimated Kilowatt Hours Consumed Annually
Vacuum Cleaner	630	46
Waffle Iron	1,116	22
Washing Machine (Automatic)	512	103
Washing Machine (Non-automatic)	286	76
Water Heater (Standard)	2,475	4,219
Water Heater (Quick Recovery)	4,474	4,811
Water Pump	460	231

A 100 watt light bulb, operating 8 hours each day, uses 292 kilowatts annually: $\frac{100 \times 8 \times 365}{1000} = 292$. A two-watt electric clock runs 24 hours each day and uses 18 kilowatts annually.

Those appliances which are electrically expensive are, as a rule, those which either heat up or cool off: coffee makers, dishwashers, frying pans, toasters, irons, clothes dryers, air conditioners. Their cost to the environment, measured in terms of how much electricity they consume, varies with how often they are used. A color television on the average uses, annually, almost twice as much electricity as an iron, although the iron requires three times the wattage. Likewise, the electric clock uses as much electricity over a period of time as the sun lamp, which with average usage has a wattage 140 times greater.

Use the formula to calculate the electricity consumed by appliances in your household. Consider "saving" electricity by bypassing "extra" cycles on some equipment—like soak cycles on washing machines, drying cycles on dishwashers. On a sunny day, when the air is clean, hang the clothes out to dry. Compost garbage rather than grind it up.

Turning off the electric light—or even the microwave oven—will not by itself avert the impending energy shortage, nor will it cleanse the air of sulfur dioxide. Millions of turned off lights could, if the effort were part of a coordinated environmental action program.

mining

• *The Peabody Coal Company, a large Appalachian and mid-western concern, employs a power shovel which stands 20 stories high, scoops up 250 tons of coal at a time, and is operated by one man. The shovel, which single-handedly devastates dozens of acres a day, has been called "the nation's largest mobile tourist attraction."*

• *The Consolidation Coal Company's mine at Farmington, West Virginia, is sprawled under an area larger in size than the island of Manhattan. After a series of massive explosions wrecked the mine in 1968, it took miners and rescuers a year to reach the first of the bodies of the trapped miners. As of November, 1970, only two bodies had been found.*

• *One-half of the town of Laurel Run, a suburb of Wilkes-Barre, Pennsylvania, has been evacuated and razed in an effort to control a mine fire raging beneath the town. Residents of the district had been plagued by perpetually hot water, carbon monoxide leaks in basements, tilting houses and huge cracks in the earth. The fire, which is still out of control, began after a miner accidentally kicked over his lantern in 1915.*

Most Americans are aware of the tragic history of coal mining in the United States. Even schoolchildren know about the terrible past which has tortured the eleven-state Appalachian region and has left much of it, even today, in the clutches of a 19th century-like poverty and despair. The story of mine explosions, lung disease, abominable working conditions, greedy mine operators, widespread unemployment and union struggles is as well-known as the contrasting one of the fantastic profits and high living of the Rockefellers, Mellons, Carnegies, and Morgans.

What most do not realize, however, is that the destruction of Appalachia, far from being over, is accelerating. In fact, it is occurring at a pace hard to imagine even a few years ago. Furthermore, Appalachia is not the only region being affected by the coal miners. The Eastern Interior Field, stretching through western Kentucky and much of Indiana, Ohio and Illinois is being exploited now more effectively than the older regions ever were.

Coal, after a series of setbacks due to union problems, the fragmentation of the industry and the competition from oil and natural gas, is again "King Coal" in the United States. U. S. coal reserves are unbelievably large and Appalachia is ideally located to fuel the East Coast and the Midwest. The demand for electricity is large and growing, and coal is deemed the best fuel, at present, for electric generators. Literally every ton of coal mined can be sold—and at record high prices.

What then, is the correlation between King Coal and the impoverished Appalachian region? To any detached observer, the coal industry—huge, thriving and an important cog in the system—epitomizes capitalism and the American way of life. Just like the automobile in Detroit or chemicals in Delaware, coal should be the backbone of Appalachia. What has gone wrong?

The story of Appalachia's decline is not an easy one to recount. Harry Caudill, a Kentucky lawyer and writer, has traced many of his region's problems all the way back to the sociological attitudes of the earliest settlers. Although this explains a great deal, Appalachia actually suffers—like most exploited areas—from an abundance of natural wealth and a dearth of indigenous industry. Appalachia's wealth was originally in the land—lumber and coal—and the settlers were content to live off that wealth. After over a century of this life and the modest income it brought in, the rich timber stands began to disappear and the backwoods folk, clinging tenaciously to the old ways, became more and more destitute. Towards the end of the 19th century, the real tragedy struck.

Although the importance of coal had long been known, it was only after the railroads were firmly established that efficient use of Appalachia's reserves could be considered. After

1870, outsiders from New York, Chicago, Philadelphia, Boston, and Detroit descended on the region with the notorious "broadform deeds"—deeds which purchased mineral rights, including the use of necessary land for access roads, from the owner, generally for fifty cents an acre. Although most of the landholders who signed these broadform deeds died without seeing the effects of their ignorance, their good fortune is not being shared by their descendants. The legality of the deeds is continually being upheld in the courts, and every year witnesses more and more land falling prey to the deedholders—and to the bulldozer.

Some of the more gruesome aspects of the destruction include pollution of thousands of miles of streams and rivers by acidic run-off and silt from mines and mountainsides; pollution of the air by smoldering coal mines and coal refuse banks; destruction of fertile areas due to loss of topsoil and ground cover; and demoralization of the people. One 80-year-old woman watched as her family's private cemetery was bulldozed by a coal company. "I thought my heart would break," she told the Governor of Kentucky, "when the coffins of my children come out of the ground and went over the hill."

It is important to remember that coal is not the only mineral being unearthed and exploitation is not confined to Appalachia. Coal's value of approximately $5 per ton is dwarfed by that of copper ($950 a ton) and gold (which averages about $38 an ounce). And total coal production of 556 million tons in 1969 was greatly exceeded a year earlier by sand and gravel output (917 million tons). Iron, copper, gravel, clay, stone, gold, phosphate, lignite, manganese and other substances are being removed, and every state in the country has mining operations.

Broadly speaking, there are three types of mining in the United States—underground mining, strip mining, and auger mining. Coal will be used here as an illustration, not because the total value of its production ($2.5 billion) is greater than that of any other mineral, but because its procurement has caused the greatest ecological and human damage. The example, though, holds true for virtually all minerals—including those like bauxite which aren't found in the United States—and future development and technology could conceivably relegate coal to a minor position in the ecological destruction of our planet.

Underground mining, as its name suggests, involves digging a hole in the ground and sending miners in to bring out the coal. Most Americans think of this process when they think of coal extraction, and it is still the principal method of mining in this country.

Strip mining—euphemistically called "surface mining" by industry and government—is a relatively new technique which is growing extremely fast. Its method, simple and devastating, is to scrape off all material covering a coal seam, deposit this to one side, and cart away the coal. In mountainous areas, where coal seams are often high above the valleys, the process is called contour stripping. There, a cut or "bench" is made around the peak of a hill at the level of the seam. The covering material (called the "overburden" and including trees, shrubs, topsoil and often rock) is piled at the edge of the bench or thrown down the hill, and the coal exposed. Stripping continues as far into the center of the hill as is economical, occasionally resulting in removal of the entire top.

Auger mining is actually the second stage of a contour strip mine operation. If it becomes too expensive to remove the overburden above an exposed coal seam, massive drills are inserted into the seam, and the turning motion of the drill pulls out the coal, much as a carpenter's drill bit pulls wood chips out of a two by four.

Since any mining operation involves great tumult to the land, many individuals scoff at the idea of "environmentally sound" mining. "It is," one cynic claims, "like humane methods of killing." Although this sentiment highlights the vast environmental problems associated with mining, it is far from true. Each extraction method has certain advantages and disadvantages, and only by studying these can one begin to tackle the mining problem.

Most ecologists feel that, of the three methods, underground mining poses the fewest dangers to terrain, wildlife and human inhabitants in the area—or at least that it would pose the fewest dangers if it were practiced properly. The underground mine—theoretically—needs only one entrance, has virtually no effect upon vegetation or topsoil, is refilled after the operation with refuse stone and sulphur, and is then sealed.

Theory, however, is hard to convert into practice. Few mine operators are interested in any considerations except money, and most see no reason to "clean up" after they are finished with the profitable part of their work. Since they don't usually plan to restore the area, they see no reason to be concerned about the environment while the work is proceeding.

For these reasons, underground mines usually have several convenient entrances and many other openings for ventilation machinery. They are rarely refilled. Sealing a mine properly is both difficult and expensive, and when done badly it never permanently closes the opening. In current mining methods, supporting columns of coal are often cut out as a last step; the mines collapse causing the surface land above them to subside. (This subsistence, which ranges up to 30 feet in some cases, is difficult to predict or to plan against; in rural areas it can be merely frightening, while elsewhere it has caused millions of dollars of damage to houses, sewers, pipes, cables and streets.) Mines which do not collapse usually fill up with a "witch's brew" of noxious, dangerous chemicals—mostly sulphuric acid—which then seep into the groundtable water. Those mines which remain dry often fall prey to fires which burn slowly and endlessly through a seam, heating the ground, killing plant life and polluting the air.

Nearly all of these problems—fire, harmful chemicals and subsistence—could be avoided with careful practices and forethought; most would be solved merely by refilling the mine with crushed rock or even industrial waste. What is not so easily solved, however, is the inherent danger that underground mining poses to the miner.

The miner is threatened with numerous dangers—cave-ins, explosions, floods, fires and disease—all of which have combined to give the industry the highest injury and mortality rates of any major occupation. For instance, between April 1 and September 24, 1970, 94 miners were killed on the job. In West Virginia, through the first nine months of 1970, 3300 miners were injured, and 20 men died. (It must be remembered that during this period, there were no major disasters such as the one at Farmington which claimed 78 lives in

1968 or one at Monongah, West Virginia, which killed 361 in 1907.)

Physical disasters are not the only perils which threaten miners. A far worse danger is pneumoconiosis, commonly called black lung disease. Brought on by inhalation of microscopic coal particles, the disease causes shortness of breath, coughing, and ultimately asphyxiation. For years it was ignored by industry and government, or considered "asthma." Dr. I. E. Buff, a Charleston, West Virginia, cardiologist, estimates that 80 percent of the nation's 120,000 soft coal miners have black lung to some degree. For years he and others have been waging a campaign to publicize the terrible nature of the disease, but only recently has he had any success at all. In 1969, for the first time, the disease was included in the list of those applicable for disability claims. Even now, in the face of substantial evidence, industry officials maintain that the disease is unavoidable, taking the stand that "the miners are being paid to take risks."

Underground mining, despite its ancient origins, is now a highly technological industry. Compact but powerful machines cut the coal, intricate underground railroad systems transport it and miners, and vast ventilation networks provide fresh air and minimize the possibility of explosions. The industry has shown itself capable of conquering all roadblocks which have traditionally made coal mining a slow and tedious process. In the face of these advances, it is inexcusable that so little has been done for the health and safety of the worker. All informed sources outside of the industry agree that safeguards could be installed and care taken to curb disease, minimize risks and increase worker morale.

A standard quip in Kentucky is, "Let's you and me get a 'dozer and start strippin.'" In many cases, little else is needed. The simplicity of strip mining stands in marked contrast to the complexity of the underground mine. The average strip miner employs less than five men, has no fears of explosions, cave-ins or floods, can claim little technical knowledge, has no overhead expenses like electricity, and stands to make a great deal of money. Stripped coal, being closer to the surface, is generally of inferior quality, but profit margins offset the lower price of the coal. The average underground miner can cut 18 tons of coal a day; a strip miner averages 30 tons a day.

V

At first glance then, strip mining appears to have all the advantages over deep mining—economy, ease and safety. Miners and environmentalists, however, oppose the rapid proliferation of surface mines. The miner is incensed because employment possibilities in an already depressed geographic area are dwindling, and strip mining requires fewer men. Given a choice between a job and a welfare check, it is not hard to predict how an able-bodied Appalachian worker will react.

The environmentalist, on the other hand, is appalled because strip mining is an ecological catastrophe. In virtually every case, the end product of a flat area strip mine looks like a newly-plowed field magnified thousands of times. Mountains of sulphur- and slate-filled dirt stretch for miles, separated only by stagnant valleys of coal residue and acidic water. In the rare instances where the mine operator decided to push the mountains into the valleys, only a barren, filthy desert remains with the original fertile topsoil buried under millions of tons of rock, coal and debris.

In mountainous areas, the scars of the strip mine are even uglier and more sinister. There, the forces of nature and gravity push the waste products of the mine down the hillsides onto the valley roads and into streams, carrying with them vegetation, topsoil and sometimes even houses. Four cases have been reported of huge boulders crashing through school playgrounds on Saturday or Sunday mornings, and observers agree that it is just a matter of time before a mountain school is hit broadside on a weekday morning. Harry Caudill reports that a one-armed miner returned from a job rehabilitation program to find his home buried under tons of rock from the mine above his property.

Thousands of miles of Appalachian streams are polluted by silt from strip mines and by sulphur and sulphuric acid which yellow the creeks and harden the water. In the flat areas of Western Kentucky, a particularly striking example of Nature's ecological interrelationship is coming to light now. Surface mines have so destroyed the natural drainage system that furrows have gradually filled with stagnant water. The area is capable of supporting no life except for a particularly virulent strain of mosquito which is now terrorizing the region and has spread nearly to Louisville, hundreds of miles away. Parents are loath to let their children outside during the hottest part of the summer, and the state has invested in a large-scale insecticide program.

In the face of such immense environmental disturbances, of the type which only 20th century man is capable, strip mining begins to look less beneficial. And auger mining, as an extension and perfection of the strip mining process, appears just as bad, if not worse. The auger holes, which are virtually impossible to seal permanently, merely channel underground water through abandoned mines and into the mines' polluted runoff system.

It is quite revealing to trace the history of government-industry relations in the mining field. The Bureau of Mines was created within the Department of Interior in 1910, after a series of mining disasters brought to public attention the plight of the miner. It was charged with assuring health and safety standards, but, unfortunately for miners, it was given no power. And, unfortunately for future generations, during the Bureau's investigation of mines, it developed unnaturally close ties with industrial heads.

After 31 years of operation, the Bureau was finally granted authority to enter coal mines to inspect them, but it remained in an advisory position. Then, in 1952, under the Federal Coal Mine Safety Act, the Bureau's authority was widened to enforcing certain provisions in certain mines in the case of a "major disaster," one which killed five or more miners.

During the autumn of 1968, the Consolidation Coal Company's mine in Farmington blew up, killing 78 men. In one of the most revealing moments in American mining history, the industry, the government and even the United Mine Workers Union joined together to praise the general level of safety in modern mines. Consolidation then proceeded to inform the miners' widows that it would close and seal the mine without removing the bodies. Under pressure it changed that decision, but turned down the widows' request that the proceeds derived from the sale of the coal mined while searching for bodies be added to the widow pension fund. Informed sources estimate the profits from the search at over $3,000,000. As of November, 1970, only two bodies had been found, and Consolidation revised its "offer" to a payment of $10,000 per widow in return for abandoning the search.

As a result of the explosion, and aided by pressure from

consumer advocate Ralph Nader's organization, the Federal
Coal Mine Health and Safety Act was passed by Congress in
1969. In a spectacular switch from the earlier industry-engi-
neered legislation, the Bureau of Mines suddenly found itself
with a tough law and a lot of new-found power. The law was
so tough, in fact, that coal companies sued in court for injunctive relief, pointing to provisions which called for equipment that had not been developed yet! The Bureau, too, ac-
customed to coddling a diverse, powerful and temperamental
industry, was entrusted with so many new responsibilities
that it had to quadruple the size of its investigative force, a
task which it has not yet accomplished. While maintaining
that the "timetables of the new law are impossible to meet,"
the Bureau is apparently undergoing a change of attitude towards the coal industry and mining problems. One official explained, "We're no longer willing to pay for energy with
human life and human health. If we can put a man on the
moon we should be able to mine coal safely. I think we're
going to get where we're trying to go on this problem."

The new law, while providing much needed relief and aid
to the miner, is of little consolation to the environmentalist.
It provides stringent regulations for health and safety, but
makes no mention of strip mining devastation, zoning
changes or ecological safeguards. It does not even require the
sealing of mines, merely specifying conditions under which
miners must be excluded from a hazardous mine.

If we are to be saved from despoliation by the bulldozer,
an entirely new battle will have to be fought in Washington
and in the state capitals, a battle which will go one step
beyond safety—all the way to the right to enjoy and to protect our natural habitat. This is a battle that extends far
beyond the confines of Appalachia, far beyond the demand
for coal. Already 2,500,000 acres of land have been "disturbed" by surface operations alone. Dozens of coal fires are
now raging out of control. By 1980, an estimated 2,000,000
acres will have subsided.

This next battle will be fought with few allies. Coal miners
want safety, but will they fight against the further mining of
coal? The United Mine Workers Union, described by Thom-
as Bethel of Appalachia Information, as "the most corrupt,
inbred, unresponsive, unenlightened and unrepresentative
union in American labor," will certainly not raise its voice in

behalf of the environment. The industry, panicked by reports of fuel shortages, metallic ore shortages and power blackouts, is opening up new operations every month. The next battle will be fought alone by citizens who are concerned about the environment.

But, with the enormously destructive implications of any form of mining, where does the answer lie? Are ecology activists pressing for such innovations as electrically-run mass transit systems only to find that they are merely shifting the problem from the city to the mountains and coal fields?

As usual, the answer is immensely complicated and there are few do's and don't's. One approach is to cut down on unnecessary uses of electricity such as electric can openers and electric toothbrushes (despite the active consumer campaigns of the utility companies), thus relieving the pressure of "coal at any price." Another solution is to inform electric companies that consumers are willing to pay more for electricity in return for saner coal mining practices. (Along with steel corporations, private utilities own many of the biggest mining companies, the so-called "captive mines".)

Ultimately, however, public pressure and governmental power will have to be exerted at the root of the problem—the coal fields. Underground mines will have to significantly strengthen their safety precautions and their worker safeguards. They will have to refill and reseal mines, leaving them as they were, once the coal is extracted. They will have to survey the terrain more accurately to preclude surprise flooding and install more sophisticated equipment to detect and disperse the highly explosive methane gas present in many mines.

Surface mine operators, even more than their underground competitors, will have to consider their actions every step of the way. Miners in England and Czechoslovakia have shown that strip mining in flat areas can be conducted without leaving scars on the land. They have proven that the topsoil can be carefully scraped off and stored separately before the actual mining begins. Then, after the coal is extracted and the intermediate layers refilled, topsoil can be respread and vegetation replanted, leaving little trace of any earlier activity. This type of environmentally-aware approach must be demanded in the United States.

Finally—and this is a harsh realization—contour strip

mining and auger mining in mountainous areas must be banned by federal and state regulations. Modern technology has not, unfortunately, kept up with man's exploitative inclinations. It is, for instance, impossible to push boulders and millions of tons of dispersed topsoil up the edge of a steep mountainside. It is also virtually impossible to keep large piles of unusable coal from spontaneously igniting and burning. Nor has science devised foolproof methods of sealing auger holes to prevent acidic drainage down mountainsides.

In many instances, the regenerative powers of the fertile, stable flatlands are great enough to absorb man's destruction. This is not true where the terrain is steep, topsoil thin and weather unpredictable. The realization must come that man's technological sophistication has not reached the point where he can safely tamper with the fragile ecology of mountains. It is urgently necessary for government to intervene.

It is important to remember that Appalachia is not unique. There are vast untapped coal deposits in North Dakota, Montana, Wyoming, Utah, Colorado, New Mexico, Kansas, Missouri, Iowa, Texas, Oklahoma, Michigan and South Dakota. The Rocky Mountains could very well become the Appalachia of tomorow. Illinois, already the leader in acreage "disturbed" by strip mining, could virtually be turned into one immense strip mine south of Chicago.

The time to act is now. Congressmen should be urged to formulate sweeping new laws governing mining damage, with strict enforcement and severe penalties. The argument that mining jurisdiction lies properly with the states no longer holds true in the days of regional power grids and interstate mining companies.

State legislatures must be made aware of the consequences of succoring a fledgling mining industry. It must be pointed out that tourism cannot survive alongside contour strip mining, that agriculture cannot compete with bulldozers and derricks, that cities cannot stand on top of empty coal mines, that people cannot live without decent, unscathed recreation areas, and that legislators cannot continue to bow and scrape before monolithic steel, power, copper, gravel and sand, and phosphate corporations.

Local authorities, especially zoning boards, have to be watched scrupulously. Sand and gravel operations, in particular, are usually located near cities and towns. Make it clear that neither the gravel mines nor the highways they require are welcome in the locality. If they are necessary, compel the zoning board to demand a master plan for the mine, including blueprints for its use when the operation is completed. Also demand that the mine operator deposit a substantial bond to insure that he carries out the "unprofitable" final part of his master plan.

Above all, vigilance is necessary. If Appalachians had been more wary and less greedy, they might have saved one of America's most beautiful regions.

oil pollution

• *A study by the state of California in 1970 reveals that the annual discharge of oil into San Francisco Bay from industrial and government facilities exceeds spillage from the Santa Barbara blowout.*

• *Continued oil pollution has been instrumental in reducing the number of puffins on an island between England and France. In 1907 when the first large spill near the island occurred there were an estimated 100,000; today there are about 100.*

• *The President's Panel on Oil Spills stated in its 1969 report that if the present rate of drilling continues, by 1980, "we can expect to have a major pollution incident somewhere every year."*

The miles of polluted beaches resulting from an offshore oil spill leave an indelible impression of ugliness in the mind of anyone who sees it. In addition to stained beaches, the number of bird deaths resulting from spills is equally staggering; therefore, the public reacts with shock to a major accident. But the concern resulting from it is not enough to temper America's voracious petroleum appetite.

Yet, as the number of bird deaths resulting from spills reveals, the ecological price for the oil is tremendous. Estimates of the total number of deaths are hard to obtain since oil companies and the Interior Department appear to assume that casualties are limited to those birds treated by care centers established after major spills. The survival rates of contaminated birds treated runs between one and six percent. One estimate by the Nature Conservancy and the Royal Society for the Protection of Birds places bird deaths resulting

from the Torrey Canyon spill at more than 25,000. Not all
were killed by oil; chemicals used to treat the spill also
claimed them.

Birds are not the only ecological victims of an oil slick. Dr.
Dale Straughan of the University of Southern California, in a
study financed by the Western Oil and Gas Association,
found that marine life in the upper tidal zones hit by the
Santa Barbara oil spill was "virtually eliminated." She also
discovered recolonization was prevented by layers of oil on
the rocks. The conclusions of this investigation were supported by a study undertaken by two University of California
at Santa Barbara scientists. They found heavy biological damage to barnacles, intertidal surfgrass, and other organisms. It
is likely that when there have been extensive losses in the fish
population the primary agents responsible have been chemicals used to treat and disperse the oil. The effects of spills on
mammals have been found to be slight, though the death of
sea lion pups reported by *Life* magazine on San Miguel Island
after the Santa Barbara spill remains a matter of controversy.

With the exception of instances of chronic pollution, the
well publicized effects of oil spills such as bird deaths and
ugly beaches are short term phenomena. While they are unpleasant and costly to fishermen and the tourist industry, the
oil companies may be correct in their assumption that the
value of the oil gained is worth these occasional costs. But
this is not the total picture. Long term damage to the environment from spills is relatively unknown, but indications are
that it is subtle and potentially very serious. There have been
repeated calls for detailed and extensive studies of the long
range effects of oil pollution, but oil companies are under-
standably reluctant to finance them. Furthermore, environmentally concerned scientists are sometimes hesitant about
accepting oil grants because the companies invariably insist
on publication rights.

Most of our present knowledge of the long term effects of
oil pollution comes from the work of Dr. Max Blumer and
his associates of Woods Hole Oceanographic Institute in
Massachusetts. Their research has centered on hydrocarbons
in the marine food chain and their effect on marine organisms and man. In their opinion the impact of oil on marine
life has been seriously underestimated. Petroleum and its
products are poisons for all marine organisms and man.

Among the toxic chemicals it contains are substances known to cause cancer. The discoveries of Dr. Blumer and his associates are particularly frightening because they show that the biodegradation of oil once it enters into the marine environment is very slow, and thus it spreads well beyond the area originally contaminated.

Organisms, particularly shellfish, were found by the Institute to be unable to decontaminate themselves once infected with sublethal doses of oil. Hydrocarbons were discovered to be stable once incorporated into the marine food chain and able to pass through many stages without alteration. In fact they are not only retained by subsequent predators but actually concentrated. In addition to spills, hydrocarbons enter the food chain in other ways. Surface feeding fishes significant in the marine food chains have been found to feed off the widely spread lumps of crude oil residue which have been increasingly observed along tanker routes since 1954. Considering the extent of known oil pollution and the increasing reliance of men on the sea for protein, the threat this poses is apparent. Dr. Blumer has further suggested that hydrocarbons may lead to the failure of some species to reproduce, thus disrupting other species higher in the food chain which depend upon them for food. For these reasons he has repeatedly warned against using chemical dispersants on spills because they create oil droplets of a size more easily ingested by marine life.

Other indications of the long term effects of a spill are provided by a study done by three California scientists who observed the ecological effects of a single heavy spill. The area studied, a small estuary cove on the coast of Mexico, was visited in 1957 shortly after the incident. Only two species were observed to have survived. It was revisited each year thereafter for seven years. By the end of the study the impact on the ecology was still evident. Some species were far more plentiful than before the spill while others which had been abundant were represented by only a few individuals. Some species had completely failed to re-establish themselves.

Despite a descriptive account by explorer Thor Heyerdahl who, after crossing the Atlantic on a reed raft, reported a "continuous stretch of at least 1400 miles of the open Atlantic polluted by floating lumps of solidified, asphalt-like oil," the total extent of oil pollution has never been reliably calculated. One Woods Hole scientist estimates that at least 5 to 10 million tons of oil are spilled annually, and feels strongly it is much higher. The large spills have, of course, been totaled and the Dillingham report, contracted by the American Petroleum Institute, listed 38 major spills between 1957 and 1969. However, only spills of over 5,000 barrels were counted, so the number does not accurately reflect the true extent of pollution. The Interior Department estimates that there are 7,500 oil spills annually in U. S. waters alone. The contribution of the large spills to the annual pollution is impressive, however. Using the Dillingham list of spills, the average yearly pollution from major incidents has been nearly 700,000 barrels.

In spite of the publicity given the oil drilling accidents in Santa Barbara and the Gulf of Mexico, 75 percent of large oil spills involve vessels. Not only are they the chief source of major catastrophes, they are also the largest single source of chronic marine pollution. In terms of volume most marine oil pollution does not originate from the highly visible disasters that are the result of risks the oil industry has chosen to accept in pursuing offshore drilling. It is instead the entirely foreseeable result of tanker practices and the industry's procedures and planning.

There are a number of ways in which tankers pollute. The major source results from flushing the holds of crude oil tankers with sea water. This accounted for 15 million barrels of oil a year according to industry figures until an international convention in 1962 prohibited the discharge of oily wastes in solutions larger than 100 parts per million within 50 miles of the coasts of the signatory nations, or 10 miles of certain ports. The logic of the convention was commented on by Rear Admiral Roderick Edwards during a House hearing in 1969. "If you carry it to its ultimate ridiculous conclusion, the secret of correcting pollution is by dilution. In other words, you could anchor a tanker within our territorial limits right now and sit there, and as long as you diluted whatever your effluent was to the point where it is less than 100 parts per million, you will not violate the convention."

The same year the convention was signed, Shell Oil introduced a new method of controlling this source of pollution. Known as "Load on Top," it places the tanker's oil and water slops in one hold, allows them to separate by gravity and then discharges water from the bottom. Oil discharge using this method seldom exceeds the limits set by the convention, though, for the cleaning of a single tanker, it may amount to over one ton. However, since the oil residue has a high salt content after having been mixed with sea water it requires specially equipped refineries to process it. Furthermore, the 25 percent of the vessels which are unable to use this method contribute seriously to the pollution of the ocean by discharging approximately .5 percent of their cargoes, or an estimated 6.3 million barrels of oil annually.

Further, vessel pollution comes from that half of the world's shipping which carries oil only as fuel. When their fuel tanks are empty it is a common practice to fill them with sea water as needed for ballast. One 1964 estimate placed the potential annual pollution from this source in excess of 700,000 barrels for U. S. waters. If one were to estimate the discharge that may occur in the rest of the world, and revise both figures upward to account for the increase in world shipping since that year, the total would drastically exceed the 1964 estimate.

The underwater storage and pipeline systems used to gather and transfer crude oil from offshore wells to onshore facilities constitute another serious source of pollution. During 1968 there was a total of 10 different reported pipeline leaks in the Gulf of Mexico. One pipeline was ruptured by a propeller and two more by dragging anchors. No chart of the network of the thousands of miles of pipeline which presently cover the seabed of the Gulf is yet available to mariners. The sensitivity of the safety shutoff devices monitoring the pipelines was unable to detect several of these leaks. Another threat arises from the fact that there have not been any studies of the incidence of turbidity currents in the Gulf which could rip the network of pipes on a massive scale.

The "wanton" disposal of motor oil and similar products also pollutes waters. Until recently it was profitable for service stations to store and sell used motor oil. Now most station operators must pay for its removal and a great deal of it is dumped. Few, if any, sewage treatment plants are capable of handling this oil. A recent estimate of the nationwide volume of oil which is not reprocessed placed the amount at 14 million barrels a year. Undoubtedly a substantial percentage of that figure finds its way into the nation's waters. Perhaps a part of the failure of the petroleum industry to study the matter is due to the cut in their market which would occur if large amounts of this oil were recycled.

There are a number of other sources of pollution. The total volume of oil discharged from each of them is relatively small and the extent of the damage they do is primarily local. This is not to say, however, that the aggregate of pollution resulting from them is not just as serious as any of the previously mentioned sources. Among them are inland transportation of oil over water on barges, oil mixed with discharged industrial wastes, sludge, pollution from refineries (a great deal of which occurs at night in the hope it will go unnoticed) and the dumping of oil mixed with other toxic wastes such as drilling mud from offshore platforms.

America's consumption of petroleum, already high compared to other countries, will continue to increase. By 1980 we will consume about 19 million barrels a day, up over 30 percent a day from the present consumption of about 14 million barrels per day. There are many sources for this oil (foreign, offshore, Alaska, shale, coal, etc.) and, industry protestations to the contrary, the distribution of production among them is essentially a political question. In the late 1950's the oil industry persuaded Congress and the Eisenhower administration to limit the imports of foreign oil, resulting in a domestic price for crude oil which is nearly double the world market price. It is this artificially high price together with another government subsidy, the depletion allowance, which creates an incentive for offshore drilling, which might otherwise be prohibitively expensive. To quote Senator Philip Hart before a recent hearing of the Senate subcommittee on anti-trust and monopoly. "It may be that these carefully built incentives have created the economic incentive to wreck our environment beyond repair." While there would undoubtedly be some offshore drilling in particularly productive areas with them, these government subsidies have led to a frantic search for more oil off the coast of California, the Atlantic seaboard, offshore Alaska, and the already dying Lake Erie. Presently offshore oil production provides 16 percent of the world's petroleum. By 1980 this share is expected to increase to 33 percent.

The greatest environmental hazard resulting from these subsidies is that they will lead oil companies into drilling and production from deep offshore wells. Drilling, other than exploratory, in depths of 600 to 1400 feet has never been attempted and will require new technological developments. Despite the risks associated with this (how does one cap a blowout in 1400 feet of water?), the industry is making plans to push ahead. Humble claims to have the technological problems solved and is planning to build a platform off Santa Barbara in 1200 feet of water. A major danger of this type of drilling is the vastly increased effect of oil pollution below the thermocline (600 feet). The rate of biodegradation of oil below this temperature gradient is so slow as to be almost undetectable. Because the pollution persists for greatly increased lengths of time, the number of organisms contaminated also increases. Furthermore, the marine organisms below the thermocline are more specialized. They live in a more precarious balance with their environment, and thus the effects of its disruption are far more serious.

Even with the Alaskan discoveries and the new push for offshore supplies, the demand for oil is growing much faster than the domestic supply. Therefore, the United States will continue to import an increasing percentage of its petroleum. The resulting increase in tanker traffic over the next decade will undoubtedly lead to both an increase in chronic oil waste discharge and a number of large disasters unless rapid steps are taken to incorporate advanced safety features and tank cleaning facilities in tankers now under construction. Furthermore, there must be new ports established and old ones expanded to meet the increase in imports. This means that new areas of the country, such as Machiasport, Maine, will be exposed to the threat of oil pollution. Many old and new harbors will require dredging, a source of pollution in itself, to accommodate the recent trend toward large super tankers. They are reaching tonnages of 300,000 to 500,000, and recently Japan claimed to have achieved new shipbuilding technology capable of producing a tanker of one million tons.

A rather different and novel threat is posed by another industry trend. The present "shortage" of natural gas is promoting its importation from abroad. It is shipped from the Middle East and Venezuela in a liquefied state. Though there is little detailed information about gas spills, one of the few things that are known is that it explodes in contact with water. It is an understatement to say that the threat this growing fleet of gas tankers will create, not only to human life, but also to other tankers in congested harbors, requires careful attention.

Alaska is another area suffering from the environmental impact of our nation's insatiable thirst for oil. The reserves discovered there are potentially the second largest in the world, 40 billion barrels or more. The influx of drilling crews and their support lines, plus the explorations of petroleum geologists, have scarred thousands of miles of fragile tundra with bulldozed roads and seismic tracks. The most well known threat, however, comes from plans to transport huge quantities of oil to markets in Japan and the United States. Humble's controversial project to ship oil in icebreaking tankers, which would at long last create the fabled northwest passage, has recently been abandoned. Though the environmental risks of such a project would have been immense, the principal consideration in their change of plans was the political infeasibility of circumventing the Jones Act which requires that high cost U. S. tankers be used to ship crude oil between U. S. ports. Thus the alternative proposal, an 800 mile pipeline from the North slope to the port of Valdez, is cheaper. The original industry plans for building this pipeline were so poor that they were almost immediately rejected by the U. S. Geological Survey. Studies showed that it was likely that the oil, running through the pipes at temperatures of 180 degrees and above, would heat not only the insulating gravel, but also melt the surrounding permafrost. This could cause the pipe to shift and break. To lessen the breakage danger, recent proposals call for an undetermined length of pipe to be run several feet above ground. It is likely that pressures on the Nixon Administration will succeed in securing a construction permit and construction will have begun by the time this book appears in print.

The laws governing oil pollution are uniform in only one regard—their inadequacy to handle the problem. While the Water Quality Act of 1970 updated many of the former statutes, there are still no uniform standards on spills or liability. One reason for the inconsistency is that it falls within the jurisdiction of many different bodies—Congress, the Interior Department, and international organizations.

Regulations on offshore drilling in federal lands are in one sense the strictest. They impose absolute liability on the oil lease operators for the oil cleanup and removal costs. This provision was a reaction to the Santa Barbara spill. However, the new policy does not provide liability for damage to other parties, boats, etc. For these cases, negligence must be proven, a difficult feat when a blowout occurs while the company involved is following federal drilling regulations. As a result of the increased liability, several small independent companies, who cannot afford the risks involved, are suing the federal government for release from their lease contracts and a return of their rent bonuses. While this may aggravate the dominance of the major companies in offshore drilling, it may also prevent the oil industry from developing marginal leases where the risks are larger than the small profits to be gained. Theoretically the increased liability should also induce oil companies to take every precaution to avoid spills by installing all feasible safety and pollution control equipment. Unfortunately, this hasn't yet occurred, as evidenced by a recent Interior Department report. In 1969 a total of 294 deficiencies were discovered on offshore platforms and wells. This increased to 341 deficiencies for the first six months of 1970, well over a 100 percent increase. To meet this threat, the Interior Department should not only continue to inspect and close down the platforms and wells where deficiencies are discovered, but absolute liability should be extended to cover damages caused by spills.

Other domestic pollution is governed by the Water Quality Improvement Act of 1970. It replaced the Oil Pollution Act of 1924 which had been gutted by an amendment in 1966 requiring that the discharge be proved grossly negligent or willful in order to be unlawful. The new act provides a criminal penalty of $10,000 for knowingly discharging oil in violation of the act. Unfortunately, it provides several limitations on liability. Limits for cleanup costs are $100 a ton up to $14 million for vessels and up to $8 million for other company facilities. Furthermore, the company is not liable if the discharge results from an act of war or God, negligence on the part of the U. S. government, or an act of omission of a third party. In fact, the company can actually recover the cost of cleanup in these cases from the U. S. government.

Spills or discharges from foreign vessels represent a threat which is not easily controlled. The Convention of the Territorial Sea and the Contiguous Zone permits the U. S. to

apply the provisions of the 1970 Act beyond the 3 mile limit
up to 12 miles. Beyond the 12 mile limit the only laws governing oil pollution are the standards set by the 1954 International Convention for the Prevention of Pollution of the
Seas by oil, plus its 1962 amendments. These standards are
commented on elsewhere. Poor as they are, they are enforceable only for domestic shipping. When foreign vessels are
discovered discharging oil, a note is sent to their home countries via the State Department informing it that the vessel is
in violation of the treaty. The vast majority of tankers shipping imported oil fly flags from small countries like Liberia
and Panama. They have been very reluctant to make a
serious effort to curtail pollution resulting from the vast fleets
registered with them.

While many citizens consider oil pollution a problem for
the government to solve, there are certain tactics and campaigns available for use in combating oil pollution. The one
that will permit the broadest participation, primarily for geographic reasons, is a campaign against the dumping of motor
oil. Some communities already have restrictions prohibiting
the dumping of refuse oil. In those which do not, activists
should work for strong local regulations governing its disposal and stringent fines against dumping. Since enforcement of
any regulations will be difficult, steps should be taken to increase the value of the used oil, thus making the economic
reward for recycling more attractive. The several suggestions
which have been coming from industry are unlikely to be implemented since the incentive provided by the low rates of return they offer is practically nil. Since oil never loses its lubri-
cating properties it would be much better to place a tax on
new motor oil and similar products that would be high
enough to make the used oil competitive after cleaning costs.

There are a number of steps citizens who are faced with
the prospect of drilling off their shore can take. Drilling within the three mile limit is in state waters and the regulations
on leasing vary from state to state. All leases outside the limit
are granted by the Interior Department. First a permit is issued for geophysical work and exploratory core drilling.
Then, after companies have completed extensive investigations to evaluate the prospects for oil the department holds
an auction in which the leases are awarded to the companies
which offer the highest bonuses in addition to a set royalty on

production. Neither the procedure for the issuance of the exploratory permit nor the sale of the leases involves public hearings. However, a recent land law review commission, after five years of studying the public land laws, has recommended that public hearings be an integral part of the leasing process. During both steps, the permit and the lease auction, citizens should dramatize their lack of participation and control over land use in their community. When the companies which have acquired leases are ready to erect the platforms from which permanent wells will be drilled, the Army Corps of Engineers may hold public hearings before granting them a permit to install it. Despite the President's National Environmental Policy Act which requires all federal agencies to consider the environmental impact of programs they control or regulate, the Army Corps of Engineers refuses to accept responsibility for drilling. It claims that it need only consider the navigational and national security hazards of the platforms. A suit has been filed by a group of Santa Barbara citizens to force them to conform with the Environmental Policy Act. Regardless of its success the public hearing should be used as an opportunity to further demonstrate the lack of true ecological concern and commitment on the part of the government.

Court injunctions, if skillful lawyers are available, can be good delaying tactics. Fish-ins and continuous maintenance of boats over the platform site may slow installation but are ineffective at stopping their location by the oil companies. They can provide wonderful publicity.

If platforms are already present there are still steps which can be taken. Because they are offshore, they must regularly be supplied with men and materials. The loading point for supplies could be a good spot on which to focus demonstrations. Municipal piers could be restricted from industrial use and oil companies would be forced to go elsewhere. In Santa Barbara, the city wharf, leased for a nominal sum, was used for loading equipment to transport to rigs. Citizens picketed it and obstructed the loading operations with a sit-in.

A visit to the platforms at night can reveal what they dump under the cover of darkness. Drilling mud and other oily wastes are illegal to dump and are very toxic. If night dumping is occurring, inform the Coast Guard and ask them how often they inspect the sea around the platforms. It is also important to tip off a reporter about it so that he can publicize the story. A good source of information about a platform, such as dumping times, is the worker on it. His job is hazardous and he may cooperate with an environmental group to help dramatize working conditions.

When a spill occurs, publicity about the dangers of oil drilling will continue for several months. Because of public concern created by the black tide, this is a key time to organize. Speakers and rallies will be popular.

The Coast Guard will be in charge of cleaning up the spill. This authority is given to it by a national contingency plan to counter spills of oil and other hazardous materials. The oil companies will be very eager to clean it up, and because of the increase in slicks, they now possess expertise. About the only physically helpful thing that citizens can do at the time of a spill is to organize bird rescue squads. Check with the Federal Water Quality Control Administration, however, to find out what chemicals, if any, are used on the spill. Also remember Dr. Blumer's warning about dispersants, but let them dump anything they want to into the harbor. If it is heavily polluted the fire danger will be extreme.

Pollution occurring as a result of marine transportation is far less amenable than drilling spills to solutions through citizen action. But this does not mean, however, that its increase cannot be stopped, or, with more luck and effort, even diminished. Each cargo of oil has its own chemical identity and it is possible for the Coast Guard to analyze a spill and identify its source by comparing the oil to that of vessels which have been in the area. Photographic evidence is also permissible in court and the Coast Guard is currently developing an infrared camera which will be able to spot and identify ships leaking oil even under cloud cover or at night. Even with new equipment and the additional financing that will be required from Congress to adequately patrol the sea lanes, the Coast Guard will still be hampered by their lack of enforcement jurisdiction. The inadequacy of the 100 parts per million limitation of the 1954 Convention, plus the lack of enforcement of even its provisions for foreign vessels means that there is no effective pollution control for vast areas of the ocean. An international system of surveillance and enforcement with stiff fines for polluters must be developed. Other than write his congressman, there is not much more a citizen can do to further these goals. This may not be quite as ineffective as it sounds, because if the people in Pennsylvania, Iowa, Alabama and other states show that they are aware of the particularly important, yet unpublicized, area of tanker discharge, it may have a strong effect on the actions of men who had not previously considered their decisions on the questions a matter of public interest.

However, there are certain steps that people living near ports should take. Refineries which receive oil transported by water should be contacted. Not all tankers carry imported oil; there is a great deal of shipping among the states: from the Gulf of Mexico to New England, from Alaska to California, from California to Hawaii. They should be questioned to see if they are equipped to receive the residue from "Load on Top" slops and if they keep a record of the tankers which should be storing such a residue actually are. Depending on their replies, either thank them politely, or publicize your findings. Letters should be sent to the Coast Guard informing them of your concern. Suggest that they undertake a broad survey of nationwide refinery capabilities and industry practices on this matter. Boating associations should pressure the Coast Guard to compile and issue a map of underwater storage and pipeline facilities in order to minimize accidents resulting from lack of public information.

Groups which are determined to stop oil pollution should recognize several things. The first of these is that short of a massive reduction in the nation's petroleum use, imports and tanker traffic will continue to grow. Therefore, such groups

---

WARNING

After the oil platform is in place, no attempt should be made to destroy it with explosives or sabotage. Not only is there considerable risk to human life, but if drilling operations have begun the act could bring about an oil spill disaster.

should be strongly oriented toward lobbying for increased tanker safety devices, navigational aids, etc., which would work to minimize the chances of accidents. They should also demonstrate strong support for the proposal of Transportation Secretary John Volpe which was introduced in November, 1970, to a NATO conference on oil spills. He called for a complete halt by 1975 to all intentional discharge of oil and oily wastes by tankers and other vessels. Were all the NATO countries to support such a plan, it would be a major step toward eliminating ocean pollution.

It is politically unlikely that offshore drilling and production will ever be banned. Therefore a strategy to stop or prevent offshore drilling should be oriented toward making it as expensive as possible, by the use of delaying tactics and by lobbying for increased liability. To be fully effective such a strategy should be complemented by a drive to lower the artificially high price of oil. The effects of such a strategy, if successful, would be twofold. First, as already mentioned, the increased liability will provide the greatest possible incentive for the companies to adopt every feasible safety precaution. Secondly, as the costs of insurance and drilling significantly increase, the oil companies will subtract the additional costs from the bonuses they are willing to pay the government for the leases. It will not affect their profits but it may affect the incentive of the Interior Department to grant leases. Stewart Udall has often said that the strongest pressure on him to grant the Santa Barbara Leases, which he did in 1967 as Secretary of the Interior, came from the Bureau of the Budget, which was experiencing difficulties in financing President Johnson's "guns and butter" program.

Lowering the price of oil will also reduce the rate of return on offshore drilling and production. Because of the oil industry's close relations with government, it will be a politically difficult accomplishment. If it were not for this, the price change could be simple. By executive order the oil import quota could be removed, thus increasing the importation of cheaper foreign petroleum. New competition from international sources would drop gasoline prices about six cents per gallon. In addition to consumer benefits, the rate of return from offshore drilling would be reduced, and the less profitable drilling operations would not continue. More oil importing does not necessarily mean that the burden of pollution will be shifted to foreign countries. Their reserves of oil are extensive and are easier to tap in an ecologically sound manner. Dropping the United States oil import quota would also substantially increase the market for oil from foreign countries, thus yielding higher revenues to them.

At some point the United States must closely examine its increasing energy needs. Even with an increase in imports, drilling for oil will continue in Alaska, the Gulf of Mexico, Santa Barbara, and other areas. Increased energy consumption also enlarges the demand for other fuels such as coal and uranium. Ways must be found to curb fuel requirements. It will not only involve development of more efficient ways to use fuel, but a change to less exploitative life styles.

noise

• *In June, 1968, two persons were struck and killed by the funeral train of Senator Robert Kennedy as it passed through Elizabeth, New Jersey. The tragedy is attributed to the fact that the whistle of the slow-moving engine was covered by the noise of low-flying Secret Service and news media helicopters which preceded the train.*

• *The sonic boom of a Canadian F-104 jet fighter flying at an altitude of 500 feet was responsible for $300,000 worth of damages to the terminal of Ottawa's new airport. The boom ripped open the roof, distorted a curtain wall, tossed aluminum flashing strips across a road, smashed windows and fluorescent lights, and broke off exterior stucco from the building.*

• *Helmut Winter, a resident of a Munich, Germany, suburb, became so enraged at the American and German Air Force jets which flew low over his home that he built a catapult and fired potato dumplings at them. The harmless thud of the dumplings frightened the pilots so much that the flight path was changed.*

Noise pollution has been with man for centuries. Some 2500 years ago the Greek city of Sybarus outlawed its most noisy industries—cabinet making and blacksmithing—from residential areas. In ancient Rome, Julius Caesar attempted (unsuccessfully) to have chariot racing prohibited during certain hours because of the racket it made on the cobblestones. Noise has plagued mankind for a much longer time than has bad air or water, and it is certain to continue doing so even if some of our more publicized environmental crises are solved.

Surprisingly, although noise is a perpetual problem in our large cities and a growing nuisance in rural areas, few laws exist which are able to adequately deal with it. Far more shocking to the environmentalist is the apathy with which the subject is greeted by the general public. Nearly everyone is bothered by one or another aspect of our increasingly noisy existence, but concerted actions to stem the tide are few and far between. Even the characterization of noise as a type of pollution is greeted with ridicule by many persons.

The sorry fact of the matter is that noise easily qualifies as a pollutant, not only by being a major nuisance to everyday living, but by causing sleeplessness, reducing working capabilities, frightening humans and animals, and disrupting communications. Far worse, it has been shown to induce hearing loss and deafness, and is strongly implicated in a wide variety of other human diseases, ailments and accidents. Residents of New York, London, Tokyo and other of the world's largest cities have begun to rally behind the cry of "Quiet!" but signs on the horizon do not give cause for great optimism.

Although noise is not one of society's new problems, it can be graphed (like nearly everything else!) as an exponential curve, skyrocketing ever upward. The main source of our most troublesome noises is the machine, and the beginning of aural bedlam coincided with the beginnings of the Industrial Revolution in the 1830's. Since then, advances in technology have multiplied volume along with productivity. And although the science of creating noise-free environments has also advanced considerably, few attempts have been made to use this knowledge to save humanity's ears and nerves.

What are the major noise pollutants that harass modern man? They cover a large range, but primarily include industrial machinery, automobiles, trucks, buses, airplanes, construction and demolition companies, automobile horns, ship whistles, tractors, kitchen appliances, subways and trains, televisions and radios, refuse collection, sirens and sound-trucks. These are mostly city-related noises, but suburban and rural regions are being treated to a fair share of them, notably via trucks, tractors, power mowers, airplanes and a variety of kitchen gadgets.

As if our present life were not disruptive and loud enough, a new technological threat is now looming overhead; the supersonic transport plane, or SST. This plane, which is on the drawing boards in the United States and in existence in France and Britain, is designed to fly at speeds of 1800 miles per hour and relegate conventional jets to the junkyard. If the plane is put into production and permitted to fly, the citizens of tomorrow will look back on the 1960's as days of tranquillity.

From the moment an object exceeds the speed of sound until it slows down again, it creates a "sonic boom," a thunderclap-like noise which travels with the object and extends 10 to 30 miles on either side of it. The boom is enough to startle the hardiest of souls and can also break glass, rattle china, and weaken foundations. In France a supersonic jet has already claimed three lives when its boom sent the supporting beams of the roof of an old farmhouse crashing down on the occupants.

A high-level committee which studied the problem of the SST for the U. S. Department of the Interior noted that noise levels in this country would be generally raised once the plane was put into use, and added this analysis:

The number of SSTs expected sometime after 1975 would subject between 20 million and 40 million Americans under a path 12½ miles on either side of the flight tracks to 5 to 50 sonic booms per day. Each boom would be perceived by its hearers as equivalent in annoyance to the noise from a large truck traveling at 60 miles per hour at a distance of about 30 feet . . . An additional 35 to 65 million people within 12½ to 25 miles of the flight path would be subjected to one to 50 booms per day of somewhat lower intensity, and 13 to 25 million more would experience 1 to 4 high intensity booms. The response of the people in the 25-mile-wide swaths swept by frequent and intense booms can be expected to be similar to that of residents of neighborhoods adjacent to busy metropolitan airports under the flight paths of planes taking off.

As indicated in this book's section on airports, the reactions of those persons forced to live near them range from continual protest to more militant actions. The business world which is making the jet, pressuring the government to fund it and creating the demand for supersonic flight may conceivably be on the verge of alienating 100 million Americans at one sonic swoop.

Although new technology may currently present a big threat to the quiet-hungry citizen, there are plenty of more mundane provocations right here on the ground. In the main, these problems reside in the city.

Some aspects of the city noise problem verge on the absurd. What rural homeowner, for instance, could imagine that the whistles used by doormen to call taxis for large apartment buildings would disturb anyone? Yet this very noise rated tenth in a 1956 New York City poll taken on annoying sounds! For many apartment dwellers, the barking of a neighbor's dog has been disturbing and persistent enough to cause them to file suit—or move.

Noise, especially in cities, is a widespread phenomenon, but unlike air pollution, it is a localized problem. Newspapers have not complemented their daily air indexes with noise indexes because noise is transitory and of short duration. The man who is kept awake at night by traffic sounds may find little sympathy from his neighbor whose apartment looks out onto a back alley. On the other hand, the back apartment may face the building's central air conditioning unit which roars all summer. Chances are that they both will be disturbed by a late-night amateur drummer upstairs and that he, in turn, will be awakened thrice-weekly by early morning garbage collection.

The average city provides enough noises to disturb nearly everyone. When, then, *is* noise, what causes it, and what does one do about it?

"Noise" is in reality a subjective concept, and is usually defined as "unwanted sounds." The drummer may consider himself an artist while his disgruntled neighbor curses him as a noise polluter. Presumably some sounds, such as rustling trees and chirping birds, are enjoyed by everyone. Others, like a television or an unmuffled motorcycle, please their owners and antagonize those around them. Most mechanical sounds, however, can be rated as true noise pollution, for they disturb all who hear them. Truck drivers, for instance, have complained more vociferously about noisy vehicles than have those living near highways.

Noise levels are measured in decibels (dB), an arbitrary scale without dimension which ranges from zero to a theoretical limit of 194. The scale is not easy to grasp intuitively since it is logarithmic rather than arithmetic, but every six decibel increase roughly denotes a doubling of volume. Therefore the superficially small decrease from 100 dB to 94 dB means a reduction in noise of 50 percent. Theoretically, dB denotes the lowest audible sound a healthy youngster can hear and 140 dB represents the threshold of pain.

The ear is an amazingly accurate organ which has been likened to a ruler which can measure, with equal precision, yards and thousandths of an inch. It is capable of assimilating the sound of a falling leaf (about 10 dB) and the roar of a rocket engine (above 140 dB), as well as being able to detect minute differences in pitch (frequency). Human conversation at a distance of three feet has a value of about 62 dB; a subway train (at 20 feet) and a power mower, rate about 95 dB; and a four-engine jet (at 500 feet) hits 120 dB, as does an amplified rock music band. The jet's noise is about a trillion times as great as a quiet whisper.

Americans, on the whole, do not hear very well, and recent studies have shown what has been suspected for years—that noise causes hearing loss. When compared with primitive tribes which live in relatively noise-free circumstances (notably the Mabaans in the African Sudan), Americans were found to hear less accurately over a smaller range of frequencies. It was shown that, although the children in both cultures hear about as well, older Mabaans retain their accurate hearing whereas Americans gradually lose it. Factory workers, in particular, succumb to the noise around them, and, despite a ridiculously stringent basis for acceptance, millions of dollars are annually paid in disability insurance to aurally injured workers. (To receive insurance, a worker must leave his noisy job for six months and then demonstrate "substantial" hearing loss in the relatively small range of human speech. He must also show that his hearing loss was due only to his work, and such factors as lunch breaks and coffee breaks are counted against claims of "continuous noise." If these unfair standards were relaxed, disability payments would clearly be much higher.)

Most of us have experienced the familiar "ringing in the ears" from relatively short exposures to loud noises (95 dB and above), such as concerts, subway rides, and some sports events. Along with the ringing comes a temporary hearing loss which is short-term, but may be quite noticeable. It has been shown, though, that prolonged exposure to 85 dB and above (approximately the level of heavy city traffic at 50 feet) will induce permanent losses of hearing, first at high frequencies and gradually toward the range of human speech. Needless to say, most industrial machines and even many indoor appliances, operate at higher noise levels than these.

Our auditory sense is not the only casualty of noise pollution. As our environment deteriorates, the sciences which study the effects of the degradation begin to find many new aspects of our vulnerability. Noise is thought to bring on headaches in a variety of ways, and the high per capita sale of aspirins in New York could indicate this. Psychiatrists report that noise can lead to or worsen mental instability. Research also indicates a positive correlation between noise and increased malfunction of the heart, endocrine and reproductive systems. Noise is even thought to affect the unborn fetus.

In the realm of legal noise abatement, the citizen finds little help, either from legislators or from courts. Most cities and towns have laws which prohibit the making of "unreasonable" noise, although few have any guidelines as to what this entails. In New York City, for instance, a policeman can issue a summons for unnecessary use of a car horn, but then must show up in court with the driver and prove that the noise was unnecessary. This is often quite difficult and usually involves a day lost in court.

New York has on the books what is generally considered to be the model for anti-noise ordinances, but residents of what may very well be the noisiest city in the world find little consolation in this fact. The catch in New York's law, and the laws of those municipalities which have followed the lead, is the word "unnecessary." Necessity is a subjective concept, and is open as much to a political as a medical definition. Once necessity is established, the term "unreasonable" is usually shunted aside on the grounds that the technology does not exist or is prohibitively expensive to remedy the problem.

Residents in the vicinity of airports have additional difficulties. On the whole, cities are reluctant to crack down on the airlines for fear of losing business and harming economic growth. In extreme cases, residents will be informed that their only possible recourse is in a court of law. The courts, however, tend to shy away from establishing precedents that would pre-empt the rights of lawmakers to decide the fate of their harassed citizens. Court cases on the subject have little uniformity, and range from large settlements in favor of homeowners who can demonstrate significant property devaluation, to judicial statements that "noise and other inconveniences are merely a part of living in a city and are necessary prerequisites for a thriving economy."

Certain companies, like utilities and transit authorities (especially if they are working on subways), can add further insult to injury. Although most anti-noise laws restrict construction work to weekdays from 7:00 A.M. to 6:00 P.M., companies that demonstrate an economic or other necessity to work beyond these hours can secure permits which allow this. For example, Memphis, Tennessee, will grant such permits if a contractor claims he will suffer "loss or inconvenience" if restricted to daylight work.

As for trucks, buses and trains, there are virtually no laws governing the hours that they may travel.

The standard argument that many large noise polluters use to justify their loudness is that since there are no quieter machines, they have no choice but to use what is available. The facts behind this argument shed light upon how much consideration is given to a company's powerless "listening audience."

In point of fact, the claim may be an outright lie. New York City's Citizens for a Quieter City has provided numerous examples of machinery—much of it imported—which can do a comparable job at a comparable price (sometimes even more cheaply) with less than half the noise. Garbage cans now exist which, though made of metal, are essentially "clangless." Dramatically quieter garbage trucks are available at about 15 percent greater cost than present 100 decibel monsters—and the price is expected to decrease with greater production. Even air compressors and jackhammers can be made quieter with no loss in power or ease of handling and just a small increase in price.

In the cases where the claims of "no new technology" are true, it is often the purchasers and not the manufacturers who are at fault. A number of companies announced the creation of quiet products, only to find that, because of slight increases in price, they were essentially unmarketable. This is as true of the construction industry, which pours out unbelievable quantities of noise, as well as the housewife. For in-stance, one large company developed a near-silent vacuum cleaner which, it turned out, was rejected by consumers be-cause the silence was equated with ineffectiveness. Typewriter manufacturers, too, have long known how to make machines quieter, but it has been shown that secretaries will not use them because silence gave the impression of slow typing.

Noise abatement is a virtually untapped citizen cause. Most large cities have clean air coalitions, but few have groups dedicated to preserving peace and tranquillity. The first step for citizens who are concerned about their ears and their health is to form a citizen coalition which will begin to exert the kind of pressure that other environmental groups exert. Noise is perhaps hard to measure, but it is a perennial problem and there should be no difficulty in finding a large number of persons who are eager to investigate a particular region's "politics of noise." City governments and state legis-latures should be made aware of the magnitude of the prob-lem and the widespread interest that many people have in curbing it.

Automobile and truck lobbies are already under consider-able fire from clean air groups and this concerted attack should be augmented to include anti-noise pressure. In many ways a newly started anti-noise coalition can cash in on gen-eral environmental awareness which will provide at least a starting base of sympathy.

Citizens can push for "quiet zones" in cities, either on a permanent or a temporary basis. The concept was pioneered in certain small tourist towns in Europe, and New York and Tokyo have followed suit, by banning traffic from Fifth Ave-nue and the Ginza, respectively, one day a week. Clean air groups will give strong support for such an action.

Strong pressure may force airports to take certain steps, and may even result in the prohibition of flights after certain hours. Washington's National Airport has an 11:00 P.M. vol-untary curfew on flights, partly because the planes must fly near the White House. Citizens should demand the same treatment for themselves that the President has.

Pressure is being exerted on airports in other areas, too. Groups in various cities around the country have demanded that their airfields prohibit the SST from landing. Even though such an action is strongly resisted by the government, and may result in the loss of significant funds, Madison, Wisconsin, has denied the new jets the use of its airport. This tactic may be possible for some of the other large planes now planned or being used.

Consumers should be on the lookout for quieter appliances. Noise does not always equal power or speed, and often, even if it does, the speed or power may not be necessary. Hopefully, among the most environmentally aware, the question will arise: Is the noisy, expensive electric appliance worth it? Or, does one really require a power mower to cut a small plot of grass once every two weeks?

When moving into an apartment or a new house, it should be closely investigated for sound insulation. Most modern construction is of a very low quality and one of a builder's least worries is what it will sound like inside once it is rented or sold. Check door fittings and walls, and, if possible, have a friend go upstairs and stamp on the floor or shout. Check the premises during the rush hour to see what the traffic outside is like—and what it sounds like outside. Also, listen to whether the pipes transmit the sound of running water throughout the entire building.

Try to be quiet yourself. Speakers of hi-fi sets should be placed on insulating material or hung on a wall so as not to reverberate downstairs. Televisions, if possible, should be placed against "interior" walls so that your neighbor can enjoy his own activities without hearing your set through his wall. Electric appliances and washers should not be run late at night. Noisy dogs can be trained to bark less.

Sounds are obviously a desirable aspect of our existence, and no one is out to silence this country. Noises can be dangerous and extremely irritating, especially if they are out of one's control. Most of the loud and continuous noises we are subjected to are gratuitous—no one wants them. They may be expensive to control, but this fact of life is one which environmentalists face time and again. We have been living off our natural and human resources for many generations now, and we have reached the stage where we will have to begin to pay back what we have borrowed.

open space

- *Five hundred years are needed to create one inch of good topsoil; an average of 500 acres per day of rural and agricultural land in California is either sold or developed for urban use.*
- *By the year 2000, it is likely that 80 percent of the world's population will be crowded within 2 percent of the land surface.*
- *In the past 9 years, Delaware Wildlands, Inc. has purchased over 10,000 acres of what local farmers consider to be "useless" marshlands. Purchase of the salt marshes, however, has prevented several possible real estate development projects while maintaining the crab and fish populations of Delaware Bay.*

The necessity of carefully planned land allocation is frequently overshadowed by the critical problems of air and water pollution. Yet these areas of environmental concern are closely linked. The overcongestion of people in existing urban areas leads to increased air pollution from traffic and more waste products than existing sewage treatment plants can handle. Factories dumping wastes into a river at its source can make the water unfit for consumption, recreation, and fish and plant life the entire length of the waterway. Poor land allocation also leads to unnecessary waste of valuable resources. Low density housing in valuable forest or mountain land may necessitate miles of connected roadways and sewage pipes to service them. The best agricultural land can be buried under a new housing development. It is clear, then, that all uses of any land area and their effects on surrounding areas must be studied before development takes place.

Such studies will reveal that some areas are better left un-developed because their natural function as a protective shield, crop land, habitat for many species, or simply a source of beauty is more valuable to all living creatures than an alternative development plan. This is the idea behind planned open space as a functional area. Instead of being un-used vacant land, it serves a beneficial purpose. It can pro-vide physical and psychological rest to crowded populations, protect wildlife and maintain an ecological balance, or sepa-rate individual communities to break up an endless mass of subdivisions. In this manner, open space becomes a valid al-ternative to development and can be purposefully built into the environment instead of another building or a new com-munity.

The main problem is not that all available land will be de-veloped and populated by the year 2000. Granted, the amount of developed urban land is expected to almost double, reaching approximately 45 million acres. And if cur-rent birth rates continue, the United States population, pres-ently 206 million, will rise to over 300 million in the next 30 years. But along with the population explosion, we will expe-rience a population implosion. This is a far more critical problem. More and more people will be moving to the large urban centers with the result that there will be increasing concentrations of people on relatively small portions of the earth's surface. Increasing leisure time and growing mobility will permit greater numbers of individuals to descend on core urban areas at the same time.

Current statistics estimate that three-quarters of the earth's population now live in urban areas, but four-fifths will be liv-ing in these areas in the year 2000. In 1960, 20 percent of the world's population lived in areas of 100,000 people or more; by 2000, this figure is expected to be 42 percent. With these concentrations, maintenance of urban open space is crucial. Some areas must be left undeveloped now to provide for the physical and psychological well-being of all future in-habitants.

The disappearance of prime soil and the best quality lands across the country because of careless development proce-dures is another critical problem. Many places that are aes-thetically marvelous turn out to be environmental hazards. Beach towns dot the New Jersey shore with stilt-legged houses perched along the primary dunes closest to the sea. San Francisco majestically overlooks the northern California coast while little cable cars shift up and down the steep narrow streets. But the primary dunes and hillsides are only two examples of land masses that cannot tolerate human habitation and still maintain their proper ecological balance. The dangers of wind and water erosion greatly increase, and, more importantly, the protective covering these forms provided for inland areas is permanently destroyed. Unless plans are developed to protect those open spaces responsible for maintaining the frail ecological balance between animals and their environments, the United States may face permanent biological disaster.

Three areas where open space can serve a functional purpose are recreation, conservation, and shaping urban development. Recreational areas have probably received the most attention; as early as 1850, residents of New York supported the acquisition of 700 acres of land for Central Park. Federal, state, and local governments have all provided community park funds, and private facilities—tennis courts, health spas, lake resorts, etc.—have sprung up wherever people have settled. The major problem at this time is to evenly distribute recreation space for its most efficient use. Many existing parks are overused to the extent that their facilities are not adequate to serve all the people who would like to use them; others do not receive sufficient use because parking space is inadequate or access is very difficult.

Valuable resources that can be conserved in open spaces include forests, agricultural lands, and bodies of water. Most conservation areas can also be used for recreation. Forests and woodlands are prime examples. While these territories are vitally important in protecting against soil erosion, aiding in soil retention of water and preventing surface water runoff, their natural beauty makes them ideal locations for hiking and riding trails, camping areas, and ski resorts. The necessity of forests for many forms of wildlife and the protection the trees provide for small watersheds also add to their conservation value.

Farmlands are rapidly disappearing. In California, approximately 500 acres of agricultural and rural land is sold or developed for urban uses each day. Some of the most productive land for fruit and vegetables in California has already been developed, and communities in Santa Clara County, where the prime soil lies, are desperately trying to save remaining open space from development. Crop lands, dairy farms, and truck farms must be conserved for the food products they provide.

Wetlands are another form of non-urban land that must be protected. They are essential for absorbing excess water during floods and releasing water to streams and rivers during periods of low water flow. At the same time, these marsh and swamp areas are the habitat of thousands of fish and waterfowl who depend on the wetlands for food and protection. Yet urban communities continue to expand into these areas without consideration of the delicate balance they are irreversibly destroying. River and lake shorelines are continually dredged and filled. In Florida, land was quietly bought up for a new major airport which, if built, will block off water drainage into the Everglades that is necessary to sustain all marsh life during winter. Conservationists are still fighting the development plans.

Water sources must also be spared from urban development. Even the smallest ponds are home to a variety of water animals. But most importantly, all community water must be supplied from natural sources, and if these sources are chronically polluted they can no longer be tapped. This poses one of the most serious threats to man's survival, and still no strong legal restrictions are operating effectively. A few new developers each year will put in too many cesspools for the natural sewage system to operate effectively and waste will drain into clean water wells. Salt water supplies are being threatened just as seriously as fresh water sources. The sardine population off the coast of California has been almost wiped out. Many areas have been declared unfit for fishing as well as swimming since poisonous chemicals in the fish could endanger the health of those who eat them. Residents of the Washington, D. C., area have been warned that anyone who falls into many sections of the Potomac River must be taken to the hospital for a checkup to detect harmful bacteria.

Many of our lakes, most notably Lake Erie, are dying. Uncontrolled sewage dumpage has caused the normal aging process, known as eutrophication, to be tremendously accelerated. What happens is that the phosphates and nitrates in the waste products cause the plant life, particularly the algae, to grow in excess. They either die off or are then consumed by bacteria, in either case consuming large amounts of the oxygen that would otherwise be available to support fish life. The water is heated by the oxygen consumption. The game fish die and are temporarily replaced by tougher strains that can tolerate the now polluted warmer water. And the water supply and the recreational value of the lake are destroyed. The mounds of dead algae and fish continue to subtract from the water area until the lake becomes a bog and eventually dry land. And on top of all this, water usage is increasing. It is estimated that consumption will increase 1½ times and water use 3 times the current rates by the year 2000. And since the natural ability of a body of water to restore its ecological balance is considerably weakened every time the water is reused and returned, we can expect several serious catastrophes in the next 30 years if current water usage rates are maintained.

The final use of open space to shape urban development will become increasingly important as urban densities rise. Green spaces will not only be needed to separate individual dwellings but also to divide one community from another as metropolitan areas expand to encompass distant suburbs. New developments will probably plan residential areas around main transportation routes or in several clusters to conserve as much undeveloped area as possible for the collective use of all residents. In Europe and Canada, many major cities have already acquired rural and agricultural lands directly outside the existing urban expanse to form what is known as a "green belt" for aesthetic values as well as for recreational and farming use. Considering that many modern American cities will probably be star-shaped structures with a central metropolitan core and many satellite towns connected by major rapid transit and highway routes, green areas should be preserved now in between projected routes and developments.

An open space program should then be developed which allocates some lands for recreation, conservation, and urban development. But this program must relate to all other development programs if land is to be allocated without conflicts. Therefore, a comprehensive land use plan for future growth must be formulated. And for open space uses, a regional plan is better than a local one since most resources have regional rather than jurisdictional characteristics; natural water supplies and varieties of animal and plant life will be the same or very similar over a large area. Local governments are often unwilling to plan large areas of open space since they do not provide the tax revenue that comes from developed land; therefore, to encourage such planning, several state governments have adopted the procedure of paying local governments in place of the tax revenue. One of the best plans is for several adjoining local governments to donate part of a large open space, thereby sharing the cost and providing all inhabitants with a large recreational nature area.

The first phase of the comprehensive regional plan must always be a careful inventory of the land and the people. Existing buildings and roadways and their different categories—house, business, factory, alley, highway, etc.—are always outlined in an area plan. So are entertainment facilities, agricultural areas, and undeveloped land and water areas. But qualitative land values should also be included. Is existing recreational land active or passive? In other words, is it a school playfield, a golf course, or just an open park? How steep are the existing slopes? Is a water supply safe for consumption or swimming?

The U. S. Geological Survey has some of this information or may be of assistance in obtaining it. Population density, and the needs and expectations of residents of different communities are factors which must be considered, since they affect open space demand. Also, in this phase of the plan, it is a good idea to collect a list of all governmental agencies and affiliates which have some authority over planning procedures.

The second phase of the plan should include standards and goals. A detailed outline should be drawn up listing every area to be preserved and every change felt necessary. Often, recreation standards can be set, establishing, for instance, that 50 acres of open land has to be available per 1000 people, and of this, two-fifths should be undisturbed nature areas and three-fifths, developed park and recreational areas. Public opinion polls will be necessary to get an accurate picture of what local citizens would like to see planned. Determining factors should be outlined. For instance, transportation routes will indicate exactly what lands will be accessible to what sections of the population for recreational purposes. A scenic lake 50 miles from the nearest highway is only going to be visited by the industrious nature lovers who don't mind long stretches of curvy, dusty, single-lane roads.

It is at this point in planning that the most difficult decision between alternative demands for the same land will have to be made. Social and environmental needs can conflict. Badly needed housing can challenge urban woodlands; high unemployment rates may make new industry more practical than the protection of a rare forest. Sometimes, a compromise can be reached with half a shoreline developed, the other half left undeveloped. But for the most part, open space suffers in any trade-off decision because, unlike most other land uses, it cannot be directly measured by cost-benefit analysis. A dollar value cannot be placed on a beautiful view as it can on the tax assessment for an office building. And assured money value will often make a development more feasible than a natural area for which revenue can only be predicted. Probably the best argument for the preservation of open space is that alternative locations for a natural area are very limited compared with those for development. If there is only one natural lake or one group of mountains in the area, persuasive arguments can be developed in favor of open space allocation for those resources. Another tactic, of course, is to make the open space area into a political issue, arguing that only the candidate who realizes the importance of protecting our natural resources and effective urban planning should be elected.

The next step in the comprehensive regional plan is to decide the various ways that different pieces of land should be acquired and who should be the responsible party in charge of acquiring each piece. Finally it must be decided in what order the lands should be obtained according to available funds, amount of development, and greatest demand.

Land can be acquired through three legal methods: acquisition, regulation, and taxation. Each of these methods can be implemented through a variety of techniques, several of which will be discussed.

Acquisition is the process by which full or partial property rights are obtained for a piece of land. Some land will be donated; other land will be condemned through tax delinquency and turned over to the community for open space use. Most land, however, will be purchased. If full property rights are purchased, the land is said to have been acquired in fee simple. However, it is often possible to purchase partial property rights to cover only that portion of private land needed for public use. The section of land purchased is known as an easement, and it can range from a 500 yard grass strip on either side of a highway to a mountain path a few feet wide. In general, easements are considerably less expensive than full purchase, and are classified positive or negative according to their function. The former permit public access as in the case of hiking trails or fishing rights on a river bank; the latter restrict public usage as in the case of scenic easements along highways prohibiting billboards and dumping. Often easements are used to hide industrial and urban development; scenic easements along the Hudson across from Riverdale preserve the original view.

Regulation includes zoning and sub-division. The first zoning ordinance was adopted by New York in 1916, and after a 1926 Supreme Court ruling that zoning was constitutional, most states established zoning ordinances granting local governments the police power to zone areas of land as long as the health, safety, and welfare of the population are protected. The two major forms of zoning are natural resource zoning and development zoning.

While natural resource zoning would be the logical measure for preserving open space, all informed sources agree that it cannot be trusted since it cannot withstand development pressures. A landowner might willingly agree to open space zoning for a few years, but there is no guarantee that he won't permit rezoning of his land when he stands to make considerable economic profit. Since there is no guaranteed tax loss compensation for landowners whose property is zoned for open space, courts may declare such zoning to be an unconstitutional taking of property. Often to prevent rezoning of open space for construction, proof must exist that development in the natural area would be detrimental to the health or safety of those who would be living there. While this may be fairly easy to maintain about marsh or swamp areas, it is not easy to prove in relation to forests or hill lands. Furthermore, natural resource zoning is rarely applied to urban areas where remaining timber and wetlands most need to be protected.

Specific forms of natural resource zoning have fared little better. Floodplain zoning seeks to preserve land on either side of a river or stream that is needed to soak up the overflow of water during floods and heavy rains. Yet few states have found it important enough to incorporate this zoning in their ordinances; as of 1968, only nine states specifically listed floodplains as an area to be zoned. If a river or stream runs through an urban area, flood paths should be zoned for open space uses such as parking lots and parks that will not be destroyed by flowing water.

Agricultural lands which have been protectively zoned for years are still overcome by urban demands. People move toward a productive and picturesque farm area, and scattered farms and new communities eventually consume large quantities of valuable crop lands. In Santa Clara County, in California, agricultural acreage declined from 247,000 acres in 1947 to 165,000 acres in 1963, and is expected to decline to 61,000 by 1980. Special soil conditions may be zoned for crop use, but these conditions are usually the result of additional water, and waterfront lots are very valuable. Few property owners can withstand the lure of high market prices for developed lakeshore properties. And unless tax assessments are adjusted according to land use, farmers can be forced out of business by high taxes that can easily be afforded by residents in adjacent suburbs.

Forest lands should also be zoned for their natural resource value, but strong timber lobbies, the number of wood houses built each year, and the extraordinary amount of disposable paper products used by the American public all threaten to wipe out forestlands permanently. Most wood products—paper, pulp, cardboard, lumber, etc.—can be reused. And unless consumer practices change, with massive recycling campaigns and use of alternative building supplies, zoning of forests will be a useless precaution, overcome by public demand for more products.

Development zoning is usually used to preserve open space in urban areas. For years, the most common urban zoning practice has been large lot zoning which seeks to preserve open space by cutting down on the number of buildings per acre. Unfortunately, there are several drawbacks to this technique, the most drastic being that developers have been forced to move further and further out from an urban area to build the number of desired houses. If two houses are zoned per acre, ten acres are needed for twenty houses; five houses per acre would only require four acres. Not only is the available open space then privately owned, but service costs are considerably higher than they would be if the houses were closer together.

The alternative to large lot zoning is density or cluster zoning. The same ratio of people to land is maintained, only in this case dwellings are clustered together and the available open space is left in one large unified area. Several environmental improvements are possible. Less pavement is necessary, sewage and power lines can be shorter, and only the most suited land need be developed. At the same time, expenses are reduced. Natural environmental conditions can also be put to advantage. Wooded areas may surround different clusters, a canyon can swing around one side of the development, trees can be left standing to protect all dwellings from the noise and view of access highways and busy roads.

Another development zoning method is large-scale zoning which permits an entire community to be mapped out at one time. The planning conflicts that often plague gradual expansion are thus avoided. However, there are times when gradual expansion can be put to good use with zoning for time development. Under this regulation, certain open areas cannot be developed until already partially developed land has been occupied. Then, when an area is rezoned for development, all service lines and roads can be put in at one time to accommodate all future residents.

Several specific forms of zoning exist. Historic zoning prevents any old buildings from being changed and requires all new ones to conform with existing standards. Unfortunately, like natural resource zoning, it cannot be guaranteed over long periods of time.

Billboard legislation began in Monterey, California, where signs were first prohibited along rural roads. The Federal Highway Beautification Act of 1965 was designed to provide landscaping along state highways, and elimination of billboards was outlined. However, the project was never funded. In 1968, Virginia passed a law limiting billboards to on-the-site advertising.

Most billboard legislation is begun in conjunction with scenic easements along highways where signs are prohibited. In many cases, however, the freeway itself is the biggest eyesore

to nearby residents, and easements hiding the freeway from
view could be more effective. Certainly the freeway is a lot
more environmentally destructive, due to the required removal of homes, increasing automobile pollution, and constant
noise. A minor consideration such as billboard zoning must
not deter major efforts. Projected freeway plans should be
studied to see whether they are necessary for the community
and whether they will be built in the most suitable area.

Urban zoning can legally regulate the height and size of
buildings, the density of a lot, the density of the population,
and the use of buildings. But other important environmental
conditions are controlled by subdivision requirements.
Among these are the design of streets, the types of building
materials used, and the percentage of subdivision land that
must remain open space. Unfortunately, in most cases, developers can offer payment in place of dedicating open space.

However, subdivision controls which regulate the installation of utility lines can also regulate the density of an area.
Other controls which permit steeper than normal grade roads
can be used to protect the natural slopes of the region from
being carved to excess. Still other subdivision regulations can
prohibit the cutting of trees, thereby helping to protect the
soil, provide shade, and minimize noise levels.

A variety of tax measures can be employed to preserve
open space. Sometimes a tax deduction can serve as an incentive to a landowner to grant easements. Most public property that serves a useful open space function will be exempt
from real property taxes. Many states make provisions to also
exempt private open space lands if they are available for public use. Some lands, most commonly farmlands, are given a
preferential tax assessment; taxes are lowered because of the
use to which the land is put. While this is a valid attempt to
keep taxes on open space at a minimum, it usually works
only until the owner is ready to cash in for the market value
of his property. In effect, it allows him to maintain the lands
at a minimum cost for several years while property values
rise.

Probably the best tax measure is the tax deferral, by which
taxes are postponed as long as the land is conserved. In the
example of forest lands the owner will pay lower taxes until
he cuts down the trees, at which time he will have to pay
back taxes. The objective, of course, is to provide an incen-

tive for allowing the trees to mature. While this measure calls for the normal amount of taxes in the end, it still permits speculators to gamble with land values. And to the extent that all tax measures adjust the land assessment, they should only play a supportive role in preserving open space.

Federal, state, or local authorities, private organizations, and groups of citizens can all make use of the above methods in their attempts to conserve natural areas. Many different federal agencies offer research or project assistance for open space sites. Among those agencies assisting in water and floodplain research and setting up construction and zoning standards for water areas are the U. S. Geological Survey, the Tennessee Valley Authority, the Soil Conservation Service, and the Army Corps of Engineers. Often, however, the construction projects of these organizations have left rich valleys permanently flooded under dams and forced the removal of hundreds of homes. Within the Department of Interior, the Bureau of Outdoor Recreation offers assistance in establishing park programs, while the National Park Service purchases lands with federal funds to become national parks. The Bureau of Land Management processes state and local applications for federal lands for open space use, but most of the available lands are limited to the western United States.

Several federal funding programs exist, and local communities should take advantage of them. Section 701 of the Federal Housing Act guarantees funds to cover two-thirds of the cost of any community planning study. The Department of Interior will pay up to 50 percent of the cost of preserving an historic district. The Federal Open Space Land Program under the Department of Housing and Urban Development will cover 50 percent of the cost of securing any open space ranging from a single lot under 1000 square feet to be converted into a vest pocket park up to 4000 acres to be added to a major state park. Since 1961 when this program was enacted, over 350,000 acres of urban land have been preserved with the federal government contributing over $400 million. Ninety percent of this sum goes toward land acquisition, ten percent toward development, and there is no time limit for completion.

The National Environment Policy Act of 1969 is probably the single most important piece of federal legislation concerned with open space. Section 102 requires that every federal agency submit a public statement on the environmental impact of a proposed plan and lists alternative methods before the proposal is implemented. That citizens have a legal right to know what proposed changes are planned for their environment will be exceedingly important in future open space battles.

State environmental bills of rights exist in Virginia, Rhode Island, and New York. While requiring adequate state planning for the control and use of natural resources, these bills also guarantee citizens' rights to use and to enjoy these resources. Michigan and Texas also have constitutional provisions protecting valuable natural areas.

Many acquisition programs can be financed at the state level. Scenic highway easements, access to waterways for public recreation, and trails for hiking and riding can be set up throughout the state. Occasionally, acquired land can be paid for gradually in installment payments which ease state funding difficulties. Another plan is the leaseback. Full payment is made on a piece of property which is then leased back to the owner to be conserved in a natural state until sufficient recreation or conservation funds are gathered.

Some states have established comprehensive open space plans to be administered by state agencies. The Green Acres Land Acquisition Act was passed in New Jersey in June, 1961, and financed by a $60 million bond issue. Under this act, recreational and natural areas were to be spread evenly throughout the state, with the state government receiving two-thirds of the money to be used for acquisition and the remaining third to be granted to local governments for smaller acquisitions. Wisconsin began a thorough open space program in the early 1960's. Funds were allotted to purchase easements along roads, shorelines and streams, to protect wild rivers and wetlands, to construct dams and to develop flood control programs. Interestingly, funds are provided by a cigarette tax which taxes all out-of-state smokers as well as in-state smokers, leaving non-smokers exempt.

Most state legislatures handed down their zoning authority to the municipal governments, since it was felt that local zoning problems could best be administered at the local level. Gradually, this "police power" has been extended to the counties to provide for more regional zoning ordinances. In some cases, the cities themselves have been granted extra zoning powers, but this alternative still restricts zoning primarily to urban development. The third and best alternative has been to create a specific planning region, all segments of which are to be covered by the same zoning regulations. This extension makes the most sense environmentally since it not only permits regional regulation, but also extends zoning, enabling legislation to regulate public improvement as well as private development.

Unfortunately, practically all regional commissions have been limited to an advisory capacity, with only limited power to develop and review a regional land use plan. They are unable to zone specific areas or to reject weak qualifications. However, several regional zoning attempts have been tried with varied success, and a few case histories should provide useful examples for other areas contemplating the formation of a regional commission.

In California, the San Francisco Bay Conservation and Development Commission (BCDC) was created in 1965 to oversee shoreline development and to protect the bay waters. In an effort to coordinate development projects of various communities around the bay, this regional commission has been granted power to pass or reject all building permits that include petitions to dredge or to fill the bay, except in agreements between local governments and the Army Corps of Engineers. It is also expected to study the ecological features and economic prospects of the bay region, and to consult all local governments on their planning views. However, the 1965 law designating the responsibilities of the commission was revised in 1969, placing considerable new limitations on citizen's power. Besides reducing shoreline control from 1000 feet to only 100 feet from the water's edge, the revision required that the number of elected officials on the commission be increased, thereby reducing the number of citizens and professionals.

Another regional commission was created for the Hackensack Meadowlands, covering two counties and several municipalities in northeast New Jersey. Over 20,000 acres of valuable meadowland remain undeveloped, and it is the aim of the state to carefully control the badly needed development projects. In this instance, the regional commission functions not so much to restrict development as to insure that the ecology of the area is protected through careful planning

and construction, and regulation of all subdivisions. A special
provision places all new development property taxes in an
inter-municipal fund effectively reducing local competition
while gathering necessary money for the commission's operations. Other funds can be collected through bonds, leases,
and federal grants. Though the commission's decisions are
subject to review by a committee of municipality executives,
a vote of five of the seven commission members can override
any rejections.

One of the best regional authorities is the Twin Cities Metropolitan Planning Commission of Minneapolis and St. Paul,
Minnesota. Originally an advisory committee, the 15-man
commission received power through 1967 and 1969 legislation, enabling them to review the comprehensive plans of
each special district and each local government in an effort to
unify and make compatible all metropolitan development
projects. The 1969 legislation grants the commission specific
power to establish a complete metropolitan sewage system
regulated by a seven-man sewage board and financed through
property taxes. Also in 1969, the Metropolitan Park Board
Act granted the commission authority to establish a seven-
man park board to regulate open space and park development for the entire metropolitan area. The park board may
acquire land through various forms of acquisition, issue
bonds, charge fees, and make use of allocated state funds,
but expenditures are subject to the regional council's review.
Council members are further expected to sit on various committees concerning environmental standards such as airport
and sanitation committees.

The possibilities for future regional regulation are numerous. Inter-government cooperation and multi-disciplinary
planning teams can be encouraged. Hopefully, the initial advisory capacity of most commissions will gradually be eliminated in favor of immediate regional power to coordinate resource use and management. Government officials, because
they are the political decision makers, should be included in a
planning commission as long as their presence does not greatly compromise the objectives or conclusions of the group.
But appointment or election of citizen committee members is
even more important. As it now stands, citizen members are
usually appointed by the city council or county board of su-
pervisors, and many of them are already involved as profes-

sionals in the planning field. If the planning commission is to accurately provide for the needs of a region, the views of laymen who live there must be represented.

A few state level zoning programs have been initiated with varying results. Probably the best known is Hawaii's general state zoning plan. Prepared in 1957 by the State Planning Office (now the Department of Planning and Economic Development), it was approved first by the governor and then by the state legislature in 1961 and eventually incorporated into the Land Use Law. Because urban development seemed to be occurring either where it was uneconomical to provide adequate facilities or where it usurped valuable agricultural land, state authorities decided to classify all lands under three major categories. The districts formed were Agricultural, Conservation, and Urban, with a fourth Rural District added in 1963. County governments are responsible for administering urban land uses and regulating agricultural and rural uses, while the Conservation District falls under the authority of the State Department of Land and Natural Resources. Changes in district boundaries require a recommendation from a County Planning Commission, a public hearing held by the State Land Use Commission, and approval by six land use commissioners. Three procedures accompany the zoning plan to protect citizens' rights and to preserve environmental quality. First, agricultural use of land can be approved in any district, accompanied by a tax reduction on that land as long as it continues to be used for agricultural purposes. Secondly, a comprehensive review must occur every five years. Thirdly, citizens' attitudes are polled for recommended changes. In the first review held in 1968–69, citizen recommendations resulted in some major changes in conservation and rural boundaries and some important suggestions, one of which was to employ incremental zoning for large developments.

At least one state, Oregon, is attempting a similar program where the entire state will be zoned. However, implementation depends entirely on the state governor and no time limits exist as to when a city or county must submit its comprehensive zoning plans. Such a procedure could take forever.

Maine has created an Environmental Improvement Commission to regulate the location of industries and to enforce environmental standards by requiring industry to meet state air and water pollution control standards, to provide ample parking and loading space, to maintain the scenic surroundings, and to find proper soil conditions before development. The commission is limited to a two-week period in which to decide whether or not to pass a development plan, and it can conduct investigative hearings at any time.

Private open space actions have the advantage of avoiding the political pressures that can delay and divert government plans. Acquisitions that are deemed vitally important for the ecology of an area do not have to wait for state or federal approval or funds but can be immediately pursued with private resources. One group that has preserved many strategic natural areas is the Nature Conservancy, which was incorporated in Washington, D. C., in 1951. Presently there are 33 chapters across the country, and as of 1970 this organization had acquired through gift or purchase approximately 200,000 acres in 43 states. One of their programs has been a series of "checkerboard" purchases around the San Francisco Bay. Many different lots of varying sizes have been purchased in strategic areas to block out large development plans. Another program has been to purchase several of the Barrier Islands off the Virginia coast that provide a home to many plant and animal species and a beautiful recreational area within one day's drive of 40 percent of the U. S. population. Many other national organizations have been formed to conserve national areas throughout America.

Several statewide programs have also been accomplished by private groups. California Tomorrow, a group organized in San Francisco, is no longer waiting for the state government to come up with an effective statewide zoning plan. Instead, they have begun their own research program with funds donated by members and a 4-man planning team guided by an advisory task force. A wall-wide planning display has been set up in the main California Tomorrow office, on which a visual sketch of the state-wide zoning proposal will be created. Included will be the necessary environmental requirements and the economic, social, and political actions necessary to secure these requirements.

Another private approach is the construction of new towns. They are commonly developed on land owned by a single, private owner, usually the developer. Homes are usually built in clusters, with large areas of open space left for tennis courts, golf courses, lakes, riding rinks and other recreational uses. Apartment dwellings, common in new towns, allow a greater population density than do ordinary suburbs, and, consequently, a higher percentage of open space—as high as 59 percent in New Seabury, Massachusetts. In theory, new town land use is an improvement over the haphazard development which characterizes typical suburban and urban communities. Unfortunately, the gain is canceled out by the fact that most new towns are almost entirely geared to high-income persons. No environmentalist advocates setting aside open space so it can be used only by a privileged, monied few.

The new town concept was originally designed to provide healthy, luxurious living areas outside of a major metropolis so that industry could be confined within already existing urban areas. However, plans for Reston, Virginia, outside Washington, D. C., leave 200 acres for residential use and 900 for industrial and government agencies. The new town was also expected to cut down on commuter traffic, but studies reveal that their living conditions have attracted many residents who are willing to commute to distant metropolitan areas for work.

Because of the resort-like nature of these communities, the prime land in an area is often selected for the new town site, which claims at least some land that might best have been zoned as state or national park territory. This seems to be the case with High Meadow, a 245 acre tract in Monterey County, California. Forty percent of this area is covered by slopes and some of these will invariably have to be carved up for building space.

Citizen group actions to affect land use policy are unlimited. One of the first things a group should do is become familiar with the proper form of a zoning ordinance and the proper procedures for a public zoning hearing. All area zoning proposals should be watched and hearings attended to provide officials with the public viewpoint.

By definition, a public hearing should serve both to inform the public of proposed legislation and to hear and consider public opinion on the subject. In zoning hearings, a zoning panel decides a specific case with open testimony. Public notice of a hearing is required and it is usually placed in the daily newspaper; other media are seldom used, so those who neither buy nor read newspapers remain uninformed. Furthermore, this notice usually appears only twice in the "official notices" section of the classified advertisements beginning two weeks before the hearing, and unless a person knows where to look, the announcement may easily be missed. Notices are also frequently couched in legal jargon. Neighborhood posters or informal word-of-mouth knowledge of hearings are two possible alternatives, but the first can be limited by local restrictions against posting bills, and the second is limited because only friends and previous contacts can be reached.

Another measure which can be used to protect zoning officials is the declaration of an "emergency situation," under which hearings can be waived. Some states go so far as to consistently waive all policy-making concerning highway maintenance, relocation, and construction. The 1950 Federal Administration Procedure Act also gives agencies the right to declare a hearing unnecessary.

Several procedural problems also exist. Uninterested or absent officials who send their staff in their place, incomplete records (sometimes a panel will permit the court stenographer to take down only what he or she feels to be the most important points), uninformed citizens, and legal jargon all plague the hearing procedure.

Most hearings seem to be designed to avoid the legal hassles of opposition rather than to permit public proposals to change an ordinance. Before the normal hearing can become a legitimate airing process, several important changes are necessary. Expanded notification and coverage are needed, verbatim records, presence of officials, and identification of every speaker are all required. Prehearing conferences to educate the public and simplified language during the hearing can remove additional public antagonism against normal hearing procedures. If both sides eliminate unnecessary defenses, communication might be established that would actually permit healthy decisions about necessary changes before a bad or incomplete ordinance is shoved through.

For citizens the best advice on purchasing land is to watch out for unsuspected opportunities and take advantage of them. Get out and walk around the community; location of power and sewage lines, main thoroughfares, main housing areas, dilapidated buildings, and existing open space can provide important factual data for decisions concerning new open space areas. Tax-delinquent properties may be reasonably priced for purchase; some communities will even assume the cost of turning these properties into recreational areas themselves. Areas now serving as dumps or sand and gravel mines can easily be converted into park areas after their initial function is completed. Any farms or large areas of unused acreage close to the urban center should be investigated to see if the owners will consider selling or donating several acres for preservation. Other gifts can be solicited; civic leaders, elected officials who have shown an interest in conservation, people who are willing to give money to any worthy cause should all be contacted to see if they are willing to donate money to preserve a specific natural area.

Preventative steps can also be successful. By collectively purchasing small plots in coastal or marsh areas, citizens, like private organizations, can prevent a single industrial firm or real estate developer from developing the entire area.

Easements may also be bought or established by a group of citizens. One group of property owners along Sudbury River outside of Boston gave easements to a local conservation agency. They were thus able to protect their property from development while preserving the view from the river. Hillside easements may be inexpensive since it would be more economical for a community to preserve the natural beauty and environmental usefulness of the property than to face the high costs of developing it.

Citizens groups can set up small "vest-pocket" parks themselves, provided they have received official approval. So far, the idea of unauthorized People's Parks has not gone over too well; hopefully future spontaneous moves to create inner-city spots for rest and recreation will be received with the proper respect for the urban dweller's psychological and physical needs. Protective zoning needed for floodplains, wetlands, or forests near an urban center can also be promoted through citizens' efforts. One of the best tactics is to publicize any dissatisfaction with zoning proposals or programs. Only by registering disapproval and increasing the number of supporters can citizens hope to influence and possibly change official decisions.

The tactics discussed in this chapter have been limited to those which are available for citizen group action. The account has left out several questions which inevitably arise in any discussion of land use policy. Should titles indicating land ownership exist, and, if so, for what purpose? Does any man, corporation, or nation have the right to irreversibly alter the ecology of an area? Some answers may evolve in the efforts being made by a few congressmen to develop a national land use policy. Yet ultimately the solution may only come with an international land use policy, as far-thinking environmentalists have suggested.

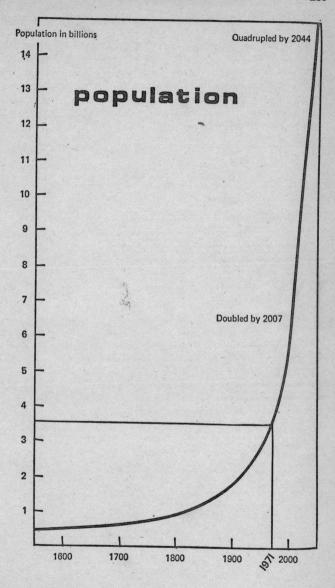

Population in billions

Quadrupled by 2044

population

Doubled by 2007

1600   1700   1800   1900   1971 2000

IV the movement: trial runs

The environmental movement is young, inexperienced, uncoordinated and lacking in money. In most instances it is still at the "beg, borrow or steal" stage, and most of its gains have been small, partial or misunderstood. Citizens often recognize problems and still feel hopelessly inadequate to deal with them.

This fear need not always be. A number of groups from various parts of the country have launched major campaigns to put a stop to the environmental depredation with which they are threatened. These are not small publicity battles or neighborhood clean-ups—they are difficult, protracted, no-holds-barred struggles against some of the strongest corporate interests in the world. And in some instances industry has lost.

This section details two of the dozens of major "trial runs" of a new movement. Although no two battles are ever the same, one of these—a dispute over a center-city freeway in Washington, D. C.—is fairly representative of a local struggle in any American city today. The other—the lobbying campaign to push a strong piece of anti-pollution legislation through Congress—gives a good idea of the work involved in political maneuvering on the national level.

Neither campaign was totally successful. They were not picked to boast of victory, but to illustrate the problems the movement faces and how dynamic action and creative thinking can make the most of a lopsided situation.

emergency committee on the transportation crisis: fighting freeway blackmail

Concrete spaghetti now threatens to strangle the cities in the United States which have so far managed to escape the highwaymen's mania for building roads. Nowhere is the citizen's plight more pathetic than in Washington, D. C., where Congress has tried blackmail to force the District to build its freeways.

Washington is quite literally the last North American colony. District tax revenue flows directly into the United States Treasury, and Congress determines how much of it goes back to the District. Citizens of the District do not vote and have no voting Congressional representative. In many cases, the Congressional committees with appropriate jurisdiction—the District committees in both houses of Congress and the District Appropriations subcommittees—also control how the money is used in D. C.

For years Washington residents have fought a plan which would pave over parks, homes, and businesses to construct a massive freeway system. For years Congress has fought to get it constructed. The public transit versus highway construction conflict began back in the 1940's with the District highway department arguing for roads and a private study urging that rail transit become the "backbone" of Washington's transportation system.

In 1957 the Highway Department submitted the comprehensive freeway plan which is still being debated today. They envisioned a downtown loop with connecting links to Maryland and, over a new bridge, to Virginia. Coincidentally, this plan was developed just one year after Congress enacted the Federal Highway Trust, which offered 90 percent government funds for highway construction.

Pressure from conservation groups and residents of a wealthy Washington area, Georgetown, finally forced planners to shelve construction plans for a leg of the freeway that would bisect that section. By the mid-1960's interest focused on the North Central Freeway, which would pave over homes and businesses in the city's predominantly black Northeast section, and on the Potomac River Bridge. The fight to prevent construction has been coordinated by the Emergency Committee for the Transportation Crisis (ECTC).

The political structure of the District of Columbia is unlike that of any other city or state in the nation since Congress exercises an unusually heavy hand in its affairs. In addition, the local public officials, because they are not elected, do not feel as responsible to the citizens as they might. Some details of ECTC's political tactics are, therefore, somewhat unique. It is their general style, structure, and degree of citizen involvement to which their success must be attributed, and in this sense ECTC can well serve as a model for other groups.

How Did ECTC Get Started?

In 1965, citizens in various neighborhoods were alarmed to discover that an interstate freeway was planned which would cut through their communities. The highway that would carry commuters from the suburbs in and out of the downtown area during rush hour would also carry the huge volume of interstate east coast car and truck traffic through their neighborhoods. Thousands of families would be displaced, parkland would be lost, the railroad right-of-way (which they hoped would be put back into use for commuter trains) would be taken for the freeway, and air, noise, and "eye" pollution would result.

In one community, a group was organized called the "Save Takoma Park Committee." In another, there was "Brookland for People and Trees." Four other neighborhoods had already banded together to form the "Metropolitan Citizens' Committee for Rapid Transit." There was also a "Committee for Urban Conservation," and a black group called "The D. C. Committee on the Freeway Crisis," and many other previously existing citizens groups which shared a common point of view toward this road and other similar highways planned for other sections of the city. A conference was held in September, 1965. From this the groups realized this multiplicity of organizations was too unwieldy for effective action which had to happen fast while the issue was hot. So the Emergency Committee on the Transportation Crisis was set up to coordinate actions for all interested groups. From that time on, any person or any group who opposed the urban freeways planned for Washington, D. C., could consider himself a member of ECTC.

Does ECTC Have Special Characteristics Which Have Contributed to Its Success?

The group is extremely broad-based. Not only does it represent all types of other groups, but in addition, its weekly meetings are regularly attended by an extraordinary diversity of people—black, white, rich, poor, suburban-types, inner-city residents, religious leaders, political activists, etc. All members of the group make efforts to get information that might be pertinent to the freeway struggle, and they circulate such information to every social sector in the city. But, the most important asset of the group is its commitment to action. They are seen and heard everywhere—operating on all levels at once.

How Is the Group Structured?

It has virtually no structure. There are various "officers," including many "vice-chairmen," but the titles are mainly for use on the letterhead. In effect, functions are assumed by whoever wants to do them or is best qualified to do them at any given moment. There are no "by-laws." The committee has come to pride itself on a rather loose, spontaneous way of doing things, remaining quite elastic so that responses to events can occur in whatever way seems best.

The fact that individuals feel free to take initiative is a major reason for ECTC's success. People are encouraged by the fact that all plans seem to be of equal worth. They are mutually supportive. Those who have felt stifled by bureaucracy in other groups feel at home in ECTC.

How Many Members Does ECTC Have?

No one knows the answer to this question. There are over 100 citizen associations involved. In a sense, all their members are also members of ECTC. As one member of the group put it: "The only membership necessary is to understand and approve the slogan—'not another inch of freeways'." Sharing in the activities of the group is the same as being a "member." There is a mailing list, but many who receive notices of ECTC activities do not consider themselves members. A routine weekly meeting draws, on the average, about 20 people. There are about 15 "regulars" and about 30 more who appear at almost all special meetings and at demonstrations. With a special effort, the group is able to get out several hundred people for an important event.

What About Leadership?

To a large extent, leadership tends to be spontaneous. Different members take the lead for different types of activities. However, the central figure in the group is Sammy Abbott. His official title is "Publicity Director." Sam, who is white, has long had an interest in politics—especially as they related to inner-city problems and the predicament of blacks. Before becoming involved in the D. C. freeway controversy, he had been active in civil rights struggles. His interest in roads may seem to be a departure from civil rights involvement, but this is not the case—particularly in D. C. Sam views both urban freeways and urban renewal as "an instrument of war" against the poor, black, urban population. This viewpoint has been the key to ECTC's success since D. C. has a black population of about 70 percent. Sam is gifted with a tremendous ability to recall political situations and to analyze them.

The chairman of the group is Reginald Booker, a young black man who is an articulate speaker and leader of the Washington Area Construction Industry Task Force which seeks equal job opportunities for blacks in the construction industry. The fact that he is involved in struggles that are purely for racial justice makes him a particularly valuable leader for ECTC because it increases the group's "credibility" in the black community.

What Is the Basic Philosophy of ECTC?

At the risk of oversimplifying, ECTC stresses the principles on which the United States' Constitution is based. They emphasize the equal worth of all people and the right of citizens to influence government decisions which will affect them. They also have a vision of a city as a place for people, for neighborhoods, for small business, for parks—i.e., a place to live. They view most road-building and urban renewal programs as big-business oriented, profit-making schemes, usually at the expense of city residents. They view the "automobile and high-rise building way of life" as fundamentally dehumanizing. To them homes, neighborhoods, and businesses should be an organic outgrowth of a decision-making process in which residents have a major role.

Transportation should be inexpensive and equally available to everyone. Public transportation is particularly important since it serves those who can't afford or choose not to own cars. In addition, it takes far less land. Each road or parking garage represents housing facilities that were not built—and housing is supposed to be a major priority of our nation. ECTC has a sociological outlook. Roads are always discussed in the context of the general urban crisis. (This puts "highway experts" on the defensive.)

Does ECTC Have a Staff, Paid Personnel, or an Office?

No. Several members of the committee work almost full-time for ECTC, but they are not paid. Working out of their homes and offices, they attend meetings of various organizations, make phone calls, write letters, prepare mailings, etc.

How Does the Group Get Money?

The group is not tax-exempt so no large sums have been acquired. Appeals for contributions are made in newsletters. A treasurer's report at meetings includes mention of any unmet financial obligations and special thanks for contributions. Individuals give whatever they can. There is no membership fee, however. The operating budget is very small, since the only major expense is payments to the printer for flyers and newsletters.

What Role Have the News Media Played?

A regular reader of the *Washington Post*, Washington's major daily newspaper, might well be unaware that a freeway controversy ever existed. Coverage of ECTC activities has been scandalously distorted, where it existed at all. The *Star*, another major newspaper, has done only slightly better. One member of the committee commented: "The real function of going to meetings was to find out what was going on, since it was not in the news." The *Afro-American,* a black-oriented publication, helped to publicize the racial aspects of the free-ways. Recently, the *D. C. Gazette,* a liberal, bi-weekly, "people-oriented" newspaper, has been outstanding. Recog-nizing the freeway controversy as a real issue, it has covered the matter with sympathy and enthusiastic support. The T.V. and radio stations have been unsympathetic for the most part, but they have recently begun to editorialize on the right of citizens to play a meaningful role in decision-making as far as freeways are concerned.

What Role Has ECTC Played in Public Hearings

An extremely active one! They call on many different or-ganizations and individuals to testify against freeways. They have brought in economists, black militants, conservationists, sociologists, etc. They challenge the testimony of the "ex-perts," exposing the inadequacies of a specialized point of view. Sometimes they upset the decorum of hearings—never suppressing their outrage when they feel that citizens are being unjustly treated. Their outspoken approach has made a few enemies, but it has made far more friends. More impor-tantly, it has kept the issues hot in the eyes of both the people and the public officials.

What Conclusions Can ECTC Draw From Their Fight?

ECTC members emphasize that quiet meetings, an organi-zational bureaucracy, and letter-writing, when not backed up by action, are not productive. An action-oriented group gets results. It gets attention from the politicians, and, most im-portant, from the people. They also emphasize the impor-tance of sharing in the activities of other organizations. (This aspect of the group's activities has not been discussed. One example will serve to illustrate the point: ECTC members joined in a demonstration to create a hospital employees' union and by that action won the support of that organiza-tion's membership in the anti-freeway fight.) Environ-mentalists are frequently accused of being "cop outs" by other social activists who charge them with "caring more for squirrels than they do for people." ECTC has never been so charged, because it has attempted to relate to the concerns of people in the communities.

Members of ECTC stress the following additional tactical points:

Keep a coalition broad-based so that different kinds of people can participate depending on what type of action is happening at the time.

Keep basic issues simple; don't allow complications to obscure the important issues or there will be little public understanding.

Always have a leaflet at special events for people who want to take something home.

Make use of slogans. ECTC's well-known mottoes are "Not another inch of freeway in D. C." and "White men's roads through black men's homes."

Politicize every issue. What happens depends directly upon politics, and usually has very little to do with technical points. Always attempt to expose the motivations of the highway-oriented politicians. Who is behind what plan and why? What connections do politicians have with highway interests?

Watch carefully for violations of laws and regulations. This sometimes takes research and checking, but such efforts are well worth it.

Stand strongly on principle as opposed to engaging in "deals" and "trade-offs." In other words, emphasize moral issues above all else.

Some citizen groups become discouraged when they find a hard-won victory quickly becoming meaningless as the highway interests simply switch tactics to get what they want. This is to be expected. For ECTC the interesting result is that the longer the battle continues, the more indefensible the tactics of the highway-men seem to become and the more the public rallies against them. One of the members of ECTC has expressed this philosophy as follows:

You just stand up and be a citizen, using your constitutional rights to make the law work for you as it should—as it must. You find out what's going on. You keep at it and you don't go away and you don't give up or get bought off. When what you are doing is fighting for human rights, then you keep standing up for them legally and morally. It's not how far the *citizens* will go—it's how far they will go to get or keep what they want. The violence is always really on their part.

Like most activist groups, ECTC's rich and colorful history resides only in the minds of participants, not on paper. A simple chronology of the struggle is not available. If it were it might take hundreds of pages; therefore, only some of the highlights of the five year fight can be shared.

March, 1966: Forced Release of "The Little Report" to the Public.

Arthur D. Little, Inc., had been contracted by the D. C. Highway Department to study the city's freeway plans. After completion, their report was kept secret. ECTC sent letters to public officials and newspapers. They then demonstrated with picket signs in front of the District Building (D. C.'s city hall). This demonstration was one of the few given good coverage by the press. The successful release of this report turned out to be a great blessing to the citizens of D. C., since the study found that the planning process had been totally inadequate and it recommended no further freeway construction in the District.

November, 1966: A Lawsuit Against the D. C. Highway Department (Final Decision, February, 1968).

The lawsuit was based on procedural illegalities in the planning process used by the Highway Department in deciding to build certain interstate freeways in the city. A large law firm, Covington & Burling, supplied the citizen groups with lawyers at a special rate. Groups raised money to pay the lawyers, whose total fee came to approximately $12,000. The portion of the case with the greatest significance concerned hearing procedures and the applicability of local statutes in Interstate project hearings. A large number of hearing procedures were challenged by the lawyers. One official public hearing notice, for example, appeared in the classified section of the paper, where very few citizens would be likely to see it. In another instance, a hearing location was changed one day prior to the start of the hearings, so that many citizens were unable to learn of the change in time.

The case was first decided in favor of the highway officials by the lower court, but citizens appealed the decision. The Court of Appeals then ruled resoundingly in the citizens' favor. All the roads in the suit were termed illegal. A precedent was set showing that interstate highway officials must still obey local statutes as well as those in the Federal-Aid Highway Act setting forth requirements for interstate projects. The courts then can be used to enjoin freeway construction until all planning laws and requirements are complied with.

June, 1968: ECTC Convened a National Conference Which Established the National Coalition on the Transportation Crisis (NCTC).

A great many American cities were represented. They included Baltimore, Boston, Brighton, Mass., Cambridge, Mass., Camden, N. J., Columbia, S. C., Nashville, Tenn., New York City, New Orleans, Indianapolis, Ossining, N. Y., Parkersburgh, W. Va., Philadelphia, Seattle, Birmingham and Montgomery, Alabama, and Washington, D. C. The chief value of this conference, and a subsequent one, was to open channels of communication between citizen groups in different cities. They have been able to benefit from each other's experience.

December, 1968: Official Planning Commission and the City Council Officially Reject the Notion of an Automobile-Dominated City.

ECTC members "haunted" their public officials for approximately two years. The meetings of the National Capitol Planning Commission had always been rather routine, private affairs, but commissioners began to find themselves constantly in the company of people who demanded the right to public participation in the planning process. Citizens persuaded the planners to hold "informational" hearings before they held official public hearings on the formal plans for the city. ECTC provided the planners with vast quantities of reports by experts on the harmful effects of too many roads and automobiles in cities. They also submitted documents and testimony showing the interesting possibilities of a pedestrian-oriented downtown area, and provided sound critiques of the highway department's claims of the "need" for new roads. ECTC also attempted to show that documents recommending freeways are often planned to justify freeways before they begin and do not necessarily have the interests of the general public at heart. Finally, they emphasized the positive aspects of public transportation.

The document for which the planners were responsible and which would have a major effect on D. C.'s future development was a regional comprehensive transportation plan. At the final hearings, big business and highway interests testified in favor of freeways, but citizen groups and small businessmen were overwhelmingly opposed. The National Capitol Planning Commission responded to the citizens' pleas by modifying their plan so as to delete freeways, and the City Council ratified the modified plan.

January, 1969: Mayor Intervenes to Stop Highway Department from Taking Private Homes.

The Highway Department began taking homes in the neighborhood of Brookland to clear an area for construction of the North Central Freeway, even though the legality of this road was being contested in court at the time. (To mention an enlightening detail—the relocation office which was supposed to help the displacees find new homes consisted of nothing but a telephone and the classified sections of the daily papers.) ECTC's first step was to send a registered letter to the Mayor asking that the homes not be taken until the lawsuit had been decided. There was no response to this letter. The next action was picketing at the Mayor's house. The citizens hoped that press coverage of this dramatic demonstration would bring them outspoken support from other city groups. Since the press had purposefully ignored some of ECTC's demonstrations in the past, ECTC used the interesting tactic of calling the police instead of calling the newspapers and T.V. stations directly. The tactic worked; word of the plans spread fast. Many different people, including priests and even fellow anti-highway people, telephoned and attempted to dissuade the group from picketing. But the action went as planned.

The Mayor responded by inviting a delegation to proceed to the District Building where he would meet with them. He even sent what one citizen described as a "warm, purring limousine" to entice the ECTC delegation to proceed to the meeting, but the group refused to bargain. They wanted all the citizens of Brookland to meet with the Mayor and the highway officials who were responsible for taking the homes. As an alternative, they publicly invited the Mayor to come to Brookland, and he accepted. ECTC thus scored a major success because they refused to "do business" in small delegations.

The next stage of the battle—to impress the Mayor with the reality of the homeowners' plight was the character of the meeting between the citizens and officials. ECTC spokesmen and others demanded that discussion of general freeway plans be replaced with attentive focus on the homes. As a result of a flier, over 300 angry people showed up and hassled the officials, refusing to allow the diversion of their attention into general issues. It worked! The Mayor sent out an order the next day to cease the taking of the homes for a road still being disputed in the courts.

August, 1969: Disorder at Three Sisters Bridge Hearing.

The City Council, which had declared its opposition to certain freeways in D. C., was threatened by Congressional Representatives Brock Adams from the state of Washington Representative Joel Broyhill from Virginia, and by Representative William Natcher from Kentucky. The Council was told that federal payment to D. C., which represented 13 percent of the city's budget, might be withheld unless the Council ordered immediate construction of the Three Sisters Bridge. This bridge had been previously declared illegal by the courts, and had been officially rejected by the National Capitol Planning Commission and the City Council itself.

ECTC members were upset, needless to say, and came to the Council meeting where the deciding vote was to be taken. The Council would not listen to the citizens' testimony and abruptly adjourned the meeting. The vote was rescheduled for a subsequent meeting which followed an unusual pattern from start to finish. The first oddity was that enraged citizens were specifically invited to attend. The predicted pro-freeway vote was much publicized ahead of time. When citizens arrived, they found what appeared to be a specially arranged reception. The room was filled with police and it was not long before the scene deteriorated into what many ECTC members refer to as a "police riot." The scuffling started after police moved to break up the crowd because they were chanting "NO FREEWAYS—NO FREEWAYS." The choruses of citizen protest resulted from a refusal of the Council to grant them five minutes to state the anti-freeway case. When the clash was over, there were 14 citizens arrested and the predicted pro-freeway vote was taken. A Councilman informed remaining citizens that for the rest of the meeting there would be "wall to wall police" and that he hoped they had been taught a lesson. In addition, it was later reported that there had been a congratulatory phone call to the Mayor on the Council vote from the White House.

October, 1969: Major Demonstration at the Three Sisters Bridge.

October fifteenth was "Moratorium Day" when thousands of students were in a mood to demonstrate. It was also the time when construction was to begin on the controversial Three Sisters Bridge, which had been declared illegal in the courts (February, 1968), and had been rejected by the planning commission and the City Council (December, 1968) in their official plans for the city. But Congress had ordered its construction and the City Council had caved in under threat of loss of federal payment (August, 1969). The issue was far from being a technical transportation issue at this point; it was a moral issue of the first order.

Students set the style of the demonstration. They "occupied" the Three Sisters Islands, over which the bridge was to cross and attracted the attention of national press with their demand that the United Nations recognize these islands as a sovereign state, thus making them immune to Congressional legislation. They also held a "sit-in" on the construction equipment, preventing its use and provoking the arrest of 141 people, which also attracted press coverage. Several national publications presented the full story, giving the citizens of D. C. a chance to gain the support of people in many parts of the nation. Once informed, several national conservation organizations and the League of Women Voters offered their support.

November, 1969: Unofficial Public Referendum Organized.

D. C. citizens do not have an elected governing body, nor do they elect Congressional delegates, but they do vote for members of the school board. About 3,000 citizens petitioned the Board of Elections to include a referendum regarding the freeways on the ballot during the school board election. Petition was denied. The citizen groups prepared their own "unofficial" referendum. Representatives were stationed at each polling place on election day, and each voter, after he filed his ballot for the school board, was presented with an opportunity to respond to the referendum question. Eighty-four percent of those responding rejected construction of the controversial Three Sisters Bridge and associated freeways. In two respects, the unofficial referendum succeeded. It increased awareness of the freeway issue among voters, and it offered proof that the citizens of D. C. did not want the new roads.

December, 1969: Bus Boycott Organized to Dramatize Inadequacies of D. C. Public Transportation.

ECTC decided on the boycott as an extremely effective way to demonstrate the plight of the bus-riding public, even though a totally successful boycott would be impossible to achieve because people could not supply enough alternative transportation. It also gave ECTC an opportunity to get the press coverage they needed to explain what was wrong with bus service in D. C. and what could be done to improve public transportation. Official and unofficial discussions continue as to what the government should do about D. C. Transit, and citizens' attitudes can form a vitally important background for these discussions. It is this last fact which made the largely "unsuccessful" boycott an important citizen action.

The Present: ECTC Has Helped Create a Climate Where the Congress Uses Unconstitutional "Blackmail" Tactics to Force Road-Building on the District of Columbia.

After the 1968 Court of Appeals decision that D. C. freeways were illegal, the city had two options: They could either appeal to the Supreme Court, or they could give up and hold proper hearings. Neither option looked promising. The Supreme Court was likely to agree with the Court of Appeals, and the hearings were likely to be unpleasant since ECTC's extensive "educational" program had left many citizens extremely angry.

But a most unlikely development provided a way out. The House Public Works Committee—Subcommittee on Roads, chaired by John Klucynski (D.-Illinois), originated a bill ordering certain of the controversial roads to be built—court decisions to the contrary! Hearings of the bill were held at which ECTC spokesmen expressed strong views, including the possibility that rioting might result if the wishes of the people were ignored. They also picketed the Mayor's home. This picketing took place on the evening after Martin Luther King was shot. It is an interesting commentary on the insight into the freeway controversy by the *Washington Post* that their newsmen accused the demonstrators of setting up a diversion, purposefully drawing police away from the downtown areas where blacks were rioting. They completely missed the point that the people were objecting to the forcing of freeways on D. C. by out-of-state congressmen.

The next day ECTC members met with several sympathetic members of the House Public Works Committee who helped by filing an extremely convincing "minority report." As a result of these efforts, that particular bill was defeated. However, the same type of mandate appeared later as Section 23 of the Federal-Aid Highway Act of 1968. ECTC mounted a massive lobbying effort just before the House vote which was successfully postponed for three days, but the bill was then passed. From there, it went into a House-Senate conference, and ECTC lobbied the conferees. Perhaps because of this, Section 23 was modified. The final version ordered the Three Sisters Bridge to be built immediately (it is now the subject of a separate lawsuit), and an eighteen month study to begin on the other roads.

The Future: A Battle for the People to Gain Control over Their Environment.

ECTC expects to carry past struggles into the future. Highway interests and thoughtless suburban dwellers are still determined to rip through Washington with a two-block-wide concrete swath, but they may learn to disguise their intentions. In other parts of the country, highways are being presented as components of more comprehensive projects that are billed as essential to urban well-being. Under these wrappings, the unwitting public may be persuaded to accept the demolition of their communities to make way for the automobile.

The three most common of the new approaches are urban renewal projects, design concept teams, and area-wide urban planning for metropolitan regions. In each case professionals pose as "experts" who have the interest of the urban public at heart—but who often act upon the values of suburban dwellers instead.

Urban renewal projects have already won a bad reputation among their victims, who with justice have labelled the approach "Negro removal." Too often these are profit-making schemes which treat neighborhoods as real estate. Large, low-rate parking lots are often designed into urban renewal projects. Availability of parking has been shown to encourage more automobilized transit. What happens in effect is that people are removed to make way for cars.

Highway planners have begun to gather landscape architects, economists, sociologists and other such professionals to study and plan new roads and neighboring facilities like roadside parks, playgrounds, and air rights housing. This grouping is called the design concept team. Its advantages over planning by politicians are obvious; when the team is brought together by the community to serve the community's interests, it is an invaluable aid. However, in some circumstances, the design team is no more than a tool for selling a highway project. This happens when the team accepts as its goal the construction of a road, not the service of the community through which the road will travel. It is under these conditions that design teams have promoted air rights housing (homes built over roads). Due to auto pollution, such housing is hazardous to the dwellers' health; the huge apartment building over the Cross Bronx Expressway on the Manhattan end of the George Washington Bridge is a notorious example.

Similarly, regional planning programs are potential enemies of urban communities, if projects are developed that are not responsive to the needs of the urban dwellers. Traditionally the inner-city resident has been least able to convince others of his particular needs. Suburban dwellers, fewer in number but wealthier, better educated, white and therefore more politically powerful, have controlled most regional decision-making. In the D. C. area this has been accomplished by a group called the Council of Governments. Each suburban government represented on the council gets one vote. The District (the city of Washington) gets one vote. Suburban interests invariably win out.

In addition to the suburban-urban conflict, the District of

Columbia is faced with direct pressure from Congress. Because of attempted congressional blackmail to force freeway construction, construction of the city's subway system has almost ground to a halt from lack of money several times. It is still being built only because of an unusual loan from the Department of Transportation. The city is in suspense to find out what will happen when the loan expires. As of this writing work on the notorious Three Sisters Bridge has been stopped by a court injunction, pending a new set of hearings.

ECTC and other D. C. citizen groups look forward to their "big day in court." The congressional mandates seem totally unconstitutional. They represent the extreme to which public officials will go when their wishes do not coincide with the wishes of the people. D. C. citizens may have to take their case as far as the Supreme Court, where they may ultimately win.

For ECTC and other urban citizen groups, the future will consist of work to gain control over their own environments. The struggle will continue until all governing political bodies make certain that human and ecological values dominate planning. The achievement of this dictates a future of hard work.

clean air bill:
analysis of pressure

In 1967, Congress passed the Air Quality Act. Although it was not the first piece of air pollution legislation, it was widely hailed as the one which would finally work. The Act was greeted with exuberant praise from all sectors, and it was assumed that the air crisis in the United States would quickly disappear. Once more, it seemed, Congress had taken a difficult problem by the horns and mastered it. Air pollution was obviously to be relegated to an historical niche in this country.

Thus relieved, Congress moved on to other pressing issues, complacently confident that the new law would soon show its effects. But by 1970, enough citizen dissatisfaction had been evidenced that the lawmakers realized that, for some reason, the air was not getting any cleaner. Even Washington, D. C., not noted for its heavy industry, was being taxed by oppressive air pollution—the Smithsonian Institution announced in that year that the nation's capital was receiving 16 percent less sunlight than in 1920. Something had gone wrong with the Air Quality Act.

The 1967 Act, modeled after its two-year-old sister law, the Water Quality Act of 1965, is a fairly complicated piece of legislation. Directed primarily against factories, power plants, and other stationary emission sources, the Act utilized a peculiar method to control their pollution. Instead of declaring absolute limits on the volume of emissions that are permitted, it based its enforcement upon what is known as ambient air standards. Ambient air is defined as the air which circulates in or passes through an area, as opposed to the air directly around a chimney, smokestack or exhaust pipe. The act authorized the National Air Pollution Control Administration (NAPCA) of the Department of Health, Education and Welfare (HEW) to set up air quality control regions across the nation (these now number 91) and then to request the various states to determine the optimum ambient air standards for each major pollutant for each region. Each polluter in the region would then be allotted a certain part of the pollution—air pollution in the U. S. would essentially be rationed!

Not only was a significant burden placed on each state by virtue of its having to determine 30 or 40 different pollutant standards, but enforcement was also complicated, tedious, slow and often inefficient due to built-in checks and balances in the law. On the books the Air Quality Act looked powerful, but in actual fact intransigent polluters were able to circumvent its force.

Although some critics may have realized the Act's shortcomings in 1967, few predicted the real reason it was destined to fail. It was doomed because it paid little heed to the chief perpetrator of our air pollution—the automobile. About the automobile the Air Quality Act made no reference. Under the Clean Air Act—as the whole bundle of federal air pollution legislation is called—the secretary of HEW is authorized to set emissions limits on auto pollutants, but this procedure has never worked adequately. By the provisions of the Act, NAPCA's testing mechanism is slow and cumbersome and the agency is not permitted to force vehicle recalls due to malfunctioning pollution control devices. Furthermore, the automobile industry is allowed to submit prototype vehicles rather than assembly line models for inspection.

A considerable amount of air pollution legislation was under consideration by both the House of Representatives and the Senate throughout 1970. The Clean Air Act was to be amended and upgraded in lieu of both new technical information and the experience in the ambient air quality regions, as well as the surge in public awareness about the cause, costs and effects of air pollution. In the House, the committee which handles all air pollution legislation, the Interstate and Foreign Commerce Committee, progressed rapidly in the study of various bills and in June reported H. R. 17255, the Clean Air Act Amendments of 1970.

Unfortunately, the bill was not all it could have been, and, in fact, contained no truly new attempts to deal with the air crisis which had steadily been getting worse since 1967. Because of the inadequacies they saw in H. R. 17255, several congressmen, led by Leonard Farbstein of New York, decided to offer four amendments to the bill when it reached the House floor within the following few weeks. The amendments called for:

1. *Substituting a more stringent provision regulating the composition of automotive fuel.* The one the committee agreed upon was strongly backed by Representative David Satterfield of Virginia, in whose district the Ethyl Corporation is located. Ethyl is the major producer of the lead in gasoline, and Satterfield pressed the committee to include provisions in the bill that would make it very difficult to ban lead from general use.

2. *Authorizing voluntary inspection of auto emission control devices in operation over 4000 miles.* Strong penalties would be assigned if the manufacturer refused to fix the defect and modify the general design if a pattern of defects was uncovered. The committee bill had no clause to this effect.

3. *Establishing as minimum national automotive emission standards for 1971, 1972 and 1974, standards already adopted by the state of California. The* committee did not propose any such modifications of the 1967 Act.

4. *Establishing auto emission standards on the basis of the cleanest feasible propulsion system.* This would involve the phasing out of large horsepower engines which could not meet the standards.

A number of national environmental organizations immediately began making plans to actively support the Farbstein amendments. These included Environmental Action, Friends of the Earth, Sierra Club, Oil, Chemical and Atomic Workers International Union, and Zero Population Growth. Other national organizations voiced their support, as did local groups from New York, Washington, Philadelphia, St. Louis, Chicago and elsewhere.

Once the loose coalition was formed, the apparatus for organized expression of citizen will was set in motion. Mailings were sent out by many of the coalition members to their constituents, informing them of the opportunity to pass a strong

piece of air pollution legislation and asking them to inform
their congressmen to support the package of amendments on
the floor. The congressmen themselves gathered sponsors for
their amendments and so informed their colleagues of the bill
itself and the improvements they proposed (known as a
"Dear Colleague" letter).

Environmental Action also prepared lobbying packets for
all congressmen. These contained basic information on air
pollution, how the situation had deteriorated in the last decade, and what role the automobile played in the deterioration. The packet emphasized particularly the fact that the
technology available for implementing stricter standards for
auto emissions did exist, but that Detroit had chosen to ignore and underplay its existence.

Hardly had the forces for strengthening the bill been lined
up and the strategy decided upon, when a parliamentary maneuver stopped them cold. Through a quirk in the procedure
by which a bill moves from committee to the House floor,
H.R. 17255 was scheduled for a near-immediate vote. The
Rules Committee, which makes this and other decisions, had
a time slot which had to be filled in the third week of June,
and the Clean Air Act Amendments was chosen.

Although it is a logical deduction that the automotive and
petroleum lobbies had a hand in the choice of the bill's date,
this is probably not the case. Observers agree that although
huge in comparison to the environmentalists', General Motors' Washington crew is relatively impotent and untrusted in
Congress. Even though other automotive interests are somewhat better organized, they probably did not affect the bill's
scheduling either. Had the environmental lobbyists exerted
pressure on Democratic leadership over the scheduling of the
bill by the Rules Committee, H.R. 17255 probably would not
have been selected for the next day's slot. But without understanding what was happening, and expecting a later date for
the bill's debate on the floor, the Clear Air supporters lost the
time needed to attempt to lobby House members.

The bill came before a House which was 99 percent unaware of its ramifications. The Committee Report, which describes the bill, translates its complicated language, and contains minority dissenting views, had been printed only that
morning and had not been read by any of the congressmen.
News of the amendments to be offered from the floor, their

contents and significance had not been circulated. Mail from home districts had barely begun to trickle in. It was an election year and a year of strong environmental concern and rhetoric, and voting against such a bill took courage most congressmen did not have.

The Clear Air Act Amendments was passed by the House 374 to 1 (Farbstein opposing) and the congressman's four amendments were all defeated. In their first major test, the coalition had scored one vote—so they turned their sights to the Senate.

Fairly early in the summer a significant contribution to the public debate on the causes, cures and costs of air pollution was published. *Vanishing Air* by John Esposito. This report, compiled by the Nader Task Force on Air Pollution, outlined the serious lags that existed with previous air pollution legislation, the generally callous disregard by industry of the seriousness of the situation, the recent scientific studies done of the dangerous health effects of various pollutants, the extent of the problem in both urban and rural areas, and particularly the lack of any real attempt to deal, either in Detroit or Washington, with the largest polluter of all, the internal combustion engine. With such a glaring revelation of gaps in legislation and the evidence of the complete lack of any meaningful action by industry, a clearer picture began to emerge of what the minimum provisions of any tough air pollution bill would have to be.

With John Esposito of the Nader Task Force acting as legal consultant, Environmental Action drew up an 18-point "Plan for Clean Air." The 18 points were enumerated and explained, and an alternate version stating the proposals in proper legislative language was also prepared. The automotive package was introduced into the Senate by Senator Gaylord Nelson and in the House by a bi-partisan group of congressmen. It passed to the Senate Subcommittee on Air and Water Pollution for consideration during its July session. Nelson added one further provision—that the internal combustion engine not be sold after 1975—in an effort to impress upon the committee his and others' strong environmental concern.

What follows is a fairly detailed summary of the Plan for Clean Air as submitted by Environmental Action. The first point was later altered to require a 90 percent reduction in automotive emissions by 1975, which is approximately the feasible limit of the internal combustion engine.

A PLAN FOR CLEAN AIR

. . . (Our current pollution problems) must be rectified as follows:

1. *Declare that, by 1975, the Secretary of Health, Education and Welfare shall set automotive emission standards which are as stringent as the emission characteristics of the Rankine Cycle Engine* (sometimes called the steam car). This engine is presently feasible and has emission characteristics which are much lower than the internal combustion engine can ever hope to achieve.

2. *Require the Secretary to set oxides of nitrogen standards for 1973, instead of 1975 as now planned.* Oxides of nitrogen contain the catalytic agent which interacts with sunlight to produce hazardous photochemical smog. The smog problem cannot be solved without early control of oxides of nitrogen. Control devices for this pollutant can be made available for 1973 model year cars.

3. *Require the Secretary to establish procedures for testing production line cars to ascertain that these cars comply with the emission characteristics of their prototypes.* (At present the National Air Pollution Control Administration tests only prototypes on a systematic basis.) A 10 percent failure rate of the production line cars would trigger a decertification of the automobiles in question so that they could not be sold in the United States.

4. *Require that the Secretary test large numbers of cars actually in use at various mileage intervals.* A 10 percent failure rate would require the manufacturer to recall and repair the defective control systems. This provision is needed to assure that cars in use do not exceed federal standards after 10,000 or 15,000 miles of operation, as has been the case.

5. A provision such as number 4 should be supplemented by a requirement that automobile manufacturers warrant the proper operation of air pollution control devices for a minimum of 50,000 miles. *A warranty provision would give automobile owners themselves legal*

standing to bring suit in the event that their devices did not operate properly and the Secretary fails to take action.

6. *Require that the Secretary's test procedures for prototypes, production line vehicles and automobiles in use be geared to differing driving and weather patterns throughout the nation.* The present test patterns are based on conditions in Los Angeles and are totally inappropriate for stop-and-start patterns in other climates.

7. *Empower the Secretary to regulate the composition of all fuels without meeting the cumbersome burden provided in the House version of the law.* HEW takes the position that it does not presently have the authority to ban lead from gasoline, despite the fact that lead is clearly a toxic and dangerous material.

8. *Empower the Secretary to permit states with special air pollution problems to set automotive emission standards for new cars where these standards are more stringent than the federal regulations.* California was granted such an exemption and experience has shown that other states have problems as unique as those of California. Those states which show an inclination to develop stronger controls should be encouraged to do so. Giving the Secretary the power to review a state's standard before it would be able to embark on its own program would avoid regulations which disrupt any national programs.

9. *Fleet vehicles such as taxicab fleets, vehicles owned by states and the federal government should be required to purchase automobiles which operate on lead-free, 91-octane gasoline beginning with model year 1971.* Detroit has announced that it will begin to build such cars in 1971 and large fleets should be required to use them.

10. *The Secretary should be required, within two years, to set emissions levels for all pollutants from all industrial sources over a certain size.* This should be done by a series of public hearings throughout the country, with an opportunity for all sides to present evidence. The standards would be based on the findings of the Secretary resulting from these hearings. These standards would apply to all sources covered by the law and would not depend upon the publication of the detailed reports

now required by law. States should have three months after the promulgation of a standard to develop implementation and enforcement plans which required that the sources applied the most effective control techniques or switched to low polluting fuels.

11. *Industrial facilities which failed to meet those standards or comply with implementation and enforcement plans should be subject to heavy daily fines and criminal sanctions.*

12. *Polluters, at their own cost and in accordance with guidelines established by the Secretary, should monitor their emissions and report them at frequent intervals to the Secretary.*

13. *The Secretary should be required to commence an immediate investigation into the availability of low polluting fuels.* Given full subpoena powers, powers to inspect sites and records, the Secretary should be required, within one year, to report to Congress on the availability of low sulfur coal and oil, natural gas and other low polluting fuels. The fuels industry has almost total control over this information and loosens its grip only when its own economic interest is served. To a large extent air pollution policy is fuels policy. The Secretary and the Congress cannot be expected to plan for clean air without total access to information concerning the availability of low polluting fuels.

14. *The Secretary must be given full power to inspect facilities, records and full powers to subpoena records and witnesses.*

15. *The term "economic and technological feasibility" must be expunged from the air pollution laws.* This term has prevented the Secretary from setting standards ahead of technology in order to spur innovation in control by the polluters themselves. Instead, the federal government has in effect been forced by this phrase to subsidize industry research through grants to develop controls which are "economically and technologically feasible."

16. *Citizens must be given standing to bring suits in federal court—either as individuals or as a class—to redress any rights given them under the new air pollution laws.* No administrative agency can ever hope to deal with every aspect of this problem and citizen interest

should be marshaled as an important supplement to administrative action. The citizen suit provision should provide for injunctive relief, damages and court costs.

17. *The annual budget of the National Air Pollution Control Administration should be raised from its present level of slightly over $100 million to $500 million annually.* Enforcement powers become hypothetical if the agency lacks the resources to use them.

18. *Court review of any administrative determinations made under the new law should not be* de novo (i.e., shall not permit the introduction of new evidence into court, thus permitting the court to judge the case a second time). Standard administrative law requires only that the court review the administrative record. This is a much more expeditious approach and would abort the polluters' standard policy ploy of delaying final action by protracted litigation.

In August, 1970, the Subcommittee of Air and Water Pollution and its chairman, Senator Edmund Muskie, reported out the proposed National Air Quality Standards Act of 1970 which contained most points outlined in the Plan for Clean Air with the glaring exception of the tenth. How did a group of environmental lobbyists who two months ago could not achieve an amendment to one bill manage to accomplish this?

First of all, the coalition which had been so unsuccessful in the House of Representatives did not collapse in the face of defeat. In fact, it became immeasurably stronger as a diversity of new groups swelled its ranks—the International Conference of Police Associations, the International Brotherhood of Pulp, Paper and Sulphite Workers, National Audubon Society, United Automobile Workers, National Farmer's Union and the Wilderness Society. Endorsements and valuable help were also received from the United Steelworkers of America, National Tuberculosis and Respiratory Diseases Association, New York's Mayor John Lindsay, the AFL-CIO, and the National League of Cities and U. S. Conference of Mayors. Finally America had rallied behind the cry of Clean Air, and this coalition was unparalleled in the history of U. S. environmental politics. The total membership of these organizations numbers in the millions.

Of course, coalitions do not just "happen." The coordina-

tion of this vast collection of groups took long hours of pa-
tient discussion, explaining, persuading, writing and telephon-
ing. The results, however, were dramatic. Local groups and
coalitions were formed to endorse the goals of the Plan for
Clean Air and worked to get local and national politicians to
take a strong stand on clean air. Letters poured in to senators
and to the subcommittee—letters which were doubly strong
since they enumerated specific points rather than merely asking support of the whole package. Mayors of hundreds of
towns added their endorsements to the list.

The coalition did not only rely on grass roots response
from the nation; it also publicized its activities and concern
through the media. Press conferences were called to announce the coalition and its various additions. Senators and
congressmen introduced parts of the plan to let the colleagues on the subcommittee know that there was a receptive
ear throughout the Senate and House for tough legislation.

In July, Nature too conspired to help exert pressure on the
subcommittee. Los Angeles was plagued with extra-strong
smog and the east coast was hit by a temperature inversion
which sent carbon monoxide and sulfur dioxide levels soaring
from New York to Atlanta. Washington, a city where over
80 percent of the air pollution is caused by the automobile,
was one of the worst hit parts of the eastern seaboard, and
for once citizens and legislators really became frightened.

The key role that Senator Muskie played should not be
overlooked. As chairman of the subcommittee and a powerful member of the full Committee on Public Works, no
strong air pollution bill could have been reported out without
his strong initiative and support. The professional staff of the
subcommittee and full committee also displayed a fervor for
more relevant legislation.

Muskie was placed in an interesting position by eco-activists. Over the previous few years he had slowly gained the
title of "Mr. Clean," at least among slogan-happy newsmen.
In terms of his Senate stature and particularly his Presidential
aspirations, this was a nickname he was particularly proud
of, and one that he could ill afford to lose in 1970. Esposito's
book, however, blasted Muskie along with many others for
using the environmental banner without realizing how far he
would have to go with it to make it carry weight. *Vanishing
Air* pointed out that heretofore the subcommittee had always

reached compromises with business on bills which attempted to save the environment.

Others were also pushed into a corner by the circumstances of the issue. With Muskie concerned about losing his leadership role, Republicans were worried that, if the bill failed, the Senator could later charge that Nixon's party was the one that was subverting legislation that all America wanted. The GOP decided that it was better to have Muskie gain credit for a strong air bill than pin the blame for a weak one on them.

It should also be pointed out that in terms of sheer numbers it is easier to deal with a 9-man subcommittee and a 15-man full committee than with a 435-member House. In this case there was time to bring together effective pressure from a single state; there were continuing attempts to have the person with the greatest credibility or influence deal with each Senator.

Upon the completion of the subcommittee version of the bill, the Committee on Public Works went into several executive (secret) sessions to change, accept or reject the subcommittee version. It was at this point that the full forces of the "other side" were brought to bear. The halls of the Senate were cluttered with almost every industrial lobbyist in town. A spot check revealed the following individuals and organizations attempting to bring pressure to bear to water down the bill:

> Edward Cole, president of General Motors
> John Riccardo, president of Chrysler Corporation
> G. C. Meyers, vice-president of American Motors
> Lee Iacocca, executive vice-president of Ford Motor Company
> Thomas Mann, president of the Automobile Manufacturers Association
> N. H. Gammelgard, vice-president of the American Petroleum Institute
> M. G. Dial, Jr., regional vice-president of Union Carbide
> Lloyd Cutler, Washington attorney and representative for the Automobile Manufacturers Association

There were also representatives from the National Lead Association, the American Mining Congress, the Manufacturing Chemists Association, the National Coal Policy Conference, and from the airline and airframe industries. Also included were Fred Bowditch (General Motors), Charles Heinan (Chrysler), and Edward Misch (Ford), the top emissions specialists of the three corporations.

On August 27, word was leaked to Environmental Action that a meeting was taking place between 20 to 30 automobile lobbyists and the staff of the Public Works Committee. It was also noted that a sign hung on the chamber door which said "Closed Session."

Environmental Action's legislative coordinator, Barbara Reid, immediately informed the coalition and called the committee to protest the closed meeting. She was told that the sign had been placed there inadvertently, and that anyone else was free to join the proceedings. Coalition representatives arrived in time to catch the last half hour of the discussion.

At the session, company representatives had rallied their most powerful resources and materials to stop the legislation from being approved. Leon Billings, one of the committee staff members, later told the *National Journal* that industry was essentially asking the subcommittee to undo everything it had done and noted that the meeting became "acrimonious." The automobile companies maintained again that the proposed deadlines could not be met, and they submitted alternate legislative materials.

Although the meeting had, apparently, not changed the minds of the staff members, the coalition protested vehemently, and demanded a similar meeting the next day during which they could reaffirm their side and resubmit arguments opposing the most recent claims of the industry. The request was granted, and marked the first time that such a meeting had ever taken place between environmental forces and committee staff members. In a larger sense, it marked the first recognition of environmental lobbyists as the equal of business lobbyists.

In the few hours they had to prepare for the Saturday morning meeting on August 28, the coalition brought together an impressive amount of material and support. Witnesses were rushed in from New York (including the city's air pollution administrator) and elsewhere, and the four-hour session was a success. It was an even greater success in the media, where the underdog environmentalists were publicized for their vigilance and their success in demanding equal congressional time.

The very nature of the legislation and the tactics used by the environmental coalition posed great problems for the industrial lobbyists. On the one hand, they were dead set against the stringent legislation; on the other, they couldn't let the public know this. When the coalition released the evidence that it had concerning the high-pressure industrial lobbying to the press, industry could only retreat further into secrecy. There was no way this anti-legislation action could be reconciled with Earth Day speeches and national advertising campaigns.

In stark contrast to the earlier House contest, the coalition this time could do no wrong. Publicity only strengthened the environmentalist hand and weakened that of the industrialist. Furthermore, publicity freed the individual senators from the common arm-twisting that industry frequently used—no senator could afford to oppose the Clean Air Bill when the health and well-being of his constituents were at stake, particularly if they were watching. The tremendous amount of publicity the coalition generated meant that little could be done in secret this time.

In the wake of the diverse group backing tough legislation, the grass roots support, the publicity attendant upon the deliberations, the full committee reported out the National Air Quality Standards Act of 1970, S. 4358, with every major provision the subcommittee recommended. The only significant change was the possibility of an extension of the 90 percent reduction in automobile emissions by one year, to be determined by the Secretary of HEW and subject to judicial review by citizen petition. In view of the fact that Detroit wanted no deadline named and a continuation of the then NAPCA guidelines calling for such a reduction in emissions by 1980, this was a real victory indeed. No one, least of all the coalition, would have predicted such success only eight weeks earlier.

The committee reported it out unanimously. Ten days later, on September 22, 1970, it passed on the Senate floor, 73-0. The only significant opposition came from Michigan's

Senator Robert Griffin, but even he was unwilling to buck the nationwide tide in support of this legislation.

Even after the unanimous Senate vote, the fate of the Clean Air Bill (still officially designated H.R. 17255) was quite uncertain. Since the two houses of Congress had passed dissimilar versions of the legislation, the bill was slated to go to a House-Senate Conference Committee where the differences would be ironed out. Fourteen conferees were chosen from the two congressional committees involved, the Senate Committee on Public Works and the House Committee on Interstate and Foreign Commerce. Under conference rules, a majority from each side is required to report out legislation.

In its configuration, the conference committee was strongly divided. The senators, who had worked for months to devise a strong bill, had a mandate from their peers to keep the legislation powerful. The representatives tended to have far less interest in the field, and were backed by the initial overwhelming House support for their weaker version.

The conferees met for the first time on October 8, 16 days after the Senate vote. Although the first meeting was meant only to be a preliminary one during which each side could "feel the other out," it was surprisingly productive. A temporary agreement was reached whereby the House agreed to the Senate's deadlines on emission reduction dates in return for a provision authorizing the National Academy of Sciences to submit an advisory study of the existing anti-pollution technology at the time of those deadlines.

Both sides were optimistic at the end of the meeting, and it was hoped that the bill would be quickly resolved. Unfortunately, two outside factors came into play. The first was the November election, which was becoming a preoccupation. The second was a personality conflict. Senator Muskie, whose strong earlier efforts had been duly noted by the press, attempted to reap additional political gains from his position on the conference committee. Although his attempts resulted in very little publicity, Republicans on the committee were angered, and they took steps to slow the progress of the bill.

On November 16, Congress reconvened to finish its backlogged business. The conference committee was scheduled to resume its discussions on November 18. On the 17th, however, a single letter threw all the proceedings into confusion. The letter, signed by Secretary of HEW Elliot Richardson, contained the Nixon Administration's views on the issue. Point by point it outlined a preference for a weaker bill: asking for authority for the Secretary of HEW to extend continually the auto emission deadline; asking for a weaker warranty section (vital for enforcement of the deadline); suggesting that citizens should not have the right to sue administration officials as well as polluters for non-enforcement; supporting a move to forbid states to set stricter emission standards for automobiles.

The committee's solidarity was suddenly destroyed. The conferees began to feel pressure from industry and government, and the momentum of the earlier arguments began to falter. This shift did not go unnoticed. Environmental activists had been watching the committee closely, despite the fact that the bill had faded from the public's eye. They countered industry's pressure, and attacked Secretary Richardson's letter. They contended, furthermore, that a weak bill would be worse than no bill at all, and vowed to actively oppose H.R. 17255 if it came out of committee significantly compromised.

The coalition made it very clear to the legislators that a capitulation to the administration position would be publicly equated with a capitulation to the polluters. In a telegram dated November 20, the coalition and other signers said:

WE VEHEMENTLY DEPLORE THE LATEST INVOLVEMENT BY THE NIXON ADMINISTRATION IN EFFORTS TO "IMPROVE THE ENVIRONMENT." WE CONSIDER THE RECENT PROPOSALS SENT BY SECRETARY OF HEW, ELLIOT RICHARDSON, TO BE A TRAVESTY. EVIDENTLY SPOKESMEN FOR INDUSTRIAL POLLUTION HAVE TRIUMPHED WITHIN THE ADMINISTRATION OVER RESPONSIBLE ENVIRONMENTALISTS. WHERE WAS THE ADMINISTRATION DURING THE PUBLIC DEBATE OF THE LEGISLATION BEFORE YOU? WHY DID THE ADMINISTRATION WAIT UNTIL AFTER THE ELECTIONS WHILE PRIVATE CONFERENCES WERE TAKING PLACE BEFORE SPEAKING OUT IN DEFENSE OF THE INDUSTRY'S CONTINUING ATTEMPTS TO WEAKEN THIS LEGISLATION? . . . WE HAVE CONFIDENCE THAT THE CONGRESS WILL STAND UP FOR THE RIGHT OF THE PUBLIC TO A HEALTHY ENVIRONMENT BY ENACT-

ING THE STRICT LEGISLATION THAT WILL MAKE
THAT POSSIBLE.

The conference committee met eight more times in the
following three weeks. On December 16, after a morning and
an afternoon session, a bill—modeled closely after the Senate
version of H.R. 17255—was reported out of committee. Two
days later, the bill passed both houses on voice votes and
was sent to President Nixon for his signature.

Some very important progress has been made, but the Clean
Air Act Amendments are not considered the last word in air
pollution legislation. Environmentalists presented to Senator
Muskie's Subcommittees on Air and Water Pollution the minimum requirements for such legislation in this first year of the
"Environmental Decade," and Congress responded with a bill
which accepts the right to pollute and goes on to debate only
the levels. Specific points which reflect this basic weakness include: (1) a loophole for polluters in which their clean-up
deadline can be extended for two years on the basis of technology; (2) the lack of any phase-out of the internal combustion engine; (3) weakening language and requirements
dealing with the 50,000-mile warranty of automotive emission
control devices; (4) language casting doubt on the citizen's
right to bring suit against the Administrator to enforce the
law. Nothing prevents an early re-examination of the Clean
Air Act Amendments of 1970 in order to rectify any defects.

Now law, the Clean Air Bill creates new anti-pollution weapons in the federal arsenal and increases citizen power against
polluters. But the fight for clean air is not over. History has
shown that industries' lawyers and "experts" will utilize any
possible loophole to protect their corporate clients. This legislation will only be successful if vigilant citizens force adher-
ence to both the exact letter and the spirit of the Clean Air Act.

appendices

APPENDIX I

personal inventory

CONSUMPTION PATTERNS

Reduce your general consumption level.

Recycle every product that can be reused; this includes newspapers, aluminum, tin cans, steel, and glass.

Buy returnable bottles and return them.

Avoid use of paper products where reusable products can be substituted. Use instead cloth napkins, towels, tablecloths, placemats, handkerchiefs, and diapers.

Use china dishware.

If you must use throwaways, use paper, not plastic, which is very slow to decompose.

Use a cloth or basket container to shop.

Use a lunch box for food. Extra paper bags are unnecessary.

Store food in reusable containers.

Share magazine subscriptions.

Keep a blackboard near the phone.

Reuse gift wrappings and advertising mail.

Don't throw hangers away.

Avoid individually wrapped cellophane packages.

Build a compost pile.

Separate trash and be careful with what you throw away. Film scraps can kill fish and wildlife.

Avoid trashmashers.

Use only the amount of detergent required—no extra.

Use baking soda and washing soda as alternatives to all-purpose cleansers.

Don't use phosphate detergents; pure soap is best.

CHEMICALS

Read all food and chemical labels.

If you have to use pesticides, use a product designed to kill one type of pest. General bug or insect killers will be harmful to many forms of animal and plant life and might destroy the balance between other species and create a new pest. Always read fine print when spraying and avoid inhalation of fumes. When you can, investigate biological cures for a predator or an odor that is offensive to existing pests and will keep them away.

Investigate crops before planting. Some vegetables growing next to each other will keep away each other's pests; others will be prey to the same pest and both crops are likely to suffer.

Avoid "No Pest Strips" made by Shell—use a flyswatter.

Wash and peel all fruits and vegetables to guard against DDT intake.

Avoid chemically laden commercial alternatives; eat real fruit.

Grow your own vegetables.

Avoid spray cans which rely on chemicals to eject the contents.

Reduce fat intake of fat meat products which are likely to have the highest level of persistent DDT and other pesticides.

Don't buy clothes and commercial products made out of real animal skins.

Buy a Christmas tree with roots—not one that is dying or made of aluminum.

WATER
Practice using less water.

Turn off the faucet while brushing your teeth.

Set a shower time limit, or take one shower with the plug in the drain to see if you can save water by taking a bath.

Try a quick wet down, no water while lathering, and a quick rinse off.

Place a brick in the toilet to raise the water level in the tank. Less water will be needed to control the flushing mechanism and less will be consumed with each flush.

Use clothes washers and dishwashers only when filled to maximum capacity.

A cold water jug in the refrigerator can provide a refreshing drink without having to run tap water until it gets sufficiently cold.

ELECTRICITY
Conserve electricity particularly during the peak hours of 5–7 P.M.

Avoid electric "gadgets": toothbrushes, shavers, can openers, scissors, knives, frying pans, and hair curlers.

Dry clothes on a clothesline.

Use low watt bulbs in areas where high visible intensities are unneeded.

Turn off all lights and lower heat during the day.

Proper insulation can greatly reduce the amount of needed heat. Weatherstrip joints, insulate the ceilings and walls, use storm windows, plant tree protection to shield against winter winds, use blankets rather than your thermostat to keep warm. Clean radiators.

Awnings, trees, and a clean air filter will reduce summer heat. If you insist on an air conditioner, use it only when people are at home.

AUTOMOBILES

Keep your car in shape; it will emit less pollution.

Drive in carpools; better yet, walk or bike when possible.

If possible, buy a 4–6 cylinder car.

Using salt to rid sidewalks and roads of ice also lessens plants' ability to resist pests. Use sand instead.

NOISE

Use your auto horn only when absolutely necessary. We're all in this together.

Avoid high noise levels; keep televisions, radios, and stereo equipment at a tolerable level that won't offend or ruin your eardrums.

community inventory

INDUSTRIAL PLANTS

Where are the industrial plants located in your area?

What are the sources of their raw materials?

What types of effluent are produced at each plant?

Are controls being used to regulate the effluent?

What means of disposal are being used?

Are other means of disposal available?

Do any of the plants emit large quantities of smoke?

Are smokestacks working at night that don't function during the day?

Are there air and water pollution standards for your area?

Are they enforced?

Is there a feasible alternative production method?

Is the plant unionized?

Are the workers satisfied with in-plant environmental conditions?

Are adequate health and safety regulations provided to cover workers?

Are pollution control devices being used?

Who is the plant manager?

What is his telephone number and address? (They could be useful for direct confrontation tactics.)

Is the plant a subsidiary or part of a conglomerate?

If so, what is the main company?

What products are produced by each subsidiary and the main company itself? (A product from the main plant may be boycotted if the local products are not suitable.)

POWER AND SEWAGE LINES

Are power lines overhead?

Are all future power lines zoned to be underground?

Are current or projected power lines blocking scenic views?

What kind of power plant serves your area?

If it uses fossil fuel, is it low-sulfur content?

Is the nuclear reactor of a new "no-release" design?

Does the company advertise "live better electrically"?

When are the peak hours for electricity usage in your area?

Where does the community water supply originate?

Are sewage lines adequate for the neighborhood needs?

Is there a primary sewage treatment plant? Secondary? Tertiary?

Are sewage plant by-products re-usable?

Are they being reused?

Are local residents being encouraged not to dispose of garbage in the disposal systems?

Are there septic tanks in your area?

Do they drain properly?

Are adequate precautions taken to prevent the septic tanks from draining into clear water wells?

Are all drainage projects prevented from draining into the good water supply?

How many chemicals are used to make the water suitable for drinking purposes?

Is there a shortage of local water supplies?

TRANSPORTATION

Where are the main thoroughfares located?

Is the bus service adequate?

Are pavement conditions and lighting adequate?

Are there scenic easements protecting the community from the noise and view of freeways and major highways?

Is billboard legislation in effect?

What new roads are being planned?

Have alternate transportation systems (rail rapid transit) been considered?

Are freeway hearings well attended by local citizens?

Do the people have a voice in approving or disapproving methods of transportation?

If new routes are deemed necessary, will they be constructed in the least disruptive location?

PROPERTY

Who owns what lands within the community?

What urban renewal projects exist?

How are the renewal projects funded?

What areas of open space exist within the urban area?

Are they protectively zoned?

Are zoning hearings well publicized?

Do citizens attend these hearings?

Are any agricultural lands zoned against development?

What pesticide spraying programs exist?

Are any efforts being made to ban them?

Are there any historic districts?

Will they be maintained?

What recreational areas exist?

What properties have been tax-condemned and can be used for community purposes?

Are there any dilapidated structures that should be torn down?

Are rent conditions satisfactory to residents?

What future development plans exist?

Will they attract new residents and increase the population?

Are cultural and educational facilities adequate?

PEOPLE

What is the current population of your area?

What are the main cultural groups?

What are the main religious groups?

Are these groups located in specific sections of the community?

Who are the community leaders?

Do the majority of the leaders come from any one cultural or religious group?

What is the financial structure of the community?

Do a few people control property?

Is there a local university?

Are there university groups that can assist with an ecological inventory?

Are there any local conservation groups who can offer assistance?

Will workers in the factory provide information as to plant conditions?

Are local officials willing to listen to citizen opinions?

Can they be of assistance in collecting community information?

national eco groups

Center for Law and
  Social Policy
20008 Hillyer Place
Washington, D.C. 20009

Center for the Study of
  Responsive Law
Box 19367
Washington, D.C. 20036

Conservation Foundation
1717 Massachusetts Ave., N.W.
Washington, D.C.

Environmental Action
Room 731
1346 Connecticut Ave., N.W.
Washington, D.C. 20036

Environmental Defense Fund
1901 N Street, N.W.
Washington, D.C. 20036

Friends of the Earth
451 Pacific Avenue
San Francisco, California 94133

Izaak Walton League
1326 Waukegan Road
Glenview, Illinois 60025

National Audubon Society
1130 Fifth Avenue
New York, New York 10038

National Parks Association
1701 18th Street, N.W.
Washington, D.C. 20009

National Recreation and
    Park Association
1700 Pennsylvania Ave., N.W.
Washington, D.C. 20006

National Wildlife Federation
1412 16th Street, N.W.
Washington, D.C.

Nature Conservancy
1522 K Street, N.W.
Washington, D.C.

Planned Parenthood
515 Madison Avenue
New York, New York 10022

Sierra Club
Mills Tower
San Francisco, California

Wilderness Society
729 15th Street, N.W.
Washington, D.C. 20005

Zero Population Growth
330 Second Street
Los Altos, California 94022

local eco groups

ALABAMA
Greater Alliance to Stop
    Pollution—G.A.S.P.
900 S. 18th St.
Birmingham, Alabama 35205
(Dr. Dan Prince, Pres.
    (205) 323-7766)

Pollution Action League—P.A.L.
University of South Alabama

Mobile, Alabama 36608
(David Langang, Pres.
(205) 460-7191)

ALASKA
Alaska Conservation Society
Box 5-192
College, Alaska 99701
(Robert Weeden (907) 479-6689)

ARIZONA
Arizonans in Defense
of the Environment—A.I.D.E.
1431 Jen Tilly Lane
Tempe, Arizona 85281
(Harry Tate, Pres.
(602) 967-7924)

Arizonans for a Quality
Environment
P.O. Box 17717
Tucson, Arizona 85710
(Juel Rodack, Chmn.
(602) 623-0287)

ARKANSAS
Society for Environmental
Stabilization
P.O. Box 252
Fayetteville, Arkansas 72701
(Andy Covington,
Episcopal Student Center)

Arkansas Ecology Center
316 Chester Street
Little Rock, Arkansas 72201
(Pratt Remmell, Dir.
(501) 374-6271)

CALIFORNIA
Ecology Center
2179 Alliston Way
Berkeley, California 94701
(David Graber (415) 548-2220)

Ecology Action Educational
   Institute
Box 3895
Modesto, California 95352
(Cliff Humphrey (209) 529-3784)

Earth Action Council
UCLA Box 24390
Los Angeles, California 90024
(Frank Steen (213) 384-2714)

Ecology Action—ZPG—
   San Diego State
6271 Madeleine St., Apt. 158
San Diego, California 92115
(Clay Kemper (714) 286-5200)

Citizens Against Air Pollution,
   Inc.
193 Bangor Avenue
San Jose, California 95123
(P. B. Venuto, Pres.
   (408) 227-8153)

COLORADO
ECO Center
1424 Pearl, Rm. 7
Boulder, Colorado 80302
(Sandy Cooper (303) 442-3652;
   or John Liebson (303) 449-0525)

Environmental Action Committee
   of Colorado
University of Colorado,
   Denver Center
1100 - 14th Street
Denver, Colorado 80202
(George Hovey/Morey Wolfson
   (303) 534-1602)

CONNECTICUT
Environmental Education
   Committee
University of Connecticut
Avery Point,

Groton, Connecticut 06340
(David McKain (203) 536-8773)

Protect Your Environment—P.Y.E.
40 Highland Avenue
Rowayton, Connecticut 06853
(Elizabeth Byers (203) 762-3824)

Pollution Control Committee
P.O. Box 281
West Hartford, Connecticut 06107
(Anita Pericolosi, Co-Founder
   (203) 523-0779)

DELAWARE
Delaware Citizens for Clean
   Air, Inc.—TB & R.D. Assn.
1308 Delaware Avenue
Wilmington, Delaware 19899
(Jacob Kreshtool, Pres.
   (302) 655-7258)

DISTRICT OF COLUMBIA
Ecology Center
3256 Prospect Street, N.W.
Washington, D.C. 20007
(Bill Painter, Dir.
   (202) 338-5010)

Metropolitan Washington
   Coalition for Clean Air
1714 Massachusetts Avenue, N.W.
Washington, D.C. 20036
(Jack Winder (202) 234-7100)

FLORIDA
Environmental Action Group
323 Reitz Union
University of Florida
Gainesville, Florida 32601
(Allen Sandler (904) 392-1635)

Conservation 70's
319 S. Monroe Street
Tallahassee, Florida 32304

(Loring Lovell, Exec. Dir./
  Jack Hanway, Admin. Asst.
  (904) 224-9992-3)

GEORGIA
Consumer Action
Box 2414
University Station
Athens, Georgia 30601
(Mrs. Virginia Mullen
  (404) 542-1661)

Georgia Conservancy
1025 Chandler Building
127 Peachtree Street
Atlanta, Georgia 30303
(Norman C. Smith, Pres.
  (404) 525-1828)

HAWAII
Environment Group Hawaii
P.O. Box 1618
Honolulu, Hawaii 96806
(Jane Proctor/Mark Cockrill,
  Chmn. (808) 531-1357)

ZPG
P.O. 11127
University of Hawaii
Honolulu, Hawaii 96822
(Paul Brundage (808) 944-8111)

IDAHO
Idaho Environmental Council
P.O. Box 3371
University Station
Moscow, Idaho 83843
(Jerry Jayne, Pres.
  (208) 885-6417)

Citizens Environment Council
855 S. 8th St.
Pocatello, Idaho 83201
(Dr. Donald Roberts
  (208) 232-1443)

ILLINOIS

Students for Environmental
  Controls—SEC
1001 S. Wright Street
Champaign, Illinois 61820
(Don Yon (217) 344-1351)

Campaign Against Pollution
611 West Fullerton
Chicago, Illinois 60614
(Paul Booth (312) 929-2922)

Clean Air Coordinating
  Committee—TB & R.D. Assn.
1440 Washington Street
Chicago, Illinois 60607
(John Kirkwood (312) 243-2000)

INDIANA

Citizens Council for Cleaner
  Air
615 N. Alabama St., Rm. 335
Indianapolis, Indiana 46204
(Miss Lynn Stevens, Co.
  (317) 635-4538)

Lafayette Environmental Action
  Federation—LEAF
P.O. Box 2103
West Lafayette, Indiana 47906
(David Page, Pres.
  (317) 463-2415)

IOWA

Iowa Confederation
  of Environmental Organizations
40 Physics
Iowa State University
Ames, Iowa 50010
(Dr. David Trauger, Coord.
  (515) 294-7252)

Citizens for Environmental
  Action
P.O. Box 1149

Iowa City, Iowa 52240
(Ron Zobel (319) 338-9809)

KANSAS
Reno County Environmental
   Action Committee
Rt. 3
Hutchinson, Kansas 67502
(Mrs. Betty Davis, Pres.
  (316) 662-5620)

Citizens for a Better
   Environment
Division of Biology,
   Fairchild Hall
Kansas State University
Manhattan, Kansas 66502
(Daniel Bowen, Pres.
  (913) 539-2156)

KENTUCKY
Environmental Awareness Society
Box 878
University of Kentucky
Lexington, Kentucky 40506
(Larry Geisman (606) 257-1567)

Action for Clean Air, Inc.
1817 S. 34th St.
Louisville, Kentucky 40211
(Tina Heavrin
  (502) 774-4401, ext. 48)

LOUISIANA
Council on Environmental Issues
1025 Carrollton Avenue
Baton Rouge, Louisiana 70806
(Paul H. Templet, Chmn.
  (504) 926-8015)

Ecology Center of Louisiana,
   Inc.
Box 15149
New Orleans, Louisiana 70115
(Ross Vincent (504) 895-5784)

MAINE
Natural Resources Council
   of Maine
20 Willow Street
Augusta, Maine 04330
(Marshall Burke (207) 623-3452)

South Maine Environmental
   Action Committee
University of Maine Law School
68 High Street
Portland, Maine 04101
(Cliff Goodall (207) 775-5691,
   Ext. 23)

MARYLAND
Ecology Action, Inc.
P.O. Box 4661
Baltimore, Maryland 21212
(Florence Kobernick
   (301) 655-4132)

Citizens for a Better
   Environment
7004 Dolphin Road
Lanham, Maryland 20801
(Dr. Robert F. Mueller
   (301) 552-3584 (h)
   or (301) 982-4860 (off.)

MASSACHUSETTS
Environmental Action
c/o King Council
207 Hampshire House
University of Massachusetts
Amherst, Massachusetts 01002
(Paul Segel/Gene Petit
   (413) 545-0648)

Boston Area Ecology Action
   Center
925 Massachusetts Avenue
Cambridge, Massachusetts 02139
(John McGrame (617) 876-7085)

MICHIGAN

Environmental Action
  for Survival—ENACT
146 F, School of Natural
  Resources
University of Michigan
Ann Arbor, Michigan 48104
(Toby Cooper, Secy.
  (313) 764-4410)

Committee for Environmental
  Preservation—CEP
148 Mackenzie Hall
Wayne State University
Detroit, Michigan 48202
(Ken Hahn (313) 577-3480)

MINNESOTA

Metro Clean Air Committee
1829 Portland Avenue
Minneapolis, Minnesota 55404
(Mrs. Janet Garrison, Dir.
  (612) 333-5463)

Minnesota Environmental
  Control Citizens Assn., Inc.—
  MECCA
26 East Exchange St.
St. Paul, Minnesota 55101
(Joan Minchesty (612) 222-2998)

MISSISSIPPI

Committee to Leave
  the Environment of America
  Natural—CLEAN
Box 643
Starkville, Mississippi 39759
(Boyd Gatlan (601) 325-5872)

MISSOURI

Citizens Environmental Council
c/o Lakeside Nature Center
5600 Gregory Boulevard
Kansas City, Missouri 64132

(Mrs. R. O. McWhinney
  (913) 649-2755)

Coalition for the Environment
St. Louis Region
8505 Delmar Boulevard
St. Louis, Missouri 63124
(Mrs. Dorothy Slusser
  (314) 968-0682)

MONTANA
Montana Environmental Council
410 Woodworth
Missoula, Montana 59801
(Don Aldrich (406) 543-6945)

Montana Environmental Task
  Force
Box 14
Montana State University
Bozeman, Montana 59715
(Gordon Whirry (406) 587-8243)

NEBRASKA
Citizens for Environmental
  Improvement, Inc.
P.O. Box 30322
Lincoln, Nebraska, 68503
(Dr. Norma Johnson
  (402) 466-0910)

Quality Environment Council
Box 7025
Omaha, Nebraska 68107
(Dr. Larry C. Holcomb, Chmn.
  (402) 536-2811)

NEVADA
Ecology Action—Southern
  Nevada
c/o Dept. of Biology
University of Nevada
  at Las Vegas
Las Vegas, Nevada 89109
(Bruce Mitter (702) 736-6111)

NEW HAMPSHIRE

University of New Hampshire:
  Improve the Environment—
  UNHITE
Wolf House
8 Ballard Street
Durham, New Hampshire 03824
(Dennis Strong (603) 862-2448)

Center for Human Concerns
136 West Street
Keene, New Hampshire 03431
(Joseph Phelan (603) 352-8622)

NEW JERSEY

Atlantic County Citizens
  Council on Environment, Inc.
137 S. Main Street
Pleasantville, New Jersey 08232
(Beverly D. Rehfeld, Pres.
  (609) 646-6604)

Plainfield Area Coalition
  for the Environment—PACE
1454 Maplewood Terrace
Plainfield, New Jersey 07060
(Jasmine King, Pres.
  (201) 754-3945)

Princeton Ecology Action
1 Murray Dodge Hall
Princeton University
Princeton, New Jersey 08540
(Larry Campbell (609) 452-3627)

NEW MEXICO

New Mexico Conservation
  Coordinating Council
433 Maple, N.E.
Albuquerque, New Mexico 87106
(Cliff Crawford, Pres.)

New Mexico Citizens for Clean
  Air and Water
113 Monterey Drive, N.

Los Alamos, New Mexico 87544
(Mr. John R. Bartlit
  (505) 672-9792)

NEW YORK
Citizens Committee
  for the Hudson Valley
P.O. Box 146
Ardsley on Hudson,
  New York 10503
(William Hoppen (914) 962-3332)

Cause
699 Elmwood Avenue
Buffalo, New York 14219
(Dr. John Howells
  (716) 833-0783)

Environment!
119 Fifth Avenue, Rm. 600
New York, New York 10003
(Tom Stokes (212) 673-8740)

Citizens for Clean Air, Inc.
502 Park Avenue
New York, New York 10022
(Robert Kafin, Pres.
  (212) 935-1454 or PL 5-3300)

NORTH CAROLINA
ECOS
Box 4787, Duke Station
Durham, North Carolina 27706
(Jeannette Luccas, Bd. of Dir.
  (919) 684-5795)

Organization for Environmental
  Quality (Raleigh ECOS, Inc.)
Box 5536, College Station
Raleigh, North Carolina 27207
(Michael Baranski, Chmn.
  (919) 755-2524)

NORTH DAKOTA
Students for Environmental
  Defense

Room 105, Law School
University of North Dakota
Grand Forks, North Dakota
   58201
(Dave Stoeneman, Pres.
   (701) 777-4360)

OHIO
Citizens for a Clean Environment
1297 Sweetwater Drive
Cincinnati, Ohio 45215
(Mrs. Frank Etges
   (513) 761-0603)

Air Conservation Committee—
   TB & R.D. Assn.
4614 Prospect Avenue
Cleveland, Ohio 44103
(Mrs. Richard Fleber
   (216) 361-0545)

Environmental Conservation
   Organization
Kent State University
Kent, Ohio 44240
(Tom Dietz (216) 673-4154)

Ohio Valley Environmental
   Council
c/o Jefferson County TB
   and Health Assoc., Inc.
224 N. 5th Street, P.O. Box 399
Steubenville, Ohio 43952
(Ben Weber, Pres.
   (614) 385-9900)

Ohio Students Environmental
   Council
Environmental Studies Center
Antioch Union
Antioch College
Yellow Springs, Ohio 45387
(513) 767-7331, ext. 475
   or 767-9010

OKLAHOMA

ECCO
c/o Dept. of Human Ecology
School of Public Health
Oklahoma Medical School
Oklahoma City, Oklahoma 73104
(Victor L. Jackson, Vice Chmn.)

Oklahoma Coalition for Clean
   Air
P.O. Box 53303
2442 N. Walnut
Oklahoma City, Oklahoma 73105
(Lois Blanche (405) 524-8471)

OREGON

P.U.R.E.
409 E. Greenwood
Bend, Oregon 97701
(Bill Ellis (503) 382-2811)

Environmental Action
2216 S.E. 180th Street
Portland, Oregon 97233
(Weldon Wellingham)

PENNSYLVANIA

Environmental Action/Zero
   Population Growth
414 Schenley Hall
Pittsburgh, Pennsylvania 15213
(Marc D. Hiller (412) 687-7271)

Citizens Committee
   for Environmental Control
   in Montgomery County
1108 Rock Creek Dr.
Wyncote, Pennsylvania 19095
(Shirley Merkin, Chmn.)

RHODE ISLAND

Humans to End Environmental
   Deterioration
P.O. Box 9

Kingston, Rhode Island 02881
(Steven G. Zelenski, Ex. Dir.)

Ecology Action for Rhode
   Island, Inc.
281 Thayer Street
Providence, Rhode Island 02906
(Mike Ireland (401) 274-9429)

SOUTH CAROLINA
Concerned South Carolinians
   for Better Environment, Inc.
Box 5844
Columbia, South Carolina 29205
(803) 254-1657

WASTE
Dept. of Biology
Winthrop College
Rock Hill, South Carolina 29730
(John Freeman (803) 328-2471)

SOUTH DAKOTA
Environmental Teach-In
Medical Bldg., Biology Dept.,
   Rm. 104
University of South Dakota
Vermillion, South Dakota 57069
(H. L. Goodell)

TENNESSEE
Birth Environment Movement
P.O. Box 8470
University Station
Knoxville, Tennessee 37916

Environmental Action Council
   of Memphis
2789 Sky Lake Cove
Memphis, Tennessee 38112
(S. Henry Hall (901) 527-9033)

PURE
Box 898
George Peabody College
   for Teachers

Nashville, Tennessee 37203
(Walter Heerschap
  (615) 291-1500)

Environmental Council of Oak
    Ridge—ECOR
105 Monticello Rd.
Oak Ridge, Tennessee 37839
(Robin Wallace (615) 483-1921)

TEXAS
Environmental Action Group
Rt. 1, Box 124-A
Big Spring, Texas 79720
(James Ream)

Ecology Action
123 W. Park Avenue
San Antonio, Texas 78212
(Ted Field (512) 227-2789)

Environmental Action Group
Box 138
Texas Wesleyan College
Fort Worth, Texas 76105
(Arthur G. Cleveland, Coord.
  (817) 534-0251)

UTAH
ISSUE?
P.O. Box 728
Cedar City, Utah 84720
(Loraine Juvelin, Chmn.
  (801) 586-6308)

Ecology Center
Student Activities
University of Utah
Salt Lake City, Utah 84112
(Brian Mason, Dir.
  (801) 322-6263)

VERMONT
Committee for Environmental
    Action

Box 99, Billings Center
University of Vermont
Burlington, Vermont 05401
(Anne Ehrlich (802) 864-4511)

Environmental Awareness
   Committee
Green Mountain College
Poultney, Vermont 05741
(Patricia G. World
   (802) 287-9313)

VIRGINIA
Committee for Environmental
   Action
7825 Accotink Place
Alexandria, Virginia 22308
(Mrs. Doann Haines
   (703) 765-0981)

ECOS
Biology Department
Old Dominion University
Norfolk, Virginia 23508
(Andy Damalas (703) 489-8000)

WASHINGTON
Avert Man's Extinction Now—
   AMEN
Central Washington State
   College
Ellensburg, Washington 98926
(Curt A. Wilberg (509) 963-1111)

Clean Air for Washington
1000 Aurora Ave. North
Seattle, Washington 98109
(J. Porter Relly
   (206) AT 4-2484)

WEST VIRGINIA
Citizens for Environmental
   Protection
1564 Virginia St. E.

Charleston, West Virginia
   25311
(Carol Wilcox (304) 343-3594)

Citizens League
   for Environmental Action
   Now!—CLEAN
College of Engineering
Dept. of Civil Engineering
University of West Virginia
Morgantown, West Virginia 26506
(Terry Elkins, Chmn.
   (304) 293-4391)

WISCONSIN
Capital Community Citizens
1109 Gilbert Road
Madison, Wisconsin 53711
(Donn J. D'Alessio, Secy.
   (608) 231-3157)

Environmental Information
   Center, Inc.
3207 North Hackett Avenue
Milwaukee, Wisconsin 53211
(Dave Cook (414) 962-2557)

WYOMING
Wyoming Environmental Group
1754 S. Conwell St.
Casper, Wyoming 82601
(Dan Tolin (307) 234-3179)

Environmental Action
Box 3095
University Station
Laramie, Wyoming 82070
(Dennis Knight)

APPENDIX IV

glossary of eco words

This glossary was prepared by the Department of Research and Education of the International Brotherhood of Pulp, Sulphite and Paper Mill Workers.

abatement—the removal of unwanted materials.

absorption—process by which one substance is dissolved by and distributed throughout the body of a second material, as a soluble gas, such as ammonia, is collected in water droplets.

activated sludge—a process that removes organic matter from sewage by saturating it with air and biologically active sludge.

adsorption—process by which gases or vapors are collected on the surface of a solid phase, by reason of the attraction between the surface and the adsorbed material. Collection of organic vapors on activated charcoal is an example.

aeration tank—serves as a chamber for injecting air into water.

aerosol—a suspension of particles (either liquid or solid) in a body of gas, of such particle size that they tend to remain suspended for an indefinite period.

air contaminant—any "foreign" material in the air, that is, material other than oxygen, nitrogen, and noble gases, water vapor, and carbon dioxide. Air contaminants include, but are not limited to, the following examples:

smoke—solid and/or liquid particles formed by the incomplete combustion of fuels, and discharged suspended in the gaseous combustion of carbonaceous fuels.

soot—solid particles containing carbon formed by the incomplete combustion of carbonaceous fuels.

flyash—mineral residues from the combustion of fuels that become suspended in the combustion gases.

fume—fine solid particles formed by the condensation of materials that were gaseous at higher temperatures.

dust—solid particles small enough to become airborne, formed by attrition of larger particles.

mist—suspended liquid droplets.

vapor—gaseous material which results from dilution with fixed gases, but which, if pure, would occur as a solid or liquid at the ambient temperature (such as water vapor).

gases—materials that can be condensed to liquid only by pressure, or at temperatures below ambient (such as oxygen, methane, hydrogen).

oxides of sulfur—products of the oxidation of sulfur; they include both sulfur dioxide (SO_2) and sulfur trioxide (SO_3), and the acids formed by their combination with water. Of these, sulfuric acid (H_2SO_4), is of principal interest.

airshed—a region that shares a common air supply. Because of the nature of air, an airshed is not a precise physical division like a watershed. It is more of a political convenience for dealing with air problems that cross municipal and state lines, such as the New Jersey fumes that poison the air in New York City.

algae—plants which grow in sunlit waters. They are a food for fish and small aquatic animals and, like all plants, put oxygen in the water.

ambient air—the surrounding outdoor air.

ambient air quality—definition of the outdoor atmosphere as it exists around people, plants and structures—as contrasted to that in immediate proximity to emission sources.

ambient air quality criteria—a scientific relationship between particular concentrations and durations of specific air contaminants, and the effects they produce on persons, animals, plants or materials. "Criteria" in this sense has a connotation distinct from "standard." Although the dictionary lists the two as synonymous, care must be exercised not to confuse them in any consideration of air pollution control. Criteria, as provided in the Federal Air Quality Act of 1967, refers to varying concentrations of pollutants during periods of exposure at which specific adverse effects to the environment and human health occur. The criteria, which after nearly three years are still incomplete, were intended to form the basis for establishment of *air quality standards* in different regions of the country.

ambient air quality standards—legal statements of ambient air quality that are subject to enforcement by law. Standard may specify maximum peak concentration of contaminant allowable, maximum average concentration, and/or frequency and duration of excursions above a given concentration.

asbestos—a fibrous mineral with great resistance to heat. Asbestos particles in the atmosphere are a widespread environmental hazard which can severely damage the lungs and throat and which can also produce cancer. Asbestos is used in approximately 3,000 products. When asbestos fireproofing is sprayed or painted on surfaces of buildings under construction, one-half to two-thirds by volume can be released into the air. Diseases associated with asbestos inhalation are rarely observed sooner than 20 years from the time of first exposure.

assimilative capacity—capacity of a water body to receive, dilute, and carry away wastes without harming water quality. In the case of organic matter, also includes the capacity for natural biological oxidation, which may be expressed in pounds of BOD per day at a specific river flow rate and temperature.

bacteria—the smallest living organisms which literally eat the organic parts of sewage.

biochemical oxygen demand (BOD)—quantity of oxygen used in the biological oxidation of organic matter, in a specified time and at a specified temperature, determined by its availability to serve as food for the microorganisms. BOD can be related to the oxygen resources of a stream. For example, after dilution and mixing in a stream, one part of BOD will consume one part of oxygen in the stream.

biodegradable—decomposing due to bacterial action. Plant and animal wastes are biodegradable, but many man-made waste products, especially plastics, and metals are virtually indestructible in the natural environment.

biosphere—the biological community which includes all living organisms of the earth.

bronchitis—disease characterized by inflammation of the bronchial passages, excessive secretions of mucous, and recurrent coughing. It appears to be aggravated by air pollution, particularly *sulfur oxides*.

byssinosis—a pulmonary disease caused by the inhalation of cotton dust and the foreign materials contained within it, including bacteria, mold, and fungi.

carbon monoxide (CO)—an odorless, colorless, toxic gas emitted during the incomplete combustion of substances containing carbon. It is almost exclusively a man-made pollutant; the most common source is the automobile engine. CO has an affinity for hemoglobin—the substance in red blood cells which carries oxygen to all tissues in the body—which is 200 times greater than oxygen. A small amount of CO in the air may affect the heart and the brain, which are especially sensitive to oxygen deprivation. As little as 10 p.p.m. in the air may aggravate heart disease, and 15 p.p.m. can impair vision and judgment. Above 1,000 p.p.m., CO can be lethal.

carcinogenic substances—cancer-producing.

catalytic converters—device attached to an exhaust system which aids in the complete combustion of various waste products (hydrocarbons, CO, NO_x) that result from an incomplete initial combustion.

chlorinated hydrocarbons—a class of insecticides including DDT, chlordane, aldrin, and dieldrin. They are highly persistent; they may remain effective for more than ten years after application. They cause serious damage to certain birds, fish, and other non-target organisms.

Clean Air Act—an act passed by Congress in 1967 which requires the federal government to establish air regions for use throughout the country. It is the states' and local governments' responsibility to establish and enforce air quality standards.

closed system—a system which recycles waste products rather than disposing of them.

coagulation—the clumping together of solids to make them settle out of the sewage faster. Coagulation of solids is brought about with the use of certain chemicals such as lime, alum, or polyelectrolytes.

coliform bacteria—a group of bacteria whose presence in water is evidence of contamination by human or animal waste. Since their survival is short-termed, high coliform levels indicate relatively recent pollution.

combined sewer—carries both sewage and storm water run-off.

compaction—crushing; primarily used to reduce the volume of solid waste.

DDT—a colorless contact insecticide, discovered in 1939 and first used commercially in 1945. It is still one of the most widely used insecticides in the world, though U. S. production (103 million pounds in 1967) has been declining since 1963 as substitutes have been found. More than half of this country's annual production is exported for use in controlling malarial mosquitoes. DDT remains active in the environment for years, passing from the air and water to plants, animals, and humans. Traces of DDT are almost invariably detected in human tissues but concentrations vary among different groups: Blacks show significantly higher concentrations than whites; people in Southern states have higher DDT residues than people in Northern states. Minute amounts of DDT in the environment can adversely affect fish and wildlife. Oysters have been found to accumulate DDT to 70,000 times its concentration in surrounding waters. DDT can cause birds to lay thin-shelled eggs and it has been blamed for drastic population declines in several species, especially the peregrine falcon, which is near extinction.

decibel—a logarithmic unit to measure sound intensity.

defoliation—the removal of leaves, especially by chemical spraying.

digestion of sludge—it takes place in heated tanks where the material can decompose naturally and the odors can be controlled.

disease vector—an animal (usually an insect) which transmits disease from infected to non-infected individuals.

dissolved oxygen (DO)—extent to which oxygen occurs dissolved in water or wastewater. It is usually expressed as concentration, in parts per million, or percent of saturation.

distillation—in waste treatment, it consists of heating the effluent and then removing the vapor or steam. When the steam is returned to a liquid it is almost pure water. The pollutants remain in the concentrated residue.

ecology—science of the relationship between organisms and their environment. The word first appeared in the English language in 1873. One of the first conservationists, John Muir, explained the concept as follows in 1892: "When we try to pick out anything by itself, we find it hitched to everything else in the universe."

eco-system—pattern of balances between organisms and their environment. Man often upsets the balance by destroying a link in the food chain (for example: DDT applied to apple orchards to control pests destroyed lady bird beetles which ate red mites; the mite population which was not affected by DDT flourished, causing severe damage to the trees). Man may also upset the eco-system by helping one organism in it to thrive excessively.

effluent —(1) a flow of wastewater to its receptor; the wastewater may or may not have been subjected to waste treatment, and the receptor may be a river, municipal sewer, or the like, (2) the liquid that comes out of a treatment plant after completion of the treatment process.

emission standards—legally enforceable limits on the quantities and/or kinds of air contaminants that may be emitted into the atmosphere. For example, limits expressed in maximum concentration of contaminant in the discharge, either as an hourly rate or in relation to the quantity of material being processed; or in terms of the appearance of the discharge.

emphysema—disease of the lungs characterized by shortness of breath. Tiny air sacs in the lungs enlarge, reducing the lungs' ability to transfer oxygen to the blood. Air pollution, especially *smog* and *sulfur dioxide,* increase the intensity of the disease. It is the fastest growing cause of death in the U. S.

enzyme—any of a class of complex organic substances, as amylase, pepsin, etc., that accelerate specific chemical changes, as in the digestion of foods, in plants and animals, without themselves being changed in the process. Used in detergents to loosen dirt from fabrics; some workers in enzyme plants have developed severe cases of dermatitis.

eutrophication—over-enrichment of a quiescent body of water by nutrients, tending to produce excessive plant growth. Commonly associated with accelerated "aging" of lakes, namely progressive change in the indigenous plant and animal life supported therein.

external combustion engine—an engine in which combustion occurs outside of the cylinder or cylinders. An example is the steam engine, which is externally fired by kerosene burners that heat pressurized liquid within the engine to create power.

fission—the splitting of atomic nuclei into smaller nuclei, accompanied by the release of great quantities of energy.

floc—a clump of solids formed in sewage when certain chemicals are added.

flocculation—the process by which certain chemicals form clumps of solids in sewage.

fossil fuels—coal, petroleum, and natural gas. Created eons ago from fossil plants, they have remained buried in the ground, like money in the bank, ever since. Incompletely burned (as they always are), they pour sulfur into the air as well as smaller amounts of other pollutants. Their sulfur content varies considerably. It is high in oil from Kuwait and West Texas, for instance, low in oil from Libya and East Texas, and lower still in natural gas; low in gasoline, high in crude oil.

fusion—the combining of small atomic nuclei into larger nuclei, accompanied by the release of even greater quantities of energy than produced in the fission process.

GNP—Gross National Product, the market value of the goods and services produced by the nation's economy each year. It includes all purchases of goods and services by consumers and the government, private domestic investment, and net exports (exports less imports). While GNP measures the level of economic activity, it does not indicate whether the economy is allocating resources for socially desirable pursuits. Military expenditures, spending on activities that damage the environment, as well as expenditures on cleaning up the environment, are all included in the GNP. According to one estimate, .005 percent of the U. S. GNP is spent on environmental problems.

greenhouse effect—absorption of heat by the atmosphere. The air, acting like glass in a greenhouse, allows sunlight to pass through it to the earth, but prevents the earth's heat from escaping out into space. Some scientists believe that increased amounts of carbon dioxide will trap more heat, resulting in the melting of the polar ice caps and the flooding of coastal regions (See *icebox effect.*)

half-life—the period required for the disintegration of half of the atoms in a sample of some specific radioactive substance.

hard pesticides—pesticides which do not readily break down in the eco-system; especially the class of chlorinated hydrocarbons.

herbicides—plant-killing chemicals. Nearly 100 chemicals are used as herbicides, mostly in agriculture, though considerable amounts are used to maintain rights-of-way, waterways, and industrial areas, and in home lawn and garden care. Herbicide use is growing more than twice as fast as use of other production pesticides; increased from $200 million to $800 from 1964 to 1969, and according to government predictions will reach $1.5 billion by 1975. First developed by military, herbicides are now widely used to destroy vegetation in Vietnam, where about 100 million pounds have been sprayed over 14 million acres. Scientists have linked several herbicides—including 2,4-D and 2,4,5-T, which have been used in Vietnam and in commercial home garden sprays—with birth defects in laboratory animals.

Highway Trust Fund—the source of revenue for all federal highway-building programs. Money collected from taxes on gasoline, tire rubber and other automobile-related products is fed into the Highway Trust Fund; by law these monies cannot be used for anything but building and maintaining roads.

hydrocarbons—compounds of hydrogen and carbon produced by the incomplete combustion of substances containing carbon. Some hydrocarbons are major air pollutants. They may produce cancer, and are a key component of *smog*. The largest single source is the internal combustion engine.

icebox effect—cooling of the earth resulting from air pollution, especially *particulates,* matter which filters out heat from the sun. Some scientists believe this will overcome *greenhouse effect* and lead to another Ice Age.

incineration—it consists of burning the sludge to remove the water and reduce the remaining residues to a safe, non-burnable ash. The ash can then be disposed of safely on land, in some waters, or into caves or other underground locations.

indicator organisms—organisms which by their reactions reveal an alteration in their surroundings; as detected by change of color, death, etc.

insecticides—insect-killing chemicals. U. S. farmers use around 2.5

million pounds per year, two-thirds of it on three crops: cotton, corn and apples. Insecticide sales in this country were about $300 million in 1969 and are expected to double by 1975. (See *pesticides*.)

interceptor—sewers in a combined system control the flow of the sewage to the treatment plant. In a storm, they allow some of the sewage to flow directly into a receiving stream. This protects the treatment plant from being overloaded in case of a sudden surge of water into the sewers. Interceptors are also used in separate sanitation systems to collect the flows from main and trunk sewers and carry them to the points of treatment.

internal combustion engine—type of engine used in most automobiles. Relies on a series of explosions within cylinders to drive pistons. Since explosions are far less efficient than a steady flame, the ICE produces much more pollution than the *Rankine Cycle Engine*.

inversion—a stagnant air condition in which a layer of hot air sits on a layer of cool air and keeps it from rising. With no chance of moving upward and no wind to blow it somewhere else, the daily accumulation of poison from car exhausts, factory chimneys, town dumps, and other sources is trapped at ground level for us all to breathe.

landfill—a place where earth or solid waste is dumped, usually to create new land for development or to dispose of garbage.

magnetohydrodynamics (MHD)—an energy conversion technique which generates electricity directly from high-temperature ionized gases passed through a magnetic field, and which uses only two-thirds as much coal to produce the same amount of electricity currently gotten from combustion of coal in steam-electric plants.

microbes—minute living things, either plant or animal. In sewage, microbes may be germs that cause disease.

micron—a unit of length in the metric system, one-millionth of a meter, equal to about 0.0004 inches. Frequently used as the unit in which to express the dimensions of aerosol particles. A particle of about 100 microns in diameter is the smallest that can be resolved by the human eye without optical aids.

microorganism—minute organism, either plant or animal, invisible or barely visible to the naked eye. Aerobic organisms require oxygen for growth. Anaerobic organisms grow in the absence of free oxygen and derive it by breaking down compounds which contain oxygen combined with other substances. Facultative organisms can adapt themselves to growth in the presence, as well as in the absence, of dissolved oxygen.

mutagenic—capable of producing genetic damage.

nitrogen oxides—gases produced when combustion takes place in the presence of atmospheric nitrogen and oxygen. The principal source is the automobile engine; coal and oil burning power-generating plants contribute about 25 percent of the nation's nitrogen oxide emissions. Nitrogen dioxide, in particular, is a major air pollutant which may cause nose and eye irritation, lung damage, and death. It also absorbs ultraviolet rays from the sun and interacts *hydrocarbons* to form *smog*.

NTA (sodium nitriloacetate)—a chemical which may be used as a phosphate replacement in detergents. Research is now being conducted to determine its cleaning effectiveness on the environment.

nutrients—elements, or compounds, essential as raw materials for organism growth and development, e.g., carbon, oxygen, nitrogen, phosphorus, the dissolved solids and gases of the water of an area, etc.

octane number—a number used to measure the anti-knock properties of a liquid motor fuel. It is the percentage by volume of a certain octane (iso-octane) in a mixture of this octane and another hydrocarbon (heptane) that matches the fuel being tested in the property of knocking. The higher the octane number the less is the likelihood of knocking.

organic matter—anything coming from living organisms. It includes coal, for instance, as the product of long-dead plants as well as nearly everything that empties into a septic tank, except detergents and other chemicals. It is also the waste from homes or industry of plant or animal origin.

oxidation—the consuming or breaking down of organic wastes or chemicals in sewage by bacteria and chemical oxidants.

ozone—a form of oxygen (O_3) produced in the reactions of photochemical smog and in electrical discharges. A powerful oxidizing agent and toxic to both plants and animals at relatively low concentrations.

particulate—any liquid or solid particle capable of becoming windblown or being suspended in the air. Tiny particles in the air may carry such harmful chemicals as sulfur dioxide deep into areas of the lung which are unable to expel contaminants. In heavily polluted urban areas, more than 100 tons of particulates per square mile may fall each month. Particulates play a key role in the *icebox effect.*

parts per million (P.P.M.)—number of parts, by volume, in a million total parts.

PCV (positive crankcase ventilation)—a system by which unburned hydrocarbons from the crankcase of automobiles are recycled back into the engine to be burned. This technique leaves untouched, however, the nitrogen oxides and the heavy-particle pollutants (lead).

persistent—in reference to pesticides, remaining active under normal environmental conditions for several years following application. Most of the *chlorinated hydrocarbons* are persistent. When such pesticides came into wide use after World War II, their ability to control insects for an extended period after a single application was considered a major achievement; however, their very persistence has had serious effects on non-target plants and animals for long periods.

pesticides—chemicals including herbicides and insecticides used to kill non-human organisms considered by man to be pests. Marco Polo is said to have brought pyrethrum back from the Far East, where it was used as an insecticide. The first insecticides were organic materials of natural origin; preparations of the plant sabadilla have been used as louse powders for centuries in South America. As early as 1763, ground tobacco (the active ingredient in which was later found to be nicotine) was used in France to kill aphids. Production of pesticides became a major industry after World War II; there are now in the U. S. 900 active pesticidal chemicals formulated into more than 60,000 preparations. Production in the U. S. which manufactures from 50 to 75 percent of all pesticides in the world—was $440 million in 1964, increasing to $1.2 billion in 1969.

phosphate—a salt or ester of phosphoric acid found in heavy synthetic detergents which, when dumped in excessive amounts in water, speeds up eutrophication.

photochemical smog—the modern Los Angeles mixture whose main ingredient is carbon monoxide. This smog is manufactured by the sun from auto exhaust and other pollutants. Sunshine cooks the old familiar poisons and converts them into new, complicated, and still mysterious substances. Photochemical smog occurs only in heavily-motorized cities where the air is stagnant and the sun is strong. It is uncommon on the east coast.

pneumoconiosis (black lung)—a disease of the respiratory tract caused by inhalation of dust particles, especially coal dust.

primary treatment—treatment of sewage by removal of solid material. Floating matter is caught in screens; heavy matter is settled out in tanks.

Rankine Cycle Engine—low-polluting external combustion automobile engine thought by many experts to be a feasible alternative to the *internal combustion engine*. It burns low-grade gasoline or kerosene in a steady flame which heats liquid in a coil to produce a vapor. The vapor drives pistons or turbine. The continuously burning flame uses fuel far more efficiently than the explosive combustion in the ICE. As a result, *hydrocarbon* emissions are 20 p.p.m. (for the ICE they are 900 p.p.m.); *nitrogen oxides* emissions are 40 p.p.m. (for the ICE, they are 1,500 p.p.m.).

raw sewage—untreated sewage.

receiving waters—rivers, lakes, oceans, or other water courses that receive treated or untreated waste waters.

recycling—the process in which natural resources are conserved by reconverting used products into usable ones again. This is usually accomplished through a technically sophisticated operation involving separation, melting, pulverizing, etc.

Ringelmann Number—a scale of values, ranging from zero through five, variously used to quantitate roughly the color or density of a stack plume. Originally proposed to evaluate the darkness of coal smoke plumes as a shade of grey. Its application to other types of colors or plumes involves an assumed "equivalence" of some related optical property, such as its opacity or its ability to obscure a target behind the plume.

salts—the minerals that water picks up as it passes through the air, over and under the ground, and through household and industrial uses.

scrubber—a device using a liquid spray to remove pollutants from a stream of air. A common anti-pollution mechanism.

secondary treatment—the second step in most waste treatment systems in which bacteria consume the organic parts of the wastes. It is accomplished by bringing the sewage and bacteria together in trickling filters or in the activated sludge process.

sediment—soil and mineral solids of small particle size conveyed in water.

sedimentation tanks—they help remove solids from sewage. The waste water is pumped to the tanks where the solids settle to the bottom or float on top as scum. The scum is skimmed off the top and solids on the bottom are pumped out to sludge digestion tanks.

septic tanks—used to treat domestic wastes. The underground tanks receive the waste water directly from the home. The bacteria in the sewage decomposes the organic wastes and the sludge settles on the bottom of the tank. The effluent flows out of the tank into the ground through drains. The sludge is pumped out of the tanks, usually by commercial firms, at regular intervals.

sludge—the solid matter that settles to the bottom of sedimentation tanks and must be disposed of by digestion or other methods to complete waste treatment; black tarry stuff left at the bottom of sewage-treatment settling tanks. It makes excellent fertilizer—sold as Milorganite, it pays for much of Milwaukee's sewage treatment. It is so combustible that it can be turned into a gas and used to run machinery.

smog—brownish haze resulting from the complex interaction of *nitrogen oxides, hydrocarbons,* and other gases in strong sunlight. Nitrogen dioxide, absorbing the sun's ultraviolet rays, breaks down into nitric oxide and atoms of oxygen. The oxygen atoms react with molecules of oxygen in the air to produce *ozone;* ozone, nitric oxide and hydrocarbons interact to form peroxyacylnitrate—PAN—a brown gas. First found in Los Angeles, smog is now common to most major cities. It irritates the eyes, restricts visibility, damages mucous membranes and destroys plant life. Smog has produced cancer in laboratory animals. It has also decreased the fertility of experimental animals and the survival rate of their newborn.

sonic boom—shockwave produced by a vehicle or other object (such as a meteor) flying through the atmosphere faster than the speed of sound. Sonic booms, such as those which will be produced if the *SST* is built, have cracked windows, plaster, building foundations and art objects.

source reduction—reduction of pollution emissions at source of production.

spaceship earth—metaphor for the earth as an eco-system in which resources must be husbanded and balance between man and his environment preserved, if life is to survive.

suspended solids—solids that either float on the surface or remain suspended in liquids; removable by filtering. The wastes that will not sink or settle in sewage.

synergism—the cooperative action of separate substances such that the total effect is greater than the sum of the effects of the substances acting independently.

teratogenic—capable of inducing development of severely deformed fetus.

tertiary treatment—advanced treatment of waste water for removal of traces of organic materials and dissolved solids.

thermal pollution—pollution from heat, which is the inevitable byproduct of the energy conversion process. The addition of large amounts of hot water into lakes, ponds, rivers and waterways which serve as "cooling ponds" of power plants, intensifying the effects of other pollutants already in the water besides lowering the amount of dissolved oxygen and others, killing heat-sensitive aquatic species (trout and salmon), and encouraging growth of heat-resistant organisms.

tolerance limit—the point at which resistance to a poison, or a food or drug which may be harmful if taken in excess, ends.

water quality criteria—scientific data relating the concentration of one or more substances in water to the effects produced therefrom.

watershed—land area from which water drains toward a common watercourse in a natural basin.

glossary of organizational abbreviations

AEC —U.S. Atomic Energy Commission

AFL-CIO—American Federation of Labor–Congress of Industrial Organizations

ASHO —American Association of State Highway Officials

CAP —Campaign Against Pollution (Chicago, Illinois)

CEP —Council on Economic Priorities

Com. Ed. —Commonwealth Edison (Power Company, Chicago, Illinois)

CRF —Citizens' Research Foundation (Princeton, New Jersey)

DOD —U.S. Department of Defense

DOT —U.S. Department of Transportation

ECTC —Emergency Committee on the Transportation Crisis (Washington, D.C.)

EDF —Environmental Defense Fund

EPA —Environmental Protection Agency

FAA —Federal Aviation Administration

FCC —Federal Communications Commission

FPC —Federal Power Commission

FTC —Federal Trade Commission

FWPCA —formerly the Federal Water Pollution Control Administration; now the FWQA

G.M. —General Motors

HEW —U.S. Department of Health, Education and Welfare

NAPCA —National Air Pollution Control Administration

OCAW —Oil, Chemical and Atomic Workers International Union, AFL–CIO

PRD —Pesticides Regulatory Division (of USDA)

SEC —U.S. Securities and Exchange Commission

UAW —United Auto Workers Union

USDA —U.S. Department of Agriculture

USDI —U.S. Department of the Interior

APPENDIX VI

contributors

WILSON CLARK coordinated Environmental Resources Energy Research Group in the summer of 1970. He is currently a freelance writer specializing in environmental problems and contributed the section on power plants.

PETER HARNIK is the former editor of Johns Hopkins University's undergraduate newsletter. Currently working with the staff of Environmental Action, he served as assistant editor for this book and is largely responsible for the sections on noise, pesticides, and mining.

JOAN KNIGHT works with the National Committee on the Transportation Crisis and with the Wilderness Society. She contributed the section on highways and the ECTC case study.

ERIC LITTLE is interning with Alliance for Labor Action. He has been conducting independent research on public policy and the petroleum industry and contributed the section on oil pollution.

SAM LOVE graduated from Mississippi State University, and was a member of the Mississippi challenge delegation at the 1968 Democratic Convention. He is the former City Editor of the *Delta Democrat-Times* in Greenville, Mississippi. For Earth Day he worked as the Southern Coordinator, and now is co-editor of Environmental Action's newsletter. Sam is the editor of this book.

MARIE NAHIKIAN is a staff writer for the Institute of Scrap Iron and Steel, Inc., in Washington, D. C. She was the conference coordinator of the College Editors Conference on Ecology and the Environmental Crisis in February of 1970. Marie contributed the section on solid waste.

BARBARA REID has a B.A. in political science from the University of Michigan (1968). She spent the summer of 1968 on Robert F. Kennedy's presidential campaign and worked a year with The Conservation Foundation in Washington, D. C. Barbara was the Midwestern Coordinator for Earth Day. She's presently the Legislative Coordinator for Environmental Action, and wrote the sections on political involvement.

MARC REISNER is a staff member of the Council on Optimum Population and Environment. He has a B.A. in political science from Earlham College. Marc wrote the airport section.

KATHY STONE is a recent graduate of Radcliffe College. After leaving school she worked with Ralph Nader's summer research project. She's now on the staff of the Oil, Chemical and Atomic Workers Union. Kathy wrote the section on factory versus the worker.

JAN SCHAEFFER is the co-editor of Environmental Action's newsletter. She contributed the automobile section.

AVERY TAYLOR is a 1970 graduate of Swarthmore College with a B.A. in English literature. She is currently working with the staff of Environmental Action. Avery is assistant editor of the book and wrote the section on open space.

Environmental Action needs your help . . .

. . . to continue to investigate the main sources of environmental abuse, corporate as well as governmental, and to bring them to the public's attention;

. . . to press for legislation to stop these abuses, and to work against laws which allow them to continue and multiply;

. . . to inform the public about which products are safe, and which are dangerous to the environment, and what action government and business are taking (or not taking) to get rid of dangerous products;

. . . to bring lawsuits against those who are wrecking the environment;

. . . to keep citizens informed about what actions they can take, individually and collectively, and to help coordinate those activities at the local, state and national levels.

Because Environmental Action does not believe it can do its job effectively if it enjoys tax-exempt status (which would allow funding through public and foundation grants), it must depend on the generosity of its friends across the country. Won't you become a Supporter?